HOMING

A QUEST TO
CARE FOR
MYSELF AND
THE EARTH

HOMING

ALICE IRENE WHITTAKER

Freehand Books gratefully acknowledges the financial support for its publishing program provided by the Canada Council for the Arts and the Alberta Media Fund, and by the Government of Canada through the Canada Book Fund.

This book is available in print and Global Certified Accessible™ EPUB formats.

Freehand Books is located in Moh'kinsstis, Calgary, Alberta, within Treaty 7 territory and Métis Nation of Alberta Region 3, and on the traditional territories of the Siksika, the Kainai, and the Piikani, as well as the Iyarhe Nakoda and Tsuut'ina nations.

FREEHAND BOOKS
freehand-books.com

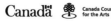

LIBRARY AND ARCHIVES CANADA CATALOGUING IN PUBLICATION

Title: Homing : a quest to care for myself and the earth / Alice Irene Whittaker.
Names: Whittaker, Alice Irene, author.
Description: Includes bibliographical references and index.
Identifiers:
Canadiana (print) 20240411234
Canadiana (ebook) 20240411579
ISBN 9781990601743 (softcover)
ISBN 9781990601750 (EPUB)
ISBN 9781990601767 (PDF)
Subjects: LCSH: Whittaker, Alice Irene. | LCSH: Sustainable living. | LCSH: Human ecology. | LCSH: Mental health. | LCGFT: Autobiographies.
Classification: LCC GE196 .W45 2024 | DDC 304.2—dc23

Edited by Deborah Willis
Design by Natalie Olsen
Author photo by Brittany Gawley
Printed and bound in Canada

FIRST PRINTING

For Owl, Wren, and Heron

CONTENTS

"We want the wild soul
and a shadow-dwelling wood thrush
heaps it on us in self-harmonizing sonata
—We revel in wildflower bloom—
marvel in the migratory sojourns of birds dodging falling stars."

J. DREW LANHAM

"In trying to give voice to motherhood,
I am trying to give voice to mammalhood."

KERRI NÍ DOCHARTAIGH

FLEDGLING

Prologue

Spiders' silk stitches together the walls of a hummingbird's nest, constructed carefully with building materials of dandelion and thistle down. The mother hummingbird had woven twigs and leaves into the walls, lined the structure with woolly lamb's ear and down of milkweed, and quilted the outside of the shelter with moss and green-grey lichen. This miniature architecture stands as tall as a small thimble, and forms an unassuming bump on a branch. Cradled in the velvety nest lay two eggs, each the size of a pea. Silver threads saddle the small cup to the fork of a tree branch, ninety feet in the air. The silky fibers bind the first home of these tiny birds to the forest where their twin hearts begin to beat inside their shells. How this nest and their fragile occupants survive the rain, wind, beaks of woodpeckers, and fast footprints of squirrels is a mystery, known only to the mother. Above the pair of eggs she sits, vigilant and hungry, a small protector facing the formidable task of building the nest and ensuring that her babies survive.

Below the nest, my feet pound against the gravel road, my Great Pyrenees dog, Bear, running loyal at my side. We quicken, two wet creatures running across a canvas of fringed forest. The rain falls, hard. My hair streaks into my eyes, and Bear's normally-majestic mane drips flatly against his face. Not in the habit of talking out loud to myself, I bluntly ask the questions I ignored for years. "What would it take for you to be kind to me? Why don't you love me? Why don't you ever let me rest?" I break into sobs as I run through the downpour, Bear keeping a steady pace, offering me unwavering love, even as I heave and weep. Afraid to stop moving. Afraid to answer my own questions. *What would it take to love myself enough that I began to take care of myself?*

THE SWALLOWS LEAVE IN SEPTEMBER

Migrations

"My God has feet of Earth. / We are flickering moths in migration." **TERRY TEMPEST WILLIAMS**

The long winter before we started a new life in the woods, we resided in an old farmhouse in a quintessential rural town. The hamlet was built on free land given to American loyalists, and the place slowly grew around a popular travellers' hotel. Our home was built in 1876, only a few years after a railway connected the town with other cites, causing the population to grow. More than a century later, surrounding farmland turned into developments, large limbs extending out from the backbone of Main Street with its two pizza shops, a post office, a coffee shop, and churches. The grocery store sold beer and the variety store sold ice cream by the scoop. Our house boasted a curved wall around the primary bedroom, and handmade spindles in the stairway railing. Large gaps between the wide maple floorboards collected dirt for over 130 years, dusty traces of families' lives. The floors and walls slanted dramatically, so a toy car could roll on its own from one side of the main floor to the other. Lush grapevines surrounded the back of the house, and grew fruit every summer. We kept bees — or rather Nik did, and I reaped the rewards of the honey from their backyard hives — until we learned he had an anaphylactic allergy, and we sold the bees to a local farmer.

I commuted for four hours a day, which left me drained and filled me with shame. I prided myself on caring deeply about the planet. Connection to nature came naturally to me and felt integral to my identity. I knew the issues. I took personal actions to make my home and lifestyle more eco-conscious and worked in international development and social justice. I founded and led an environmental charity called Mother Nature Partnership, which worked at the intersection of waste reduction and gender equality by providing reusable menstrual supplies and training to girls and women so that they could fully participate in school, work, and community life. I made my own cleaning supplies, used a reusable mug, and read tomes about mass extinction. I didn't want to be driving for hours a day and running myself into the ground, but I couldn't see another way. Guilt plagued me as I burned gas and ran on fumes, taking endlessly from both myself and nature.

Maternity leave with my second child gave me a brief respite from the commute, but I struggled with postpartum anxiety and depression, made worse by spending twelve hours alone taking care of a toddler and baby while my husband, Nik, worked in the faraway city. My two-year-old daughter, Owl, struggled with growing anxiety and stimulation overwhelm, which eclipsed the needs of her quiet newborn brother, Wren. When I first moved to that old rural house, I expected excitement about the promise of the future. I jarred apples from the tree in the backyard, wallpapered the bookshelves in Owl's first bedroom, and showed her the wonder of the bugs living in the grapevines. I also paced around the house, cried when alone, and worked hard to convince myself of my happiness. I felt isolated in the strange, small town, and my body wouldn't let me ignore my unhappiness as years stretched onwards. I strained, bent, and cracked. I finally admitted what I had denied since moving day: *this was not the life I wanted for myself. This was not home.* Voicing the despair strengthened the sentiment, allowing it to grow more powerful. This commuter life was not the dream of my childhood, in which I aspired to dance professionally in the glitter of the city. Nor was it the dream I craved as an adult: living with my family in a cabin surrounded by trees.

We waited for someone to buy our house, and for months no one did. Maybe people were dissuaded by the roof that needed to be rebuilt, or the dramatic slope of the old floors. My hopes rose but, over and over, potential buyers' interest fell through. I felt guilty to be upset at all, knowing how many people struggled to find housing. We didn't know where we were going to move to, but I couldn't stay put. We tried to move closer to the city, at least to cut down on the drive, but we could not afford anything. We eventually found an inoffensive home beside a gas station construction project, and the place greatly exceeded our price range, but less so than everything else. Seeing the house as our only option, we put in an offer conditional on the sale of our home, and went to the town hall to pore over blueprints and zoning maps, researching how close children can sleep to gas station pumps without adverse health effects. Despite its obvious failings and an uneasiness in my gut, I wanted to move to that house to escape from my feeling of being trapped.

One night, we received the call. "Another sale of your house fell through." I panicked and cried. My hopes had climbed higher than I realized, and I hadn't expected to be so deeply disappointed at the news that we were stuck indefinitely. My face red and mottled, I drew a bath to try to calm down. Stepping into the tub, the water shocked me with its coldness. We'd run out of hot water. I sat down in the nearly overflowing icy bath and, in a microcosm of my whole life in this place, I tried to make it work and then gave up. Climbing out of the bath shivering, something caught my eye: a grey-brown moth, winging at our bathroom window, erratically flirting around the edges of the pane, trying to get to moonlight. A nighttime creature, like me. A nocturnal insect that a nightjar could catch on the wing, snatched out of the thick, dark air. I sat naked on the cold lid of the toilet, hopeless, watching her flit ominously at the inside of the window. Soft wings, hard glass.

Ten years earlier, I hopped on my blue, too-small bicycle, listening to "All I Need" by Radiohead on my no-name MP3 player as I sped through a yellow light, weaving around the Toronto traffic inching across the Danforth towards Cabbagetown.

My loose helmet shifted on my head, falling down to my eyes, as I crossed curving streetcar tracks. My backpack bounced in the front basket, heavy with the weight of textbooks, tights, ballet shoes, a thermos of green tea, and a change of clothes for my restaurant shift. I sped up to the theatre school, locked my bike hastily to a rack, and threw open the front door. Classical piano floated down the stairwell, and the exhilarating sound of live drums crept through the hallways from a studio on the opposite side of the old building. I raced along the hallway, the wooden floors creaking, and ran up the stairs and into the main studio. *Only three minutes late,* I tried to reassure myself, adrenaline racing as I threw off my clothes, revealing pink tights under a black long-sleeved bodysuit with a deep v that intentionally showed my bony sternum and ribs. Twenty dancers stood at the barre around the edges of the studio, eyeing me, wondering if the teacher would chastise me for being late. Embarrassed, I pulled on my tight ballet slippers and walked quickly to the last spot at the barre against the mirror, forcing my classmates to shift and make space for me as they prepared for pliés. I pulled my hair into a practiced bun as the piano repeated the same expressive song, and we started the exercise on the second side. Out of the corner of my eye, I watched my classmates on the opposite side of the room, copying the exercise with a split-second delay. I descended into a grand plié, and moved by the soaring music, lifted my sternum to the sky and inclined my head to follow the arc of my arm down to bras bas.

"Pelvis in! Shoulder down!" the teacher told me for the hundredth time as she walked past, and I worked to follow her instructions while also returning my heels to the floor as quickly as possible. My best friend Andrea and I smiled at each other, and I shrugged while dancing, though the correction bothered me. My shoulders always tensed up by my ears, no matter how hard I pulled them down. I glanced sideways at the mirror, and instead of watching my form as I finished pliés, I frowned darkly, fixating on the slight curve of my stomach and the flesh at the back of my left arm.

Ballet ended ninety minutes later, and we travelled as a class to a different studio for modern dance, taking off our ballet shoes to instead dance with bare feet. I swapped my pink tights for black shorts in the washroom, and pulled on a pair of oversized knit overalls that I rolled down around my waist with studied precision, letting the roll of the fabric sit on my waist where it shrank my appearance. People ate snacks before continuing training, and I eyed a classmate's celery and peanut butter jealously, counting down the minutes until the next class began. The drummer walked in while we stretched, and soon he played pulsing, soulful music while we perfected an intricate and physical sequence, sweat dripping down our necks and chests. Bare, calloused feet turned in unison on black marley vinyl. Pelvises pushed us across the room, as we worked to cover ground. Shoulder blades instigated powerful turns, three at a time with our heads spotting, before we all threw our heads down to the ground and then flew back up, arcing towards the fluorescent lights on the ceiling. Lightheaded, I spun.

When the day in the studio concluded, I left my bike at the rack, hoping it would make it through the night. Too tired to bike, I dropped a dime into the cash box at the subway station, pretending it was a $2.50 token, and took the train a few stops, studying my anatomy textbook, memorizing muscle origins and insertions. In the evenings I worked at a fancy Italian restaurant, and on weekends I worked at a pointe shoe shop until five p.m., the same time when I technically started my restaurant shift, meaning fourteen- or fifteen-hour days of work. After selling dance shoes all day, I ran in from the bright summery glare of the well-off neighbourhood and ducked down the stairs into the oppressive mahogany and Frank Sinatra of the restaurant. *Only five minutes late*, I reassured myself. Black H&M $19.95 pants, black Value Village shirt, and Payless shoes on, and then into the dining room. I took coats at the door, handed out menus, and presented a pepper grinder when pastas arrived from the servers. "Seen, not heard!" and "Turn on a dime!" had been my instructions on the day the manager hired me, and I made myself invisible and efficient, as instructed. At 10:30 p.m. I brought two coats out to a table of two, and the man slipped three coins into my hand. I sighed in relief. *Subway fare.*

After I walked home from the station in the middle of the night from my restaurant shift, I drank a glass of cheap port and cracked open my computer to work on grants to perform social justice work with small grassroots charities. Three lives, stuffed into the hours for one. I filled every available corner of the day and night with productivity, and yet I still went to bed in the wee hours of the morning with my alarm set for two or three hours later, chastising myself for being unaccomplished. Hungry, tired, and broke, I repented for not managing to do more with less. I played "All I Need" on repeat, always comforted by the repetition of shows and songs until I couldn't stand them anymore. I am a moth . . . trying to get out of the night. At three a.m., I opened a box of cereal to pour myself a bowl before collapsing in bed, and small moths flew out of the box into my face. I dropped the box, and Os of cereal scattered across the already-dirty floor, rolling into corners and under the counter.

Exhaustion plagued me for years, a result of perfectionism and workaholism. A thorny and transformative decade took me from five city apartments to a rambling house on an island to that century home in a small country town. I never rested and I barely ate. My relationship to food and my hurting body changed gradually, with many false starts at healing, as if my inner wisdom and my unrelenting mind wrestled with each other. Just when I thought I'd emerged into a state of health and nourishment, I backtracked into self-induced starvation, like a tree that grows sideways to integrate a trauma. But when a tree grows sideways, looking injured, it is actually growing towards the light. Despite my illness, over a long timespan, I kept gradually growing towards the light.

Interspersed with dance training, I solo-travelled throughout Africa, Asia, South America, and Europe, visiting twenty countries in a few years. I gravitated to wild, green spaces and animal sanctuaries wherever I voyaged. In the Amazon in Peru, I found myself surrounded by birdsong amidst the towering trees. A platform in the highest reaches of a soaring hardwood tree became my bed in Ghana. The snowy evergreens of Rocky National Park in Colorado and a moss-draped, misty forest in Scotland welcomed my wanderings. I paddled alongside the clouds of green rainforest on the shores of Lake Bunyonyi in Uganda, looking up from a dugout canoe, small and safely held in the cupped hands of the universe. I reveled in the jungle habitat of Gombe Stream National Park in Tanzania, where Jane Goodall did her research. I would only understand years later how that rainforest changed my life. When I went far away from home, it was not the slate cities that captured my attention, but rather the feathered forests.

Back home between travels, I graduated from the dance conservatory, despite a traumatic injury that altered my sense of self. The injury also rerouted my life path, and I started to build a fulfilling career in fundraising and then communications, on a fast track to leading large teams in non-governmental organizations focused on poverty reduction, gender equity, and environmentalism. I still felt torn between being a professional dancer and building success in my new career, so I tried to do both, with my sanity and health as the casualties of doing too much. I spent the days in meetings talking about strategy and key performance indicators for donation campaigns, and in the evenings, I biked up the road to choreograph dance works with talented artists for residencies and tours. Rest, a foreign concept, flashed of failure. So I kept running. Through illness, through injury, through the hungry, wakeful nights.

My environmental awareness and guilt grew, me being the ideal candidate for environmental shame. Perfectionist, empathetic, stretched thin, informed. I had first learned about my personal responsibility for recycling as a child, and remembered walking around the school grounds, swinging a skipping rope above my head and under my feet in a continual loop. I called out, "Reduce! Reuse! Recycle!" to any child within earshot, as though elementary school children needed to hold the responsibility that ought to lie with the adults making decisions. Through my twenties, I learned more about extinction, climate change and waste. I watched the documentaries, read the nonfiction books, and stewed in statistics, experiencing the first waves of a crushing doom that told me hope was lost.

Through the noise of those years of repeatedly abandoning myself, hectic overachievement, and persistent guilt, trees rooted me despite my best intentions to remain rootless. My soul sought lessons from the trees, which my bristling ego wasn't yet ready to hear. Something wise and ancient in me drowned out a cruel and unforgiving part of myself, and I gravitated towards the patient, soaring trees, which were imprinted in my genetic material.

The purchase of the ill-advised house near the gas station finally fell through, and I felt free to ask the question I kept ignoring: where did I *actually* want to live my life? Trying to answer the question, I thought of all the trees I had known. The solitary elms growing out of the sidewalk in the city, the ones I kissed under neon strip-club lights, walking home from late-night restaurant shifts. Later, the eastern cottonwoods, growing on the island that would eventually force me to leave, rendering me nestless with a newborn. The lush Miombo woodlands of Gombe. These trees seeded the idea in me for years, quietly inviting me to live in the forest. My inner voice gently guided me through those years, managing to speak calmly through the frenetic busyness of my life. Whether the message came from my inner voice or an invitation extended through the roots of trees, I finally listened.

We decided overnight to move to a cabin in the woods.

Starting a new life in Québec would mean leaving our jobs and living far from loved ones, a leap of faith with no employment in hand. A conditional offer on our home mercifully came through. We handled endless logistics in a precarious few weeks, including a quick and joyful search to find the right home. I made decisions led by my intuition and my body, rather than rational thought, listening to my inner voice in a way I never had before. Scared of the unknown, the notion of staying put tempted me with its ease and safety. But the trees carefully wrapped their knowing roots around me, inviting me to return home.

The night we made the decision, I again drew a bath and climbed in. This time, the water steamed and soothed, filled with lavender and chamomile. My skin turned red as I lay in the water, sweating in its heat. I brushed out my hair, dreading the unhealthy, matted knots that formed under the back of my ponytail. They grew from neglect over the course of weeks, carefully hidden under a tidy top layer of hair, thickening every time I swept my hair into a functional bun, trying to ignore their presence. I brushed and brushed and brushed. Yanked the knots, pulled and clawed through them, working through the nest of hair with pain and patience. The only way to get through to the other side was to make a mess, to unearth the hidden knots, to shed. The once-lovely flowered bath turned yellowish from the chamomile blossoms, and long strands of hair floated around me in the sweltering water. Too hot and slightly dizzy, I leaned back into its depth, dreaming of living in the woods, which scarcely seemed real. Listening to my intuition and needs for the first time in my life offered a deep and unfamiliar relief. Revelling in a decision made for me and no one else, something caught my eye: a delicate spider softly lowered herself from the ceiling, hovering halfway between the ceiling and the floor, suspended from an invisible thread. Between two worlds, she moved up and down the silk, expertly and without hurry. Both safely held and falling freely.

"Barn swallows perform long migrations, some that breed in North America winter as far south as Argentina," write the authors of the 1977 edition of *The Field Guide to North American Birds*. "Like other swallows, they migrate by day, often feeding as they travel. They are swift and graceful fliers, and it is estimated that they cover as much as 600 miles a day in quest of food for their young."

Our migration also stretched over the miles, long and good. I covered distance not in quest of food for my young, but rather for my own happiness. I was on a quest for care, but I was also fleeing something: perfectionism, overwork, self-extraction. What is the opposite of a quest? What do you call the purposeful and beneficial fleeing of that which you know so well, but which you must abandon through a journey? Perhaps a liberation.

We moved to our shy cabin in the woods in the early autumn. The olive oak leaves turned turmeric. The heavy, rented moving truck full of our family of four's worldly possessions curved with the road and jostled down the steep hill to our hidden valley, surrounded by forest but minutes from a town, and close to a city. A romantic and rousing French song tumbled out of the radio as we drove over the culvert that passes the creek and turned left onto our road. My cells rushed with joy at the sound of the music mixing with the lilting birdsong, which drifted from the treetops' through our open windows. The birds welcomed us.

Unfolding myself and my children from the car, I walked around the moving truck and stood in front of the cabin with baby Wren on my hip. I exhaled, as though I'd held my breath for years. Maybe here, in the woods, I might begin the hard, messy work of letting go of guilt and a lifelong, destructive attachment to perfection. Maybe I could stop chastising myself for the weight of a world in crisis. Maybe here I could balance the sorrow of wildfires with the beauty of wildflowers.

I inhaled, sipping the exhalations of spruce and red oak and paper birch into my lungs. In conversation with each other, we passed breath between our bodies, my own lungs opening to the aliveness of the trees that made up this northern jungle. One particularly grand pine tree caught my eye, with paint-bristle needles and a soaring, crooked trunk that arced over our house. Two large scars marked the side of her bark, like the two long scars that marked the side of my own left arm — body evidence of that traumatic dance accident that pleaded with me to stop pushing too hard. I hoped the imperfect pine would now take care of me, offering support that I traditionally refused so vehemently, giving me breath through her needles and holding the ground with her thick roots. As my family and I extended our own roots into this gracious geography, the least I could do was learn how to take care of her, too. But I couldn't quell the uneasy question: How could I possibly nurture the Earth when I was struggling to take care of myself?

I moved to find home in the woods — but really, I needed to find home in my own body and self. I needed to find home as a welcome, good, and worthy part of an exuberant Earth.

Living in an overwhelming culture of consumption and extraction, I found myself inflicted with the destructive wounds of human systems that demanded too much productivity, and with a deeply internalized misconception that my worth came from my performance. I would have to repair what had been damaged in my own self. I would have to start new cycles, ones that take care of, and give back to, the Earth — in my own house, in my own body.

I resolved to learn everything I could about how to live in a way that aligned with nature's cycles, and to understand how that might impact my personal and planetary homes. My curiosity led me to alternative approaches to homebuilding, homemaking, consumerism, farming, food growing, clothing, and the economy. I began an obsession that would last for years, surrounding myself with piles of books, reports, and podcasts, and deciding those would not be enough: I needed to speak with farmers in their fields and homebuilders in their houses. Mine would be an eclectic learning journey rather than a comprehensive one, following my constellation of interests, with each conversation leading me to new places and people, eventually amounting to dozens of interviews with farmers, ranchers, climate activists, designers, economists, scientists, conservationists, and community leaders. I put pressure on myself to know everything, partly because of my earnest nature and partly because I felt deep responsibility on account of my privilege to be living in this home in the woods.

I would take everything I learned, and change my practices to be a good steward of the Earth. I knew that I wanted to, but I had no idea how. I decided to embark on a journey to find out in the only way I knew how: aiming for perfection, and with headlong obsession.

3

BIRDSONG CABIN
Unpacking

"Wilderness brings us back home to our bodies."
TERRY TEMPEST WILLIAMS

I fell in love with our new home the way you fall in love
with a person, a whole-body experience that awakened me,
making the world more beautiful. Our home sits on a few
acres of generous land, held together by the constant curve
of a large creek to the east. These beautiful acres lay at the
bottom of a valley surrounded by forest. The creek flows
through the culvert up at the end of the road, after which
it pools in a large, rock-bottomed swimming hole. From
there, the water spills over rocks and ridges, lapping up onto
the soggy, wild-grown banks after a heavy rain. The creek
winds back and forth, meandering messily, gliding along
a wide expanse of meadow before cutting dramatically to
the east, defining the landscape. Up from the creek, across
the meadow, and over a small hill, stands a red-roofed barn.

A workshop and garage occupy the ground level, and upstairs is a converted apartment with Wi-Fi and heat, but no running water. Over from the barn, a woodshed is half-filled with a pile of last year's logs and kindling. Twenty or so steps from that woodshed rests our small cabin.

Home became synonymous with this cabin nestled safely between the treeline and the curving creek. Soon enough, we could find our way to the bathroom in the middle of the night without bumping our shins, and we learned the locations of all the light switches. A resident ferret, apparently accustomed to the previously unoccupied state of the cabin, quickly realized that four people and three cats had moved in. After a couple of dramatic encounters with the felines, he found new lodgings elsewhere, and stopped sneaking out from under the stove in the middle of the night.

We organized the dishes in cupboards and lined the books up neatly on bookshelves, in our last week before I started a new job in a new place. We had just enough money from the sale of the old house to set up the new home with some second-hand furniture and treat ourselves to a new couch, and sustain ourselves until my first paycheque. Belongings placed on shelves, and carpets rolled out on floors, muted the lonesome echo of empty rooms. Hoisted up a flight of stairs, my grandmother's old upright piano took up residence in the apartment on the top floor of the barn. My grandfather honoured me with the piano after Nana died, and generous friends, parents, and movers carted it around on my decade-long journey from city apartment to island rental house to country century home to woodland cabin. On top of the piano, we placed our old globe, rickety on its faux-gold base, which collected dust in every home. The big dining table and oversized wooden chairs, around which we luxuriated in so many nighttime conversations, took their place between new walls for a continued tradition of meals and community and staying up past our bedtimes. We set up our broken old record player for some eventual, faraway day when we might find time to repair it. I debated where to put my best Underwoods, which I had kept from a heavy collection of typewriters that I had amassed for a dance work I'd choreographed about women writers like Sylvia Plath and Virginia Woolf. I tucked away one sacred box of old pointe shoes, legwarmers, and bodysuits at the back of my otherwise sparse cupboard. A box of the most sentimental baby onesies and sleep sacks was placed lovingly in the crawl space. I brought with me carefully selected items that meant something about where and whom I had been before. I wanted symbols from my past — music, travel, intellectual conversation, writing women, dance, motherhood — in my new life in the woods. The cabin began to feel lived in.

A one-and-a-half-storey structure, the house itself is small by modern standards, especially considering how many creatures we squeeze into its comforting walls. A red front door interrupts the rows of cedar shingles, which are starting to show their age. A main bedroom juts off the front entrance, scarcely big enough to fit our dressers and large bed which, throughout any given night, sees a mix of grown-ups, children, and cats. The dining room and kitchen are combined, and the window over the kitchen sink looks out to the barn and, beyond that, the meadow. Past the meadow you can see the creek, if the water flows high enough. The kitchen centres around an island, ideal for children to run around during that witching hour after dinner, as Nik and I enjoy the noisy pause before the bedtime routine. This is where we sit, savouring the moments of motionlessness for too long, until a child starts falling to pieces and we begin the bedtime routine thirty (or sixty) minutes too late.

The living room is both grand and cozy, with a small footprint and a soaring ceiling that acts as an umbrella over a wood stove surrounded by grey stone. Off the kitchen, a screened-in sunroom looks onto the barn and the meadow. We live in that room during warmer months, and in the winter, it stores soup and leftovers, acting as an overflow from the packed family fridge. A single grapevine that we planted grows upwards along the screen, beside a hanging bed.

"It's a daybed, not a play bed!" goes my refrain when the kids leap onto the bed and rock it back and forth with feral excitement, banging it repeatedly against the wooden wall.

Inside, a narrow, metal spiral staircase connects the living room to a small, cottage-like upstairs with slanted ceilings. In this attic-like half-storey, the children share one cozy bedroom, and their toys and books live in the other upstairs room. Because the cabin is a small space with a lot of creatures, mess and chaos seem to crawl in through the cracks in the walls. An eclectic rainbow of Keens and Crocs tumbles across the front hallway, no matter how many times I tidy them. Pale blue-grey footprints of mud trail into the house, becoming fainter as they approach the kitchen. The front hall table, my Sisyphean headache, clutters itself with sunscreen bottles, muddy hats, goldfish crackers, cheap plastic sunglasses, crumpled receipts, lichen, feathers, and treasured rocks. Next summer's clothes and less-favoured toys are stored in boxes in the backs of cupboards and in a crawl space in the corners of the roof. What the home foregoes in storage space and tidiness, it makes up for in wild places.

That first fall, I explored new spots with Owl and Wren, those two beings I thought of as the hummingbird mother's pea-sized eggs, relying on her for warmth and survival. We acquainted ourselves with the fairy tree up the road, a mammoth, moss-covered trunk of a very old tree that the municipality recently felled. The tree appeared rich with mysterious nooks and crannies, and creaked with eeriness, which transformed a walk into a mystical adventure. "I'm scared!" exclaimed Owl, and the children scrambled down in fear when the chirr of a branch and a howl of wind startled them on the top reaches of the old, spooky trunk. The fairy tree offered itself as one of many woodland delights to explore, both that inaugural autumn and over the course of a childhood. Soon enough, my children rode on a tractor when once they had ridden a streetcar. Compost-coloured leaves hanging over the creek drifted into the wandering water below, during a few fleeting weeks before winter.

The more I walked, the more I realized how long I needed until I truly knew the place. I suspected a lifetime, and still I'd be surprised by a type of wildflower that escaped my notice last year. Humbled to realize how little I knew about the forest, I could barely identify any of the trees, or the difference between coyote and wolf scat. I did not know why all sorts of birds preferred the old white pine to the branches of the cedars or paper birch. I had yet to meet my creaturely neighbours — bears, deer, snakes, herons, coyotes, and wild turkeys — but I started to notice the clues to their existence that they left around our cabin. I couldn't name most of the flora that surrounded me, but I started to pay attention. I had yet to see the seasons turn, and with them, the remaking of the land. Just when I knew this place, I suspected, the seasons would change again.

Every morning, I breathed deeply, looking out on the novel forest. My new and wild home. I surveyed the woods where spruce, cedar, oak, and birch grew freely, and I noticed how the mustard-gold glow of the sunlight dripped through their veined leaves. Their soaring trunks cast olive shadows onto drenched, autumn Earth. I looked at those trees, morning after morning, and started to observe how they transformed with nature's cycles. These lush, ecological guardians of life possessed a whole network of interconnected roots that extended deep into the ground beneath me.

With my cabin at my back, I walked up through the woods onto my neighbour's land. No one lived there. The forest up there grew wild, with few human witnesses. I started up the overgrown path, its edges lined with burdock, the tenacious burrs catching on my pant legs. My path traced alongside an offshoot of our creek, with just a faint trickle of water moving through the landscape, through the angled walls of the shallow ravine. I walked around a fallen trunk, one of many trees that criss-crossed the forest due to eroding hills and loose clay soil. Arriving at a wooden plank that connected one side of the ravine to the other, I walked cautiously across it, about six feet above the rocky ground below. Cautious and curious, finding a path to somewhere for the first time. Unsure. Attentive.

On the other side, the path steepened and my breath grew shallower. I made my way up along the side of a ridge, and looked at a basin of trees and understory to my left. What looked peaceful at first glance was a mess of life. Fallen trees, crooked roots, dead snags. Large limbs hanging from branches. Lacy lady ferns with crispy brown edges, and patches of moss with chunks missing. Scattered seeds and ripped leaves. The misshapen hole a woodpecker carved, half-filled with yellow sawdust, spilling out to the ground below. My eyes welled up. The forest was imperfect, and I loved her still.

Somehow, I could revel in the imperfect beauty around me, yet demand flawlessness from myself.

Perfection embedded its dark self in my bones. I carried the heaviness of perfection to the bathroom sink when I brushed my teeth. Perfectionism dragged me through my eating disorder, illness, injury, exhaustion, missed opportunities, voicelessness, and loss of identity. Perfection grew with me, like a tree that has grown in and around concrete, as though the cement were in fact a part of the tree. But it is not. The tree has never known itself without that hard, unforgiving surface. I, like the tree, feared I would not be able to stand without the rigid concrete. I feared that without perfection I would miss a necessary part of myself, when really, without my addiction to perfection, I might finally be whole.

I came to the top of the ridge, to an expanse of land where the trees had been cut down a couple of centuries ago. People lived up here until it was abandoned about fifty years ago. The land, in a process of rewilding, grew grasses to the height of my shoulders and small trees emerged in the relative barrenness. I swatted at the bugs in the long meadow grasses, and tucked back into the merciful forest to make my way back down to the valley. Signs of people who occupied this land in the past made themselves visible: the rotting lumber of the old family farmhouse; a fallen tree with a sign nailed to it; a rusted pop can from decades past, its dated logo and metal unyielding to the elements.

I wondered who walked over this trail before — the humans, the animals, the birds, their footprints and hoofprints overlaid on each other, in one geography and over many eras. Fur, skin, hair, feathers. Imperfect creatures, like me.

The sun set and the woods grew dim. I walked through an arbour where the path closed in and I faltered, doubting whether I could find my way home in the dusky sameness of the forest. I felt a soft shame, not knowing my way through the darkening twilight, getting lost so close to home. Someone more intrepid would be able to navigate her way. Weighing my options, I turned left, thinking I saw a soft-trodden path that might lead to the cabin. The incline of the forest became steeper, and I stumbled gracelessly down the hill, little silly steps as I lost my balance, holding onto the tree trunks for support. Night approached. The ground held me up. Afraid to let the Earth and the trees keep me standing, I couldn't hold myself up by my own shoulders anymore. I resisted it, but I needed support. I sat at the base of a cedar tree.

I saw our cabin. Smoke puffed from the chimney, like a drop of ink billowing in a glass of water, but in reverse. The living room window glowed with a warm, comforting light, framing the kids as they watched *Paw Patrol*, the saccharine action momentarily mellowing them as they snuggled. Finding my home through the pines, surrounded by the lovely, dark, deep woods, I made my own promises.

The bare bones of the forest revealed themselves, stripped clean of their leaves, their decorations. Dead trees lay in the woodshed, chopped and piled by our own hands, as tidily as two people can muster while two little ones help stack the wood. The chopped logs, collected and cut from fallen trees, waited to warm our family in the first winter in our forest home. (It made sense to me that the word *hearth* — that threshold of the fireplace, and symbol of home — holds the word *earth* within it. The word also shares an ancestral linguistic root with *carbon*.) In the quiet, undefined space between late autumn and early winter, we tried to do too much in a few short weeks, revelling in the duties of our cabin, puzzling out what activities we needed to complete before the first snowfall.

Like the seasoned woodland animals that surrounded us, we prepared for the barren months ahead. The mice moved into the barn to stay warm and build their nests. We stacked wood, aired out bedrooms, removed window screens, and cleaned out the sooty wood stove. Squirrels in the stand of pines beside our front door collected and buried a harvest to tide them through the winter months. We dried herbs from the garden, and prepared frozen stocks for soup. Bears became more reclusive, moving higher into the woods for their hibernation. We tidied outdoor toys to save them from freezing into the ground until the spring melt, swapping sand-castle buckets and Frisbees for sleds and skis. The deer and their grown daughters foraged in gardens for the hardy crops that they ignored during more fruitful summer months. We looked at our own growing children and dug out the snowsuits, hats, and mittens, taking stock of items they had outgrown. The box of outdoor wear from last year served as a time capsule, measuring my children's growth and the swift passage of time.

Before I moved to the woods, I mistakenly thought that only four seasons existed. Living in the forest, though, I watched the distinct subtleties that come forth in those liminal spaces between spring, summer, fall, and winter. When the coltsfoot leaves are still bright green but wild-flower leaves crisp and curl. When snow lies on the ground, with dried wildflowers preserved in mid-air. When night falls early and you need to bundle up in warm sweaters to go outside, but the creek flows freely for a little while longer. In-between spaces as worthy as any season. A friend later told me about the traditional Japanese calendar, which, instead of the blunt instrument of four basic seasons, has seventy-two poetic microseasons throughout the year, each only a few days long. The mist starts to linger in February, the wild geese fly north in April, the evening cicadas sing in August, the swallows leave in September, and the north wind blows the leaves from the trees in the week that knits November to December. Observing my ecosystem's specific seasons evolve in the woods, I marvelled at our massive quilt of a planet, made up of regions each with their distinctive microseasons, personal to us and our places. In that Japanese calendar, the succinct season around the winter solstice happens when an edible wildflower plant called self-heal, or heart-of-the-Earth, begins to sprout. Midwinter in the woods had me beginning to self-heal, too. Beginning.

Grey frost lay in the thinnest layer over thorny bushes and leafless branches, a pointed reminder of winter drawing nearer. The once-green meadow turned silver. Seeing the frost as a sign of hope, three-year-old Owl pressed her nose against the front window and whispered impatiently, "I can't wait until the snow flies." Her wishes must have elicited some effect, because that year, the snow flew, and flew, and flew. According to our neighbours, we saw one of the heaviest snowfalls in recent memory. The white stuff piled up at our doors and windows, and spilled over the tops of our boots.

We ventured down to Vermont to adopt Bear, the dog who later ran alongside me in the rain. Seeing his massive size and impressive paws, his name stuck. Abandoned after being a farm dog down in Texas, a foster rescued him from euthanasia and brought him up north. A regal white mane framed his head, and he boasted a grand tail and human-like brown eyes. Not housebroken when we brought him home, Bear perched terrified on a dresser, all 115 pounds of him. As we got to know him, we learned that he was a gentle and loving soul, and our loyal protector. We also learned that his wild heart sometimes called him to run away, and when it did, nothing could stop him.

We sat on the frayed blue, red, and gold living room carpet that first night he came home, weary after our trek to and from Vermont. As we let ourselves relax, a chill drifted through the house. We suddenly noticed the side door gaping wide open, with Bear escaping into the woods as snow continued to fall. Without throwing on our coats, and as our children slept unattended upstairs, we ran into the cold night and began searching for the animal we hadn't even known for twelve hours, in a forest we hadn't yet lived in for two months. After an hour, Nik tracked him down in a cave-like enclosure in the woods and dragged him back home through the creek, both of them soaked with freezing water. This was not the last time that Bear wrestled between his domestic life and the forest that surrounded us.

After Bear joined our family and returned from his escape unscathed, heavy snowfall continued unabated outside, and the dark days of midwinter descended. The sun set in the afternoon, and six p.m. felt like ten p.m. We hibernated inside, warmed by the steady fire. Smoke floated out

of the chimney, in swirls and puffs, like a signal to the surrounding woods that someone lived here again. As the kids
slept, I slipped out of the cozy cabin into the clean bite of the
winter night to take Bear for his bedtime walk. I clipped a
leash to his collar, lest he run away. We stepped into the icy
darkness, with the chimney smoke at our backs, and the tall
black mess of forest behind that. We plodded along the road:
me lost in thought, him eyeing the allure of the unkempt
woods. At the end of our road, for the first time I noticed
a wooden sign nailed to a tree. The light of my headlamp
illuminated two words hand lettered onto the sign: *terrain
privé*. Private land. Difficult to spot in the autumn because
of lush foliage, in winter the sign announced itself, clearly
visible. The words gnawed at me, made me uncomfortable,
in a beneficial way. They reminded me of my privilege to
be living here, and the suffering that occurred for me to be
here. They counselled me that this was not, in fact, private
land, but rather shared land. They asked me about my relationship with and responsibility to this place, as a white
person on stolen land.

Many creatures depended on this valley for survival,
boxed into an island of nature by the developments being
built in every direction. The sign reminded me of my new-
ness here, and that this ecosystem and its inhabitants lived
here for much longer than me. Indigenous peoples lived
here, on this unceded land, living in respect and reciprocity with nature over long arcs of time. It reminded me
that I had yet to root deeply, repair past wrongs, and prove
myself to be a worthy caretaker. My name etched itself on
the papers alongside Nik's, but the very premise of those
documents cracked as a vestige of an old, crumbling way of
thinking. A mindset of ownership, of control, of domination.

This place is terrain partagée, shared land. And I am not the benefactor: this place is shared with, not by, me.

I wrestled with guilt. I bumped up against my immense privilege, uncomfortable with being able to own a home. I moved around the world with the comfort and benefits of whiteness and "sameness" — heterosexual, able-bodied, with a finely-honed ability to operate within our dominant system. Even wrestling with my privilege, examining and reading about it and trying to learn, felt indulgent, when many people learned about oppression and racism as small children through experience, while I chose when and how to engage with it. Usually, my guilt started a spiral of self-contempt. *How did I stumble into such privilege?* New thoughts took root, though, instead of self-loathing, maybe prompted by the forest, or by the space to be myself and hear my thoughts. Instead of staying frozen in guilt, I could learn about my privilege and my place in the capitalist, white supremacist system, and how I upheld it, and then begin the hard, endless work of dismantling what harm I could. Lifelong work.

Lost in thought, I turned and walked away from the end of the road and the wooden sign. Seeing something in the dark, Bear bellowed a wild call. I planted my heels, as deeply as the frozen ground would allow, and held on for dear life to my lovely beast. Just as autumn had finally lost hold of her season, I struggled to hold onto Bear, knowing full well that an inconsequential golden chain was all that stood between him and the wilds.

I caught my breath and held the leash tight, and managed to prevent another escape. After dragging him back to the safe enclosure of the cabin, I thought about my own separation between so-called "wildness" and domesticity.

I'd followed the rules in a linear world for so long, and it was all I knew. From childhood, I learned how to survive in it, how to get good grades, how to be promoted, how to be celebrated for adhering obediently to its linear laws. I struggled to even imagine what rewilding myself would look like. Rewilding, according to the organization Rewilding Europe, means, "[L]etting nature take care of itself, enabling natural processes to shape land and sea, repair damaged ecosystems and restore degraded landscapes. Through rewilding, wildlife's natural rhythms create wilder, more biodiverse habitats." Rewilding meant returning to a more natural or wild state, and to make or become natural or wild again. What would it look like to return myself to my natural state, to my own wilderness?

Local rewilding efforts across the globe let nature take the lead on regenerating landscapes, with humans as helpful supporters. At Knepp Farm in the United Kingdom, Isabella Tree and her husband rewilded a 3,500 acre area from what had been a longstanding industrial farm. Within a few short years, harmful chemicals disappeared from the soil as it regenerated itself, and endangered animals and birds returned after decades of absence. They reintroduced grazing animals to the landscape, like longhorn cattle, pigs, and deer, with the animals' disturbances aiding the return of rivers and woods that had been tamed by past human efforts. Some rewilding proponents advocate for the return of predators like wolves to help keep balance in ecosystems. In Ireland, there are calls to rewild natural parts of the island in an attempt to restore vast swatches of temperate rainforest. Eoghan Daltun has fostered the rewilding of thirty-two acres of woodland in southwest Ireland. He called the return of native plants and trees, as well as birds and insects, an "ecological resurgence." Rewilding efforts like these show how relatively quickly landscapes can restore themselves, and how human beings and non-human animals can help shepherd in the hopeful return of nature.

—

The alluring idea of capital-W Wilderness drew me in, as it has done for many environmentalists, but I started to learn that it proved to be problematic. In *Behind the Colonial Silence of Wilderness*, Malcom Ferdinand outlined how the false notion of wilderness was created only by the forced removal of Indigenous peoples, "coming at the expense of local peoples who had been living there for centuries if not millennia." Wilderness, he showed, does not consider worldviews of Indigenous and Black peoples, and instead excludes racialized people and cultivates an imaginary place that is occupied by whiteness and dominated by men. William Cronon in *The Trouble with Wilderness* writes how wilderness is in fact a human invention, reflecting a particular moment in human — especially American — history when human beings held a particularly broken relationship with the natural world. The emergence of the notion of wilderness came alongside the myth of the frontier, including the creation of modern society, the forced removal of Indigenous people, and then the use of force and the legal system to keep inhabitants from reentering their homes. Wild spaces were upheld as places of American identity, as well as redemption and renewal from the fraught, artificial modern world. Wilderness became a playground of the urbane, white, and wealthy. It fed settlers alluring fantasies about sacredness and salvation, in the face of an increasingly destructive way of life. We romanticized wilderness as our real home.

In Cronon's words, "By imagining that our true home is in the wilderness, we forgive ourselves for the homes we actually inhabit. In its flight from history, in its siren song of escape, in its reproduction of the dangerous dualism that sets human beings somehow outside nature." Wilderness pitted humanity against nature, with the former considered a parasite and the latter pristine. Here I thought wilderness brought me closer to nature, but the concept reconstructed the problems I wanted to escape.

Cronon wrote:

> We get into trouble only if we see the tree in the garden as wholly artificial and the tree in the wilderness as wholly natural. Both trees in some ultimate sense are wild; both in a practical sense now require our care. We need to reconcile them, to see a natural landscape that is also cultural, in which city, suburb, countryside and wilderness each has its own place. We need to discover a middle ground in which all these things, from city to wilderness, can somehow be encompassed in the word "home." Home, after all, is the place where we live. It is the place for which we take responsibility, the place we try to sustain so we can pass on what is best in it (and in ourselves) to our children.

Neither Malcom Ferdinand nor William Cronon want to remove the idea of wilderness entirely. Ferdinand suggests we need to resist holding one worldview and historical experience above all others, expecting all people to follow the lead of the white experience of wilderness. He challenges wilderness advocates to recognize and engage with many cultures, theories, and histories, and to include the voices of women, the poor, and people of colour in conversations about wilderness. He says, "I simply call for the recognition of the other as one who has their own standing, as one having equal dignity of voice and power of theory in the stage of the world. In listening to these voices, the word that is powerfully cried out is not wilderness but justice." Cronon acknowledges that we learn from wild places and respects the idea of *wild nature*, but not when we alienate ourselves in relation to that nature. He calls on us to honour the wild, including acknowledging its autonomy and striving for conscientiousness in our actions. Honouring the wild means reflecting on and respecting our use of nature, choosing non-use when appropriate, and practicing remembrance and gratitude.

"If wildness can stop being [just] out there and start being [also] in here," Cronon wrote, "If it can start being as humane as it is natural, then perhaps we can get on with the unending task of struggling to live rightly in the world — not just in the garden, not just in the wilderness, but in the home that encompasses them both."

Fear visited me, threatening that if I honoured the wild in myself for the first time in my life, I might lose the identity and accolades I spent a lifetime carefully crafting. I feared losing my ability to follow the rules. Obedience and people-pleasing worked well for me, at least on the outside, and worked brilliantly for others. More powerful than my fears, though, was the call to uncover my wild natural self, by creating a culture of regeneration and care that could only start *in* me.

I started the winter eager to learn more and start living in this new way. But my body gave me different information; it told me to rest. My mind pulsed with springtime energy, while my body resisted with the dark quiet of midwinter.

In wintertime, seeds lie, unseen, fallow, and — like when we take time to rest — we wrongly assume nothing is happening. Over years of perfectionism, I'd wrongly thought of rest as a weakness, and perpetual productivity as the ideal state for human beings. Burnout and busyness gleamed as points of pride, while rest indicated laziness and defeat. Shame swelled in my body when I needed to stop achieving in order to succumb to illness or exhaustion. *It's time to rest*, my body whispered, yet still I pushed through. *It's time to rest*, it declared again and again, more adamant with every repetition. Co-creating positive cycles and new ways of being could only emerge with space to breathe and think. I could break my back striving and taking actions, but the true work had to happen in my internal wilderness, with meaningful transformation rather than superficial actions. The act of healing the damage in myself required that I first unravel the shame associated with doing nothing and see the beauty in retreat. I needed to acquaint myself with the power of rest, if I was going to do the transformative and regenerative work that called me. *It's time to rest.*

That winter, I slept surrounded by the forest as never before, tucking into bed early with profound fatigue. This fertile, tender tiredness was familiar, and I recognized the bone-deep exhaustion. I was pregnant again. My third child found me, a small being, veiled in the heart of winter. I built a home inside my pregnant womb, experiencing these concentric circles of home, from my belly out to myself to my cabin to my community to my ecosystem, and onwards.

These dwellings were like nesting dolls, distinct and individual parts of one wide whole.

This new creature, which would grow steadily over the coming months, lived as a seed unseen in the warm quiet. I had arranged my dark skirts, and reached deep into my pockets to find them full of seeds and lichen. Though I struggled to, I did not believe I deserved unconditional acceptance and care. Nested in my home, and homing in my new nest, I wanted to believe that the Earth would take me back tenderly, in all my pull between regenerative ideals and extractive behaviours, in all my uncomfortable imperfection.

4

BELONGINGS

Houses and Home Making

"You do not have to be good. You do not have to walk on your knees for a hundred miles through the desert repenting. You only have to let the soft animal of your body love what it loves." **MARY OLIVER**

The world around our cabin looked cold and bare, a brittle beauty, mostly white, with evergreen trees and the faded copper of dead milkweed that gave the landscape some subtle colour. It seemed impossible that the lush, leafy ecosystem to which we had moved would grow again the following spring, thrive throughout the summer, and turn rust-coloured again the next fall. The frigid outside crackled with ice and snow, but inside the belly of the cabin glowed with warmth. Life lay in wait under the icy top layer of the creek, under the surface layer of frozen soil, and under the soft rise-and-fall of my own warm belly.

We worked to set up our home with as little environmental impact as possible, starting with the size of the home. We know that bigger homes have an outsized effect on the environment. As a house's size increases, so too does its use of resources, the amount of land it occupies, and the storm water runoff that it produces. A smaller home that is built only to moderate environmental performance will often be more environmentally-friendly than a large home that has all the high-quality environmental performance retrofits, though they are beneficial too. The amount of square footage per family member has tripled since the 1950s, and we build and buy massive homes that are too big for our ever-smaller families, and then fill them with stuff we don't need. Renting, buying or building a smaller house are options towards a more sustainable home. More compact homes, or tiny homes, are often intentionally built, and they encourage us to limit our belongings and excessive consumption tendencies, and work more efficiently within the boundaries of nature. We had downsized from a four-bedroom house to a small cabin. Aware of how fortunate we were to have a home at all, I felt guilty that our new home, while smaller, was not tiny.

Moving to the woods also cut our driving time, gas bills, and greenhouse gas emissions dramatically by ending our commuter life. The closer our homes are to our workplaces, schools and communities, the less the environmental impact. As newly rural folk, we mostly drove, but as we watched temperatures climb upwards we also experimented with a mix of carpooling, transit when downtown, biking, and working from home. Nik rode Owl to her school in the Thule on the back of his bike, wrestling his way heroically up the steep winding hill out of the valley.

I still felt guilty, though. We continued to use two fossil-fuel cars as a part of daily life, our kids eating puréed fruit from plastic fossil-fuel pouches in their car seats. After looking into electric vehicles, we resigned ourselves to the fact that they were unaffordable for us, a family of four on one salary.

I turned inward in the home, and focused on our stuff. We passed on piles of furniture, toys, and clothing when we moved, and I felt noticeably happier and lighter with a less cluttered home. The kids seemed calmer, too. Beyond the mental health benefits, reducing stuff and excessive consumption also meant reducing greenhouse gas emissions in the creation and transportation of items, and then reducing excessive waste when we finished with items. Everything we brought into our home, every free toy given out at the grocery store that ended up in a pile on the floor, I imagined where it would be in ten years, or a thousand years. We shopped at consignment and thrift shops, and tried to limit buying new objects unless we had no other choice. Despite my best efforts, items started collecting again and spilling out of the baskets, shelves, and drawers that I kept organizing and reorganizing with Lady Macbeth-like obsession. Online photos of simple, uncluttered playrooms and flawless minimalist mothers made our home look chaotic in comparison, with our small kids' rooms cramped and colourful with the plastic treasures they adored along with the wooden toys we chose.

The zero-waste movement soared in popularity at the same time as we moved into the cabin. Zero-waste influencers, through hard work, good intentions and good advice, modelled a photogenic, unachievable waste-free practice that put pressure on people like me, the model prey for perfection and shame. I posted recipes and zero-waste cleaning tips at the same time that I learned them; they looked idyllic but I didn't measure up. I knew my unphotogenic reality, especially my inner daily panic to do everything right. We made our own cleaning supplies out of baking soda, lemons, vinegar, and Borax. They worked well, and saved money, and I genuinely enjoyed making them with my toddlers and using them. We cleaned reusable straws, silicon pouches, and popsicle molds, keeping them long after they worked suitably, with broken caps and chew marks in the straws. A pile of Ziploc bags accumulated by the sink, waiting to be washed like the pile of socks I intended to mend, and I felt guilty when either one developed a hole and I threw it out, picturing its infinite future in a landfill. We loved a local, woman-owned, zero-waste grocery shop, and frequented it for a few months, stocking our jars and brown glass bottles, before we realized we could not afford it anymore. Instead, we shopped at Costco, with its formidable aisles of plastic, and at our local farms, with their cardboard boxes of nourishing locally-grown food, emblematic of a constant tension between our values and reality.

Throughout our marriage, as we grew a family and a home while dedicating ourselves to nonprofit work, we often found ourselves in debt. We worked all hours of the day, skipping big vacations, babysitters and new clothes, but still finding ourselves problem-solving the next mortgage or daycare payment after the kids went to sleep. At times, we lived more frugally, which meant cutting all non-essentials and selling anything we could, and other times more luxuriously, which meant the nice coffee and takeout. We were not alone, with many people struggling with increasing inflation and housing unaffordability as the billionaires prospered, but like many people who struggle to make ends meet, we felt alone and ashamed as we solved yet another financial problem. I was afraid. *What if this month we could not pull it off?* I'd worked full-time, or two or three jobs, consistently since adolescence, but still always fell behind financially. Still, we tried to prioritize our ecological values, which meant practices that sometimes saved money and sometimes meant spending more. Many actions, like protesting or consuming less, cost nothing, but many actions we wanted to take felt impossible, causing guilt when we fell short. *Wasn't this our individual responsibility?* We worked to cobble together an income and navigate increasingly tighter economic realities, while working hard to spend sacred time with our babies and take care of our literal and planetary homes.

Trying to convince myself that balance mattered more than flawlessness, I struggled to believe in "enough" and still experienced guilt when I drove the gas-powered station wagon, bought food packaged in plastic, and chose the non-organic mass-produced food because the budget stretched thin. I worried about my decision to resume eating meat, and my inconsistency over the years: ten years as a vegetarian, the briefest of flirtations with veganism, and then the reintroduction of hunted meats and beef from regenerative farms. Balancing these responsibilities of environmentalism and motherhood while simultaneously leading teams and organizations at my day job wore on me. I aimed for perfection, in homesteading, work, motherhood, and environmentalism, but I would soon learn my time and energy could not be sustained.

When I first moved to the city to train to be a professional dancer at age nineteen, I lived in endless fear of falling short of the impossibly high expectations at our conservatory. We revered our teachers, and I sought their approval with my whole being. For those dancers who did fall short, a speckled brown-and-white envelope landed in their mailbox, expelling them from the program. Those who were kicked out cried in the hallways, surrounded by their dearest friends, who silently thanked the stars that they had been spared this time. Our studios and stages fostered a culture of artistry, excellence, and camaraderie, but also competition and overexertion. I saw an injured knee as a badge of honour, particularly if I could muscle through the pain. Perfection measured my worth, and as it is inherently unachievable, I considered myself flawed. Never good enough.

Anorexia consumed me. It ate me. My fixation with food and my obsession with losing weight took over my life, looming more important than relationships, health, and happiness. Only making my body disappear mattered. Cells, organs, bones — starving to death, as I attempted to become enough by becoming nothing. I lay awake at night, cold and starving, my ribs digging uncomfortably into my mattress as I struggled to make it through to the next morning without food. I willfully tricked myself, because in the morning there would be no food. Maybe I could make it without food until lunch, or dinner, or the morning after that. Pounds and sizes defined my worth, and the pursuit of losing both caused the colour to drain from my life. The thought of gaining back the weight that my body struggled to find, as it tried to survive, caused me great terror. My periods stopped appearing, and my bone mass started disappearing, sending me to an osteoporosis clinic for bone scans, along with a waiting room of women in their sixties and seventies. People complimented me for becoming smaller still, and inadvertently congratulated me for my disorder. Even when loved ones saw my illness and expressed concern, their worry became the external validation I craved to confirm my right to exist. I turned every comment into validation for my pursuit of perfection. In those hungry years, I vanished.

Dinner parties, grocery shopping, family celebrations, gatherings of old friends, and lunch breaks with colleagues felt volatile and unsafe, shrouded in lies and deep craving. I couldn't concentrate on conversations, and deceived people to keep my illness somewhat secret. My fixations with my scale and mirror told me more about my value than anything or anyone else, external validations that overrode my inner pain. Clothing, meals, photographs, conversations, and casual comments contained hidden meaning that justified my destruction of myself. Hungry, cold, and guilty, I always felt deserving of the misery I inflicted on myself.

I lived with fellow dancers as roommates, and we deepened our bonds as we toiled together to become professional dancers. One dancer, Andrea, shared four apartments over seven years with me, and we became kindred spirits. Our rentals grew progressively less derelict with every move, situated across various stops of the subway line and their streetcar veins that brought us to our homes du jour. We often saw two a.m. together, and supported each other through the bumps, breakups, family losses, decisions, and life changes that marked our twenties. The call of the city finally lost its sway over me, though I remained there. I felt penned in, rootbound, as though my existence missed something essential. Alice Vincent wrote, "A rootbound plant will push at its boundaries, come to take on the shape of the container it inhabits, even pushing out at the holes in the bottom where water is supposed to flow. They need more — more nutrients from more soil; more space to expand — in order to reach their full potential." I needed room to breathe. I planted Dollar Store seeds in the front lawn of our last apartment, but they never took root. From the kitchen table of our last apartment together, I frequently scoured rental listings for farms to rent, plotting how I could maintain my downtown life but take a train out each night to some hypothetical rambling old house, surrounded by trees. Dejected, I saw from the scant listings that a farm rental required high rent and a car, both of which were out of reach. I continued my search, wanting to find home.

While I waited for a seemingly impossible someday-dream of living surrounded by woods, I found solace in the trees of the city. On tipsy walks home after my restaurant shifts, I slowed down until I stumbled upon a relatively empty patch of sidewalk, and I shyly approached lone urban trees to kiss their trunks, pressing my hands to the cool roughness of their bark. The earthliness stood in stark contrast to the cement environment. These trees seemed like me: surrounded by concrete, light, and noise, without nearly enough space for our roots to grow.

⸻

I sat on a plastic chair outside a trailer, waiting at my dear friend Andrea's home for our visit. She and her family drove up, their van stirring up dry August dust on the road that curved around the old barn. Andrea spilled out of the red minivan and rushed towards me, as bright and doe-like as always. I greeted her with a huge bear hug, with years of history wrapped up in an embrace. A friend like this is rare.

Both of us had changed dramatically from when we first met at the age of nineteen. Once girlish, now we were womanly. We once filled every moment of our lives with coffee dates, rehearsals, and socializing in all corners of the city, whereas now we nourished ourselves in the scraps of time that caregivers find in the sacred corners of the day.

By the time Andrea and I hugged hello, her family emerged from inside the van. Her husband, Todd, three-year-old son, Sage, and one-year-old daughter, Vivere, smiled at me, while their freewheeling dogs, Bija and Uma, wagged tails and sniffed greetings. After falling in love with a plot of land that was a mix of farm and forest, this vibrant family left their home in a small Ontario town, planning to retrofit and live in the old barn on the property that used to be a working farm. Once they made the decision, their vision grew beyond the barn. Soon they broke ground on a small round home with straw bale insulation. It would be built as a circle, with the rooms oriented around a central living room. From their couch, they would be able to look up through an oculus window to gaze at the stars.

I decided to visit Andrea partly because I missed my old friend, and partly because I sensed her new home would have something to teach me about living within nature's cycles. When I visited the building site of the round home for the first time, something magnetic about the place drew me in. Apparently everyone from the construction worker hired to dig the foundation to the company representative installing the hydro lines mentioned the power of the circular structure.

When I first saw the house-in-progress on that August afternoon, the foundation had been excavated and poured, the well dug, and the water pipes installed. Wooden beams soared around the circumference of the home. The beams of the roof fanned out from the oculus at the centre of the roof, which suspended two stories above the ground. The strong bones of the thing showed. As I watched the building process over a three-day visit with my family, pieces of plywood were meticulously measured, cut into triangles, and nailed to form the roof. As I first stepped through the frame of the walls into the circle of the home, I felt comfortably surrounded, even without the walls and roof in place. Andrea took me on a tour of the house, using her powers of imagination: here was where the kitchen sink would be, here was the main entrance, here was where the bathtub would be, here was where they would build a loft for storage and guests. The small house would have two bedrooms, a kitchen, laundry room, and family bathroom. The pièce de resistance would be the living room in the centre of the home under that soaring circular skylight.

Nested into the land and surrounded by acres of field, forest, river, and meadow, the home stood as part of nature without dominating it. Relatively small, minimalist, and energy efficient, the home prioritized the outdoor space as much as the interior. Frank Lloyd Wright knew intimately about the connection between structures and the land that they occupy, saying, "Study nature, love nature, stay close to nature. It will never fail you." The connection to nature extended beyond the circular home's physical location. Straw bales insulated the home, stacked on the foundation of the walls and plastered in place.

Andrea and Todd inspired me to learn more about straw bale insulation. This type of insulation is truly circular, in that it takes a waste product and gives it a useful life. Once the edible part of a crop like wheat has been harvested, the stalk that remains can form a straw bale. Straw bales are relatively inexpensive and can cut costs while building. They do this without harming our health and polluting our air, unlike some synthetic insulation materials that include hazardous chemicals and emit pollutants into the air, posing health risks. Straw bales boast a high R-value, which means they effectively resist heat flow and insulate well, keeping a home warm during the winter and cool during the summertime. These bales also have a low-embodied energy, so that they do not take a lot of energy to produce, which lowers the emissions generated.

In the building process, the straw bales help form desirable thick walls, support windows, and can be carved into clean straight angles to accommodate the unique architecture and design of a home. When properly used they can be more resistant to fire than a traditional wood-frame house. At the end of their hundred-year life of keeping a family warm, the straw bales are biodegradable.

I learned how insulation of any kind makes a significant difference in capturing heat and coolness in a home. It can reduce a home's environmental impact, not to mention its cost. It can stop the flow of heat and energy out of the home, and the flow of money out of our pockets.

Like most circular approaches, using straw bale insulation makes sense economically, environmentally, and health-wise. Straw bale insulation is better for humans' health than other insulation materials, while also being better for the health of our planet by reducing harmful chemicals in their production, usage, and disposal. The farmer who grows the crop earns an additional source of income, the homebuilder enjoys a high-quality eco-friendly source of insulation, and waste is diverted from overcrowded landfills.

Modelling our approaches off nature's fine-tuned cycles, people can see "waste" as useful and keep it in use.

Building and living in this sort of home is the sort of monumental life change that many people daydream about, and dreamy it is, but it is not without its challenges for Andrea and her family. For about eight months, two parents, a toddler, a baby, two dogs, and one cat shared a 300-square-foot RV trailer, with the bulk of their belongings stored in rental bins at the edge of the property. They experienced frequent ambiguity, as building times were lengthened and the practicalities of building a round home with straw bale insulation came to the fore. The circular roof proved difficult, even for Todd, a seasoned carpenter and contractor. He was hands-on with all the building and did most of the work himself, along with Andrea and a skeleton crew. This meant that as he built the new home, Andrea worked hard caring for the children and preparing meals. You were just as likely to find her digging water trenches with Vivere against her chest in the baby carrier as you were skinny-dipping and making mud pies with Sage down in the river. They all pitched in and called on friends and family for help in raising the home, as was customary in the past. Some days were marked by exhilarating accomplishments, like finishing the roof or switching on the lights for the first time. Most days, however, marked themselves with delays, surprises, interesting weather, and slow-moving progress.

Andrea and Todd navigated the process of building their straw bale round home with grace. They showed an openness to the learning curves thrown their way, bringing resourcefulness, creativity, and resilience to the process. Andrea and Todd expected to move in in October, five months after they broke ground on the foundation. October became November, and November became December. Building a circular home demanded that the builders shed some of their linear thinking. Instead of sequential processes, strict timelines, and a goal of moving into the home in autumn, the whole family moved in on Christmas Eve, revelling in their new home and taking time to hibernate for that first winter. "We are slowly turning our round home from a jobsite into a dwelling space," Andrea told me in her characteristic lilting cadence. "The circle around us affects how we live."

Learning about Andrea and Todd's home opened me to explore other ways to live and build houses. Like us, they lived in a rural home with a nuclear family, a setup that is not accessible or desirable for many people, so I wanted to seek out a diversity of eco homes. My search first brought me to other types of homes in my own area. I met with Ann, an environmental economist and writer in my community who lived ten minutes from me. After working on climate policy, Ann wanted to live in a house that aligned with her values and principles, and that desire led her to build a Passive House, a type of home that heats and cools through efficient use of sun and shade. Passive Houses are built differently depending on their geography and climate, but they are always constructed to a high-performance building standard, which allows them to reduce greenhouse gas emissions and ideally withstand extreme weather. The upfront costs are typically five to ten percent more expensive than traditional home building, but utility costs fall dramatically and save money over time. While Ann's place housed a single family, larger residential buildings can be built using Passive House principles in cities, conserving even more energy because of their multi-unit architecture.

"As they say, a Passive House requires active owners," Ann

told me. "I can keep this place cool without air conditioning, but I have to put the shading on in the summer. I open the windows at night and I'm quick to close them by seven a.m. to seal in the cool air. I am very mindful of the temperature and the sun, and it means you have to be attentive to those cycles." Outside of the home, Ann introduced rain barrels to collect water and a garden for growing food. She let the meadow grow unfettered, to provide nesting places for birds.

Next, I visited another local community member to experience his green, high-performance home built out of waste materials. Bradley Robinson, a home builder, constructed the home in a mere two months, in stark contrast to the first home he built, which took six years. With affordability and waste reduction as key concerns, he insulated the home from locally available waste material, in this case Styrofoam, though he worked with cellulose in other builds. He didn't necessarily advocate for using Styrofoam, given it is made of natural (also called fossil) gas, but emphasized the importance of using what is available and practical, with the understanding that it can take an involved process to convert waste to usable building material. On top of the Styrofoam, cement finished the home. It looked minimalist and modern, with almost white clay-like walls and abundant sunlight. Like Ann's house, it held heat efficiently, though he told me it took effort to warm in our cold winters.

"The house has a high-performance building envelope," Bradley told me, and I learned that means there is a barrier between the interior of the home and the external environment. That barrier is designed to ensure energy efficiency, as well as other benefits like healthy air quality and durability. "This home uses a digester for its sanitary, energy storage, and heating systems. The sanitary waste goes into the digester, and then it goes under the building where we store energy. It breaks it down and then it comes out as fertilizer, and then I use it in the garden. So that's how it works! The site produces the water, which runs through the system back into the site and back to the well. So it's a closed loop."

He explained it to me simply, and I felt thrilled to see a closed-loop home in person, and was fascinated by both the use of waste in the structure and in the systems he used for daily living. As we talked more, I learned more about the complex system of tubes and sand filters that allowed for the separation of grey water from black water, as well as systems designed to reduce humidity, prevent mold, and a host of other complications I had not thought about previously.

Bradley thought and spoke with the big picture in mind. "There are all of these layers, and that's what I mean about how we can look at a lot of these problems differently. You know, how we're doing things. Our forecasts are not necessarily what we think they are. You know, if we're forecasting some sort of crisis, then it doesn't make sense that we shouldn't apply all of these solutions." He paused. "If we started targeting waste with an overall view of our big challenges, it fits right in, right? We're talking about stuff entering the oceans and the atmosphere. Energy, waste, biodiversity, human resources, everything: if we're not harnessing those things, and we're not making use of it, then we don't value them. When in fact it's enormously valuable. Our options are to use the remaining emerging resources that we have, or find other materials. And so all of these agricultural byproducts, industrial byproducts, all of this stuff creates this huge solid waste stream that is ideal for building products. And the built environment is the only place big enough to put all of this material, right?"

Before building this closed-loop home, Bradley spent several years living without a home, sleeping in a tent in a forested park because he could not afford rent. He cut most expenses and washed dishes at a local restaurant for food. He likened the experience to the lives of people thousands of years ago; like our ancestors, he used geography to find a good spot to sleep at night, staying close to the lake for water, but in a very specific spot where he could access the sun for warmth.

"I guess I was romantically inclined about it all," Bradley reflected. "It wasn't very realistic, though. It was hard. I've made it this far. I'm actually pretty lucky now, you know. I'm still alive, and I'm still fairly healthy. I'm eating well. I grow sprouts in the winter, and my greenhouse produces food, and I'm not doing much right now but my gardens were beautiful." He lit up speaking about the garden. "Last year I grew watermelons. They were enormous! You should see the garden grow with the nutrients coming out of the system. It produces gas, too, for cooking. And there's another part that produces hot water from the roof, and a greenhouse produces electricity from waste heat.

"Ideally, people don't necessarily need to understand it," Bradley told me, gesturing around him at the house he built and lives in. "If it meets their objectives, their needs in life, then that's the driving force. It's not about the 'environment,' because people need to do what they need to do to support their families and put food on the table and all those other things. And unless we can deal with those issues, then it's easy for me to say that and live like I do, which actually works fairly well for me, but it might not for most people."

Bradley's remarks pointed to the fact that people struggle with housing insecurity in our current affordability and housing crises, and adding the burden of a home that is environmentally sound is unfair and inaccessible to most. The onus cannot be on individuals to build inventive, efficient homes, taking on extra costs and inconvenience. Rather, the people designing policies, buying large swaths of land for development, and building homes at large scales need to incorporate a variety of practices that reduce energy usage, keep waste materials in circulation, and provide adequate, safe, affordable, ecologically sound housing for everyone.

Andrea, Todd, Ann, and Bradley showed me various options for building homes that use waste as a resource, reduce greenhouse gas emissions through efficiency, create closed loops within the homes themselves, and connect with nature. These beautiful examples of rural living inspired me, and led me to learn about Earthships, rammed earth homes, tiny homes, and shipping container houses, all of which boast small footprints. I researched green roofs and rain gardens, which could be added around the home to absorb rainwater, reduce flooding, cool the surface temperature, and attract pollinators.

I explored approaches to houses in other contexts outside of my rural reality. One concept, fifteen-minute neighbourhoods, provided a model for more sustainable living in cities that went beyond the house or apartment to the community. Residents could access services and shopping all within a fifteen-minute walk from their home, inherently reducing dependence on cars and fossil fuels, supporting active lifestyles, and fostering more vibrant and fun neighbourhoods. Some critics said the idea was unrealistic in North American cities, while some people worried about a good idea being usurped to restrict freedom of movement. Others said the concept was simply a rebrand of good urban planning ideas that had been recommended for decades. Like the transition to more sustainable houses, the adoption of fifteen-minute neighbourhoods required decision-makers to show courage and conviction, and to protect the needs and rights of individuals rather than big businesses.

The last approach to homes I found looked not at building houses, but rather at taking them apart. Unbuilders in British Columbia meticulously deconstructed homes, salvaging the old-growth timber and other materials from the home. By saving whole houses from landfill, they reduced waste and the associated methane emissions. Homes could be built again with the precious materials, giving them another life while they housed a new set of people. Unbuilders, like fungi that compost dead matter to turn it into soil, formed an important part of an ongoing cycle.

As I set up my own belongings in our cabin, I wanted to treat the surrounding woods with that same stewardship. This desire came from a more intimate relationship with the land around me. When I stood in the cabin kitchen and ran water from the tap, which came from the well, which came from the creek, I couldn't help but notice the connections between my house and my ecosystem. When I took a shower and looked out of the window at the trunk of the soaring pine tree that grew two feet from the bathroom's exterior wall, I couldn't help but imagine the roots that grew under my very feet. To be made and sustained, our homes rely on the planet to draw resources, and when we are done with these same homes, they have an impact on the planet in how they are deconstructed and how their materials are either repurposed or wasted. The four walls that we live in are an extension of our ecosystems, and they interconnect with our planetary home. Living in the woods, I felt safe and held, as though I belonged somewhere.

5

THE BORROWED
NEST AND THE OWL

Regenerative Farming and Soil

"The soil exists in a state of constant change, taking part in cycles that have no beginning and no end." **RACHEL CARSON**

My baby and my belly grew. My hard-won recovery and healing around my body meant that I savoured the swelling of my physical body, creating a nourishing home for my third child. With my first pregnancy, I worried the dramatic weight gain would send me back kicking and screaming into my eating disorder, and to my surprise I took joy in my bigness, and in seeing the steady growth of a healthy baby reflected in my own body. The softening curves of my arms and face instilled in me a desire to model health and well-being to my babies, so they might never know hunger and shame. I grew and he grew and we grew.

In the middle of the night, I kissed my two children as they slept in their beds, climbed into a cab, and went to the airport. I flew to Colorado. Unrelenting nausea was my travel companion, but my purpose — to conduct a two-day interview with famed economist, author, and regenerative rancher Hunter Lovins at her ranch — propelled me forward.

Hunter influenced me before we even met, and I was compelled to seek her out in person. When I flocked to the woods at the insistence of my inner voice, I also listened more closely to an inner call to be a better steward of nature, and this led me to leave my career in international gender equity to land in environmental economics. While I knew a lot about international development, communications, and social movements, I knew next to nothing about economics, so I turned to books. I read Hunter's books, and listened to her interviews, as I worked to learn more about alternative approaches to economics that work within nature's boundaries. One of her podcast interviews in particular affected me, in which she talked not about supply chains and market signals but rather about soil. Hearing her talk about her work as a regenerative rancher was the first time I had heard about farming in a way that gives back to the soil. The hope of it all left me speechless: we had the capacity to give back and solve many of our environmental challenges by nourishing the soil. Amidst the reports and tomes filled with doom and destruction, soil offered solutions. Salvation, perhaps. That one interview spurred me to learn everything I could about regenerative agriculture, and to fill my shelves with books about soil. I learned that by taking inspiration from nature's cycles, hooved animals and human beings together build up healthy soil that holds carbon, reduces climate change, limits erosion, and grows healthy food. For millennia, Indigenous and Black farmers have practised regenerative agriculture, but my eyes opened to that later.

With a couple of wide-open days in Colorado before I would meet Hunter, I drove past places like Larkspur, Black Forest, and Happy Canyon on the way to Rocky Mountain National Park. I cut through the Colorado landscape on the grey highway, surrounded by lavender mountains and soaring red rocks. In impractical boots and too-thin mittens, I walked quietly through the snowy forest, getting lost enough to feel frightened and safe at once. Dusk fell and, just as I grew comfortable in the park, I knew I had to leave and find the place where I would sleep that night. When I travel alone, I always cycle through a rhythm of finding a place of comfort and then forcing myself to venture out again. In my car, I skidded on the ice on the steep downhill curves coming out of the park, grateful that the lady at the rental agency convinced me to rent an suv with four-wheel drive. There at the airport the southern air pulsed with sun, but up here winter persisted, like the ones that I knew but with an exotic mix of trees. Thousands of miles away from my small children, in the unsettling unfamiliarity of being alone, I constantly felt as though I'd forgotten something important. I missed Owl and Wren to the point of pain, while at the same time an electric freedom crept in through my longing to see them. I revelled in the joy of stopping spontaneously for tacos, slowly sipping hot coffee, easefully moving from one place to another, or reading and writing for hours with quiet focus. Life on my own rhythm.

In the dark, I found my rented solar-powered bunkie on the suburban edges of Boulder. The place boasted a small wood stove, an eclectic collection of books, and healing remedies prepared by the owner of the adjacent house. The simplicity of it hummed electric: my carry-on suitcase, a couple of dishes to wash before bed, a handful of carefully selected items in the fridge, the day's clothes folded tidily as a precursor to unfolding my pajamas. A busy working mother artfully playing the part of a lone traveller for a few sweet days — simple, sane, calm, quiet. I climbed into bed, nervous about interrupting my introvert's bliss in the morning, when I would leave the solitude of the bunkie to meet the rancher-economist.

One of Hunter's colleagues picked me up in her suv after my night in the bunkie, and we greeted Hunter at the airport, where she landed after a flight back from a speaking engagement in Asia. If the pregnancy wasn't already making me nauseous, the thirty times we circled Denver International Airport made me ready to crawl out the car window. Mercifully, the circling stopped and my discomfort dissipated when we saw a woman walk out across the tarmac towards us. Hunter Lovins looked exactly as I pictured, based on the photo on the dust jackets of her books and the gravelly drawl of her voice in interviews. A rancher personified, she wore an unapologetic black cowboy hat and a prominent belt buckle. A bolo tie tipped with aiguillettes fastened her crisp button-up shirt at her neck. She completed her look with a toothpick hanging out of the corner of her mouth. She greeted me warmly with southern charm and gracious politeness, and I was taken aback by how much attention and time she gave me, an unknown and eager writer.

We left the airport and surrounding sprawl, and drove up into the mountain towards Vail, where Hunter would make the next stop on her book tour. She told me tales from the front seat, while working on a laptop to create a presentation for the evening's speaking engagement. We drove past towns like Silverthorne and Wildernest, and mountains with names like Copper, Silver Plume, and Tenderfoot.

Bighorn sheep stood in fields as we drove to higher altitudes, and snow crept in as the roads wound around mountains.

I saw a bison, standing broad on snow-wrapped mountains. I later learned about the thirty million bison who used to live in North America before they were hunted to near-extinction. Majestic creatures, brought to their knees by humans with guns only a century or so ago, in a genocidal attempt to eliminate the food of Indigenous peoples. The more I read, the more the image of the buffalo I'd seen defined itself in my mind. His hulking frame stood out against his wide-sky habitat, fur imprinted with mud and dust, as his dusky eyes gazed from under battle horns at rest. He browsed on willows and cottonwoods, a ways from his herd, pressing sedges hard between his ungulate cheeks. His broad craggy body, an escarpment of muscles, laced together with fourteen or fifteen ribs (how could I possibly count as we sped up the highway?), and his whole anatomy bristled with long shaggy hair. His hooves stood steady, designed for this terrain. I thought of his ancestors, millions strong, with their sage woolly faces lost to history at settler hands. The record of their bones written in the earth, beneath our feet, beneath our roads, beneath our cities. A story of a species disappeared, written under Yukon ashfall and Wisconsin glaciation. Longhorn fossils were discovered in snowmass, and bison stories were told in paintings in caves. Red shoulders dripped across stone walls. Settler ancestors slaughtered them by the millions in less than a hundred years, shooting whole herds from the roofs of trains on modern railroads, which crossed the land in proud domination. We piled their skulls in mounds as tall as buildings and forced them to extinction. *Near* extinction, except for a few hundred individuals who became ancestors to the animal I saw, standing broad on snow-wrapped mountains. As though they were buffalo stories dug up from the earth, their fossils discovered and filled with oxygen. Revered paintings peeled off cold walls to lumber bravely out of the caves, to once again graze along a highway in Colorado, up in the mountains, rebounded from extinction.

In Vail, I sat shyly. Meeting new people makes me nervous, and meeting *groups* of new people makes me slightly terrified. Hunter spoke with conviction to residents dedicating their evening to gather in community, trying to protect their mountain ecosystem and rise up to the role of stewards of their local ecology. She stayed after her speech, talking with attendees and signing books, despite the international flight and hours-long drive that brought her here, and the drive back down the mountain that awaited her. We grabbed a late-night dinner from a gas station on the drive back to Boulder, and I felt guilty for the plastic water bottle, chip bag, and plastic clamshell of veggies that I used briefly and tossed in the garbage. Pregnant, exhausted, and hungry, I acted like a good modern consumer, chastising myself for my individual actions.

The next morning, I met Hunter in Longmont at a diner that looked like someone's house. Owned by a woman named Debbie, the red exterior needed fresh paint, with a narrow wooden porch out front that projected into the parking lot. A black sign hung from an iron rod at the side of the building, with yellow lettering that read *Crane Hollow Cafe* above the silhouette of a crane in flight. The diner specialized in eggs prepared a variety of ways, as well as biscuits and gravy, with hot drip coffee offered liberally from a pot brought to diners at our small oak tables. Creamers sat on the table alongside the classic diner breakfast condiments, but Hunter asked for real cream, which then came from the kitchen in a small, white ceramic jug. She was obviously a regular. Over our greasy spoon breakfast, we related to each other about atavistic connections to our respective ancestors when we visited Scotland. We talked about the origins of the circular economy, cowboy ethics, horses, cities, and nature. After we settled the bill, we drove towards her ranch — she in the unlikely rancher's choice of a compact electric vehicle, me in a rental gas-powered suv. As we drove from the cafe, she pulled over unexpectedly and I followed suit. Hunter pointed out the rookery of crane's nests that gave the road the name of Crane Hollow Road.

Sandhill cranes stand large and graceful, with long, dripping wings. A quick search online labels them *not extinct*, a worrying classification term — should they not be *living*? As though *extinct* and *not extinct* represent the only two options. The birds look almost painted, with a brushstroke of charcoal grey along their white necks, and a patch of red on their pearl-coloured faces. A handsome bustle of rust feathers decorates their bodies. Searching from the side of the road, I could not spot any of the birds. In winter, they resided further south. My imagination, though, conjured them here in warmer weather, with Crane Hollow Road bisecting their habitat. The cranes' long beaks pecked and prodded, moving back and forth over berries and acorns in the grasslands, and over insects in nearby riverbeds, soft fruit bodies pressed flat and delicious on their hungry tongues. Their long legs stepped delicately in wetland muck, the soaked earth forming a satisfying soup that squished across their webbed feet. Calling across the landscape, they declared flight, and sometimes they chanted duet songs. Large flocks searched relentlessly for open space, swivelling feathers on their heads, expanding and contracting the skin on their faces and changing colours to communicate. Downy chicks purred for their parents, who painted their feathers with mud, desperate to hide their fragile young in these hard-won rookeries. Sometimes they built new nests and other times they worked diligently to repair old ones that lasted for decades, using cattails, willow branches, sedges, and grasses from this roadside home to construct or rebuild these first homes for their babies.

We left the rookery and my imagined cranes, and continued driving to Hunter's ranch. Her solar-powered home, like the electric vehicle she drove up to its front door, seemed at odds with the stereotype of a rancher, while also reflecting her values as an award-winning environmental economist. The ranch house itself began with a narrow entrance hallway, where I left my boots to melt snow onto the tile floor. Her partner, Rob, soon after told me, "I tripped over your boots," and when I quickly apologized, he chided me, "You can just keep them on. That's why the house is so messy." The trappings of ranch life adorned the walls and shelves: copper mugs, horse reins, thick blankets, cowboy hats. The home offered refuge for human beings and animals alike. People outside of Hunter's family who needed shelter and community found a home here. Rescue dogs lived their lives on the ranch, too, with one particularly old dog lapping at his bowl of water loudly throughout our conversation. In her barns, Hunter rehabilitated horses that faced slaughter, and then rehomed them when they were ready. Hunter said to me, "I could not live without horses in my life. Without cattle, without puppy dogs, cats, all the critters that we have around. So I've arranged my life to have this home ranch."

She and I sat at her kitchen table, and we talked. I kept expecting her to interrupt me and drawl apologetically that our time was up, but her gracious gift of time continued. She shared stories about the roots of the circular economy, and about her decades of alternative economic thinking — long years in which her ideas that had been radical twenty years ago became common sense in many circles. I asked her if these decades discouraged her.

"Yes, it has been discouraging," she admitted. "I've been at this for a long time. You've got to ask, why the hell haven't we handled this a long time ago? Now it is abundantly clear that we are in a climate crisis. We are in an inequality crisis, which is causative of social collapse across millennia. We're in very serious trouble losing the insect populations, losing biodiversity, exceeding the planetary boundaries, failing to meet basic human minimums, 97 million people on the move. Those are staggering numbers. And the scientists saying the Mideast will be too hot to be habitable by 2040. Where are all those people going to go?"

In addition to questions, she had answers, too, in the adoption of renewable energy, a topic we discussed at length. "I mean, we are all going to die one of these days, but not today," she said, with a wry humour that I started to recognize as characteristic. "And we know how to solve this energy problem, and do so at a profit." She also offered hope with the idea that had first inspired me to leave my cozy cabin, fly pregnant to Colorado, and spend my precious vacation days interviewing a stranger. "You then add in regenerative agriculture," Hunter insisted. "And we solve the other half of the climate crisis at a profit by pulling carbon out of the air, putting it back in the soil."

Before I met Nik, I tolerated rocky relationships in which I searched for the wrong things, gave too much, and stayed too long. Heartbroken from one such relationship, I wrote on a piece of paper that I needed a partner who showed me warmth and reciprocity. Soon after, I attended a pizza party where I socialized and ate, well into my recovery. I met Nikolas, a very tall man in a flannel shirt with a large beard and a glint in his eye, who shared my love of language and nature. Nik, the consummate outdoorsman, loved rock climbing, paddling, skiing, and cycling. The most confident person I'd met, he seemed to be good at everything: baking bread, cooking, fixing and making things. He even beat me at Scrabble, to my great dismay. One night only two weeks into dating, we set out on our bicycles and rode along Toronto's busiest streets, and he led me on a meandering path that ended up at a concert hall: he surprised me with ballet tickets. Another time he picked me up in the lobby after a dance performance of a piece I choreographed. A van waited outside, several kayaks strapped to its roof. I climbed into the van, took off my fancy clothes, pulled on fleece outerwear, and wiped off my lipstick. We drove through the night and spent the next ten days kayaking on tumultuous waters and camping on the craggy shores of Lake Superior. We shared art, language, and nature, and otherwise were opposites when it came to most things. His practicality contrasted my emotional nature. His steadiness balanced my storminess. He was highly social, I was introverted. Mostly he showed himself to be caring and warm. We navigated a few months of dating and finding our rhythm together, and then we fell in love. We began building a life together.

A room rental opened up in a house on Ward's Island, south of Toronto. I broke my lease, and we lugged my grandmother's piano, my cats, my library of books, and my heaving typewriter collection on a ferry across the lake. The house creaked with history. I felt reverent in its silence and candlelight, with the thousands of communal meals enjoyed there and the conversations seeped into the pores of the walls. Oversized chairs that seemed to swallow you up surrounded a wooden dining table, around which you poured another glass of wine and engaged in thoughtful conversation over the sound of waves lapping at the shore through open windows. At night, I tiptoed past the bedrooms of my two roommates, en route to my bedroom that overlooked the lake. A nautical bulkhead light in a metal cage shone down from the wall behind my bed. The home looked more like a ship than a house, with a curved wall with large windows overlooking the steely charcoal lake. Upstairs, a tub sat under a large skylight, and on stormy nights I watched the trees bend over the house as rain pelted the window above me, a thin layer of glass separating the stars and the rain from a watery human being in awe.

I first listened to the whispers that told me I wanted to live a different way on that island. Perhaps relatedly, I first grew food in that place. I experimented with starting carrots and nasturtiums from seed for the first time, stunned when those first signs of seedling life broke through the soil. Small, eager shoots grew out of coconut fiber coir pots that stood in rows, covering our dining room table. The backyard garden soon brimmed with kale, peas, herbs, and tomatoes, all spilling out over the sides of raised garden beds, steamer trunks, and a bathtub my roommates filled with soil for growing food. A motley assortment of containers, nests for new life. I experienced great joy when Nik pulled our first eccentric carrots from the ground.

Beyond the garden, lake water lapped at the dock. Beyond the lake, the city skyline dominated the horizon. And beyond downtown sprawled ever-growing developments over what used to be rich farmland, and before that, forest and wetland. A ten-minute ferry ride separated the island from the city. I boarded the boat at the edge of the lake, leaving my tightly-knit community nestled amidst trees to go to work. Minutes later, I stepped into the Financial District, rattled by a daily culture shock. I held my breath, the noises and lights causing me to jump, overstimulated. At the end of the frantic workday, I blissfully exhaled when the ferry carried me back home.

Living on Ward's Island gave me a sense of belonging and abundance that I'd never before experienced. The place awakened my cells. Friends raised concerns about the cold cross-lake commute in the winter, or the curfew-like schedule of the last ferry at eleven p.m., but I didn't care. I revelled in crossing the lake, the quirky hippy community, the wintry quietness, and the connection with nature. My gut told me that I had found the right place for perhaps the first time in my life, finally surrounded by trees. Basswoods, elms, and ash created a feeling of home. The eastern cottonwoods released white ethereal fluffs every year, which carried across the island on the wind, like oversized dandelions letting their bristles fly. The grand willow provided shade for decades, and now provided shade for me.

I built a relationship with those trees, and welcomed their motherly presence when I prepared to become a mother myself. Three weeks after Nik and I got married in a field of lavender on the summer solstice, I became pregnant for the first time. I peed on a stick in a coffee shop bathroom on King Street, told Nik the news with disbelief before his work shift, and then went to a music festival. On the night that I found out I would soon be a mother, I lay awake in my sleeping bag in the middle of a field of tents, and dreamed that my child would be named after an owl. In due time that became her middle name — fitting, as she, like the barred owl, can only be truly seen by those who seek her out in dark retreat. As my Owl grew within me, one half of myself remained in the bars, theatres, and apartment parties across the lake, where I glittered with my late-twenties lifestyle. I pressured myself not to change with my growing maternity, a result of my internalized capitalist and patriarchal notions that we shouldn't let motherhood make us bigger, softer, or less productive. Another soft and insistent part of me nested peacefully in my island home, where I sometimes let myself succumb to nausea and exhaustion, but more than that, to the intimate beauty of expectant motherhood.

That winter, the icebreaker ferry cut through the expanse of ice across the surface of the lake. Looking out from the bow of the boat, a sense of adventure filled me, with the rich black emptiness in front of me and my growing child inside of me. The boat cut the frozen strata of the lake into massive triangles of ice, and the deep cracks filled with inky water as large floats scraped alongside the hull. The deafening noise made conversation with my neighbours impossible, causing us to settle into comfortable silence, bundled in scarves, cloaked in community. With the brightness of the city skyline at my back, I looked purposefully towards the dark island, lit only by wintry starlight and the occasional square of a glowing living-room window.

The birth of Annaliese Alice Owl broke me wide open, in the most beautiful and transformative way. In childbirth, the only way is through, and then there is no going back.

You leap into a dark, unknown sky, leaving on the ground parts of you to die, unsure of what will remain or emerge. When she made me a mother, she brought with her a flood of the unending bigness of the universe. When the spring equinox passed and we stood on the bridge between aging winter and newborn springtime, I held her to my naked chest for hours, marvelling at her wisdom and radiance. Her earliest weeks are the most vivid days of my life: I can still smell the inside of her co-sleeper, I know the sensation of putting a onesie on the precise shape of her little body, folding the second-hand diapers lovingly under the crusty curl of her belly button, which healed slowly from that moment of physical separation from me. I can see clearly the many-coloured tulips that people brought me in celebration of her birth. I can feel the pain in my neck and the persistent headache caused by staring down at her for hours, seeing a wondrous being worthy of adoration, and realizing that maybe I am, too. In bed, I observed her sleeping face like a piece of art, full of vulnerability and beauty. I knew her already: I'd known her forever. Love coursed through my body like water running up through the roots of a tree and out through the veins to every single leaf.

When our landlady told us that she was selling our rental and that we needed to leave, we found ourselves priced out of the city, like so many people in our generation. I felt betrayed and homesick for the house I was preparing to leave, with a mere couple of months to find a new place for our small family. Being home-insecure with a newborn devastated me, and as post-childbirth hormones coursed through my body, I faced treatment for precancerous cells in my cervix, while also resuming working full-time when

Owl reached just six weeks old. Heartbroken to return to work so soon, I explored every possible avenue but could not afford to stay home with my baby. I wondered where I would live next, and how I would do it all. I didn't want to leave the island home and the trees that I loved so deeply, yet we couldn't afford to go back downtown. Begrudgingly, we packed our boxes, in the moments between working and breastfeeding. I taped closed the envelopes of unplanted seeds, and I placed the dormant life in boxes to be opened in some foreign home at the end of an unwanted move. I looked at the seeds and packed boxes, a mother bird without a nest for her young.

————

"You can't see it now because it's covered with snow, but when we moved here in 2003, this was bare dirt," Hunter told me as we sat around her dining room table. She gestured to the land that surrounded her home as she recounted the story of her regenerative journey. "This was dry land ranching. There is an irrigation ditch that goes through, but every drop of the water is owned, and if you don't have the right to that water, even though it runs through your property, you can't use it. So everything we've done has been with no irrigation and it's entirely been through conscious grazing: the grazing animals eat grass, the roots, slough, the polysaccharide sugars. And then those sugars feed the microbiological community in the soil. It was bare dirt, and now you walk out in the pastures, and there's *grass*."

I first found out about regenerative agriculture a few short months earlier, and the more I learned about it, the more an unfamiliar and exhilarating sense of hope stirred inside me.

"Any smart farmer isn't growing corn or cattle or whatever is above ground. They're growing *soil*. The essence of agriculture is the life in the soil. Modern agriculture thinks of soil as dirt. You try to sterilize it. And then you pour artificial chemicals, fertilizers, herbicides, and pesticides on it, and you try to kill everything except whatever plant it is that you're growing. And you genetically modify the seed for that chemical treatment, so that it won't get killed by the herbicides. You pour carcinogens on it, so we have been poisoning ourselves and we've been poisoning the soil. As a result of all this, the United Nations is now saying we have sixty more harvests before the Earth can no longer support the children who are alive today."

Without thinking, I touched my stomach, where my third child grew quietly, now about the size of a fig. *Sixty more harvests.*

"We'll see that point in time, unless we change. Because we know how to grow healthy soil. Here on my ranch, for example, all of our horse manure goes on to the ground. The horses eat the grass, they fertilize it, and their hooves chop it up. And then we move them off that particular patch until it's recovered. We keep cover on the soil as much as possible. If we have to, we spread old hay, or now that we've got grass coming up, we try to ensure that we keep grass on the soil. We don't let them graze it down to bare dirt. And we keep roots in the soil. The roots are what are feeding all of the little critters that live in the soil, but particularly the mycorrhizal fungi, the interconnected network of life that connects fungus to the roots of plants. They seem to be key to fixing carbon in the soil. It's what mineralizes the carbon."

Hunter took a quick phone call about a corporate merger, adding commentary to me about a big company that faced an existential crisis because its investors were questioning their lack of sustainability. Her dog nudged me whenever I stopped petting her, and Hunter told me to tell her to go lie down, and then continued telling me about carbon.

"This ranch is part of a new citizen science effort to measure our carbon. What I've got to do is find a chunk of land, maybe my neighbour's ground, where they're not doing regenerative agriculture, and measure their carbon to see how it compares to our soil, which through our methods is effectively storing carbon. I need to measure the carbon that we have now, and then over the following ten years. What's thrilling is that there are about thirty-five of us in the Boulder Valley who are now doing this. So this notion that what you're really doing with agriculture is growing soil is starting to spread, and just in the last two years! I first got onto this in about 1985." She had been doing this since the year that I was born.

"The best peer-reviewed science shows that not only does it fix carbon in the soil, but it enhances the profitability of the ranchers who were practicing it. Gabe Brown, a farmer up in North Dakota who was going broke, was trying to grow corn soybeans the conventional way. And he said, because I'm going broke, I'll try anything. His family had no choice. They could leave the land or they could cut their costs. So, what did he do to cut his cost? He stopped breaking the soil. Then he went to planting cover crops, deep-rooted plants that would then take the carbon and the other nutrients deep into the soil. He realized that there is plenty of nitrogen in the air, because plants fix nitrogen. If you have the right plants, then you don't have to buy artificial nitrogen, right? You don't have to pay for the costs to run the machinery to till the soil. You don't have to pay for the herbicides, fungicides, and pesticides, because the plants do that themselves. And then he drills seeds. He's still growing corn, soybeans, oats, and a variety of cover crops, as well as tending cattle, sheep, pigs, chickens, and their eggs. He even does agritourism. His business is wildly profitable. And in some of his paddocks, he has gone from a little over one percent soil organic matter to now over eleven percent."

"What about grazing animals and their role in regenerative agriculture?" I asked Hunter, recalling the topic that first led me to her.

"It's called holistic management. The thesis is that what you need is dense packs of grazing animals in nature. If you've got a lion trying to hunt a wildebeest, the safe place for all the wildebeests is in the centre of the herd. So they pack up and they're all trying to get into the middle. They eat everything, their hooves chop up the soil, and they fertilize it. They can't stay on that patch of ground because they've fertilized it, so they move on to the next patch of ground, and they do the same thing. And they just keep moving all across the Plains of Africa or the steppes of middle Europe or the steppes of Mongolia, wherever the world has had grasslands.

"Our land has co-evolved with grazing ruminants, and it is this mowing and mobbing that allowed grasslands to become the world's second-largest carbon sink, after the oceans. And the oceans are apparently becoming exhausted as a carbon sink. They're now starting to give up carbon and the oceans are turning acidic because of the creation of mild carbonic acid. The world's grasslands are our hope, if we are to reverse climate change."

I interjected. "We need many solutions, but it seems like regenerative agriculture and holistic management are major solutions. So why aren't they happening more widely and taking root? What is holding us back?"

"Habit," she replied. "People say, 'I've never done it that way. I don't know how. Oh, my God. I got to put up all this electric fence. I just turned my cows out.' And what has happened heretofore is that farmers and ranchers have changed when they have no choice. Right now what's starting to happen is, as people like Gabe Brown go around sharing their story, other farmers and ranchers are starting to say, 'Maybe I could do that too.' And consumers are starting to demand this stuff, because it's healthier. Farmers who have integrated systems are showing what is possible. You graze the cattle and they have big clumps of manure. You turn the pigs out, who root the ground and break up the manure. Then you bring the chickens through, and they eat all the bugs. Nature. Nature! It's the way the system has always worked."

"We were stewarding a thousand acres of ground, and we actively managed the land," she continued. "There is this notion that people are evil and therefore, the way you manage land is to get off it, right? That is not true with Western rangeland. If humans have impacted it, it will degrade to a lowest common denominator. Maybe over hundreds of thousands of years, it will rebuild, because nature is amazingly resilient, but what we did was come in and use the tool of holistic grazing to begin repairing the land and soil. And we have endangered species reappearing that hadn't been seen on the land in twenty years. We reversed the erosion. We reversed the desertification and the invasions of noxious weeds. You ask yourself, what's the purpose of managing this piece of ground? And you then pick the tools that allow you to achieve your holistic goal. And you then operate the land consciously. You understand that piece of ground because you've studied its ecology."

I nodded. Reading about regenerative farming practices gave me hope, but hearing these stories from a rancher on the earth that she had helped restore to health made that hope real. The talk about rich soil and the return of vanished species came to life.

"This narrative where we say humans are evil and not a part of nature is destructive," I added, hoping I had it right. "We need to picture ourselves not as the enemy, but as a part of nature working with her."

"Yes," she agreed. "And learn from nature, and co-evolve as we have for a very long time."

Much later, I encountered related wisdom about land management and our human goodness in Lyla June's profound TEDx Talk, *3000-year-old solutions to modern problems*. The Diné musician, scholar, organizer, and cultural historian spoke about four Indigenous land management techniques, the first being working with nature, such as growing food at the base of a watershed to receive monsoon rains. The second was expanding habitat, such as through the use of fire to expand grasslands in a way that grows topsoil and also attracts animals like buffalo. Third, decentring human beings was critical, so that instead of hoarding for our species, we nourish a web of life. Finally, systems should be designed for perpetuity, so that they last for millennia; rather than planning for fiscal quarters or even a lifetime, the systems we create should be designed for the benefit of many future generations.

Lyla was clear that mimicking Indigenous practices is not the answer, though her stories can offer hope and inspiration. She also talked about how European settlers came across food and land managed by Indigenous people as they expanded westward, and failed to understand or respect what they saw. "They often mislabelled them as *terra nullius*, or 'virgin land,' or wilderness," Lyla explained to her rapt audience, "instead of what they really were: living heirlooms, thousands of years in the making."

"The Earth may be better off without certain systems we have created, but we are not those systems. We don't have to be, at least," Lyla June said, smiled, and continued. "What if I told you the Earth needs us?" This is the part of the video that gave me chills. "What if I told you that we belong here? What if I told you I've seen my people turn deserts into gardens? What if these human hands and minds could be such a great gift to the Earth that they sparked new life wherever people and purpose met?"

Thinking about human beings, and myself, as *good* for the Earth became a lesson I held close, a gem unearthed along my quest.

Hunter and I left the dining table, and walked outside towards the barn. She introduced me to her horses, and we prepared to say our goodbyes before I flew home.

"When I come home to Colorado," Hunter told me, "I climb off the airplane and smell the Colorado air. That cold, crisp air that rolls down off the mountains. And then I come here to the ranch, where most of what you see is not human-made. And when the weather's nice, I saddle my horse and ride west up into the hills, right up into the high country, right up to the continental divide. I pull some brook trout out, and fry them up. It's a good life. It's beautiful."

I drove from Boulder to Denver, torn about leaving my quiet, pensive days with Hunter to return to the responsibilities and balancing acts that awaited me. But I missed my Owl and Wren with the force of my whole body, missing their molecules, eager to hold them. As I flew north, I looked down at the patchwork of fields that knit this city to the next one and the next one. After my conversation at Hunter's ranch, I knew more about the soil that lived and breathed under those fields. A world of organisms and mycorrhizal fungi fed the roots of plants and fixed carbon so that it did not escape into the atmosphere. The soil did not divide neatly into the rectangles of soy and corn that peeled away under the wings of the plane, but rather it stretched in every direction, interconnected across landscapes. I left determined to learn more about soil when I arrived home, not from the pages of books but from the farmers in my new community and from the soil that surrounded Birdsong Cabin.

Drifts of snow met me when I arrived home. Snow is water holding its breath, a calm pause after a deep inhale, waiting for that great exhale of spring when, instead of air, water rushes forth with relief. I found it hard to believe that a person could ever drop a seed into this hard and frozen earth and see green life break forth. Planting seeds, though, is an act of hope, and so is dreaming of a garden in the snowiest of winters. Rooting around in the still-packed boxes that had been relegated to the barn, I unearthed the small envelopes that had been sealed shut in my earliest weeks of motherhood on the island. This assortment of seeds, of questionable age and vitality, were from my first garden, wedged between a ship-like home, a lake, and the skyscrapers of the Financial District. The seeds of carrots and nasturtiums waited patiently to express themselves, but they would have to wait a few months still.

I, on the other hand, grew impatient as always. While I waited to sink my hands into earth that seemed like it may never thaw, I continued to read books about soil and regenerative agriculture. I arranged interviews with several regenerative farmers in my own ecosystem, and learned about their interconnections to the soil and food they grew, as well as the endlessly hard work and economic challenges they faced. I stumbled upon stories of bison being restored in parks and farms across the continent, and how herds grew more quickly than anyone anticipated. These storied creatures grazed and stirred up the Earth with their hooves, improving water storage, reducing flooding, storing carbon, and strengthening the soil, in partnership with the land. Hooves and soil. Mycorrhizal fungi and plant roots. Ranchers and animals. A pregnant writer and seeds she treasured from her long-ago nest. Interconnections across the continent that, like the soil, knit places together.

6

IF RAVENS SHARE

Consumerism Alternatives

"When it comes to healing, the only path I know is straight to the heart of it: running boldly in the direction of our grief, which is our love. Perhaps Poe's winged visitor was not an agent of torment, but of acceptance — there to teach him that the only way forward is through. If so, the raven really is wise, a keeper of life's most simple and sacred secret: *it goes on.*" **WILLOW DEFEBAUGH**

Inky black birds flew around our house and up the highway, waiting for animals to be killed by our cars so they could eat. They acted out witchy scenes, calling to each other in gurgles and trills as they circled the meadow filled with last year's milkweed, its brown leaf edges curled and crisped.

"How do you tell the difference between a Common Raven and an American Crow?" I asked the children. On the dining room table, I spread out a growing collection of bird books, collected from old bookshelves, gifts, second-hand stores, and a post I made on the local Buy Nothing group in an attempt to feed my book addiction when the budget creaked.

I learned about my local Buy Nothing group a few months into living in the woods as part of my exploration into the sharing economy. I discovered an active community of neighbours giving away anything they no longer need, from suitcases to appliances to toys outgrown by their children. Some of the items on offer held great value in the market economy and received interest from dozens of community members, while other items missed parts, needed repairing, or included the ends of old craft supplies, with only one community member happily expressing interest in a niche item. Part of the gifting economy, Buy Nothing groups work to keep waste out of the landfill, save money, reduce consumerism, and connect neighbours. Built around an ethos of giving without expecting a favour in return, Buy Nothing groups operate at the hyperlocal level, often managed by a volunteer with rules customized to the specific community. Guidelines include giving freely and graciously, and trying to move away from assigning monetary value to everything we do. A reminder from the administrator of our local group states, "We're experimenting in giving and receiving because that's how we can take care of ourselves, each other, and our community, building connections between ourselves that don't carry the market economy inequalities."

The Buy Nothing Project popularized these groups starting in 2013, including through extensive media, a website, an app, and a book. The international network of local gift economies reports 7.5 million Buy Nothing members in 128,000 communities, with 2.6 million gifts a month. They express a belief that "communities are more resilient, sustainable,

equitable, and joyful when they have functional gift economies." Of course, sharing among community members
surely existed for millennia, and strong local gift economies
built on generosity and support flourish in countless places
around the world. By its very definition, the spirit of Buy
Nothing cannot be owned by a single organization, and
most gifting happens organically between friends, family,
and neighbours.

While Buy Nothing groups work to foster community
connection and free exchange of resources, a broader system of community-based support is mutual aid, a way of
living where community members pool resources, services,
cooperation, and solidarity, working towards common benefit when an unjust society cannot provide what we need.
Especially in times of crisis, like the ones we live in, mutual
aid strengthens community, reduces inequalities, and can
help people survive.

On many occasions, researchers witnessed juvenile
ravens exhibiting mutual aid. The young birds, after finding
a moose carcass in the lean winter season, communicated
the feast to other ravens in a thirty-mile radius. Counter-
intuitively, the rarer the food, such as the moose carcass
hidden in brush or under the snow, the smaller the cost of
sharing and the greater the benefit of cooperating. A group
of the black birds, referred to perhaps unfairly as an *unkind-
ness* or a *conspiracy*, is also said to share beyond their species.
Ravens communicate and cooperate with wolves to feed
their respective families, informing brethren about the
large animal so the birds can divide the feast. The wolves
tear into the carcasses with their teeth, making the food
available to the ravens. The canines provide access to essential nourishment in winter months when food is scarce, in

exchange for the birds' alerts about where to find meat. I later learned these stories of sharing and community among ravens might be exaggerated, or only one part of the story. They reminded me of human beings who can also cooperate for mutual survival and well-being, in a complex tangle of hunger, self-interest, cooperation, and altruism.

My children and I browsed the various books procured from our local Buy Nothing, searching for information that would help us glean whether the black birds circling the meadow like Ouija planchettes were crows or ravens. "The Common Raven is twice the size of the American Crow, a bird of Viking legend, literature, and scientific wonder," *Birds of Eastern Canada* informed us. The raven's Latin name, *Corvus corax*, means crow of crows. Ravens loom above crows, as big as red-tailed hawks, with a larger bill than their smaller counterparts.

Using the index of another book, *Birds of the Northern Forest*, we turned to a page with an illustration of a craggy, watchful black bird, his back hunched and claws wrapped around a branch. The book explained that a raven is like an overgrown crow, but there are other differences as well. The bill is longer, and the tail long and shaped like a wedge. In flight, they soar like a hawk, and their feathers are spread apart. At their throat, the book informed us, ravens have a shaggy beard. Their calls, deep and throaty, sound more guttural than the crow's caw.

"(A) combined effect of light absorption by melanin pigments and light scattering by a thin layer of keratin on the surface of tiny feather barbules" cause a purplish gloss to the ravens' black bodies, according to *What is a Bird?* Without this miracle of chemistry, light, and feather, their feathers would remain matte.

We read our bird books like we read the *Pokémon Super Extra Deluxe Essential Handbook* before bed, poring over surprising statistics and superpowers. Wren, obsessed with Pokémon, introduced me to the wonders of characters like Corviknight, a Raven Pokémon with lustrous black feathers and a ruff of feathers on its throat that resembles a beard. Known for high intelligence and social skills, the fictitious creature engages in territorial battles like that raven who inspired him. With mom enthusiasm, I drew parallels between the wonders of the real raven and the character that captured Wren's attention in his turbo, tattered handbook.

The intelligent ravens fascinated me. It took my breath away when I saw one, eerie and powerful in flight over the barn, or standing watchfully beside my speeding wheels en route to a meeting or school pick-up. The birds waited for me to pass, black wings hanging down their backs like capes.

With my mind set on learning about the sharing economy, I visited the Ottawa Tool Library. The wide open warehouse space housed makers and fixers. Old trades like carpentry coexisted with new technologies like 3D printing, in a place where people used their hands and ingenuity to make things. The tool library is tucked into the back corner of this large space. The library's co-founder, Bettina Vollmerhausen, walked me through the aisles of her creation. She showed me the coterie of drills and bits, the fleet of saws and hammers, and a collection of large flat, Robertson, mini, and duck bill screwdrivers. Around the corner, we saw the sewing machines and ice cream makers, all items available for members to rent for a membership fee. The sound of a carpenter's saw punctuated our conversation.

"I think there should be a tool library in every neighbour-hood," Bettina said adamantly with a trace of a German accent. "We used to live in communities where we shared. Because we lived in smaller communities, we knew that John had a ladder, and that Paula could help you out when you had cooking questions. You knew who to ask for support. Now we live in urban centres, where you don't know who lives above you in your apartment building. You don't even talk on the elevator. Having somewhere where you can go to ask for help and to ask for support should be everywhere."

Sharing among community is an old way of life that some cultures maintained while others forgot, though the practice is enjoying a resurgence of interest. Why buy new objects for each and every home, when communal use can cut down on cost while reconnecting with one's neighbours? Repair and mending are also experiencing a renaissance as people embrace these lost arts to reduce expense and environmental impact. A rejection is steadily growing against the excessive, individualistic consumption that is sold to us as our duty. People share a widespread hunger to extend the lives of our belongings through sharing and repairing, and at the same time, we reconnect with community living.

Bettina talked about her idea for five high-quality vacuum cleaners for each apartment building, rather than storing one in every unit. We talked about playrooms for families in condos, where not every family wants or has space for a full collection of toys and easels and skipping ropes in every unit. A floor in every condo building could act as a dedicated playspace where kids enjoyed toys and art supplies, neighbours shared childcare, consumption and expenses were reduced, and community came together in those isolating years of early parenthood.

Bettina first conceived of starting a tool library in 2014, and the idea grew from a small ambition to be housed in her garage to a national news story. She received overwhelming interest and demand before the tool library even found a home. "Yes, people wanted it, but where were we going to go? We wanted to be in a city centre, where most people live, and where there are people in apartments with storage issues. We wanted to be accessible by the transportation system," said Bettina.

Accessibility forms a key tenet of tool libraries. The concept emerged in the United States in the 1970s, but the model took off globally in the last decade, with hundreds worldwide in major and smaller centres.

"There's that statistic out there that a drill in its lifetime gets used from six to twenty minutes. Think about it — it's disgusting. Think of all the resources that go into making it, shipping it, storing it. Think of all the space that people are using to store things they aren't using. The first thing we need to do is refuse. Not reuse — but refuse. You don't need a drill, what you really need is a hole in your wall."

Instead of buying a drill, tile cutter, or sewing machine, a person can borrow one from the library and return it when their project is done. Tool libraries often host workshops, too, so apartment-dwellers with limited space enjoy a place to build a headboard or table. Expert fixers volunteer to give advice and teach new skills, passing on their knowledge to a society that largely lost our building and repair know-how. People collectively share tools to cut down on consumption, cost, and storage while building community.

Libraries like this don't stop at tools. A lot of objects like camping gear, board games, and bicycle repair equipment are usually only used for a few days a year. Instead of purchasing these items outright, individuals access them when they need them through Libraries of Things, reducing clutter, cost, and waste. These models hold importance for people on a tight budget, who otherwise face barriers to accessing tools or equipment. Like many similar entities, the Ottawa Tool Library offers a pay-it-forward fund that allows for free memberships. "We give away free memberships to anyone who says, 'I can't afford it, but I really need some tools.' I don't ask for income, I don't ask for statements," explains Bettina. "It is a conversation between people."

In addition to reducing consumption and increasing accessibility, libraries like these foster community and intergenerational learning. Bettina explained to me that her volunteers and members show a real range of ages. "We had a phase where there were a lot of people in their forties and fifties, but right now it's younger people. A lot of the fixers are older and come in with experience. They either have built their own house, or have been a carpenter before. It's that generation too, right? They had to learn how to build their own things, and fix their own things. They are happy to see this space as a place to pass on their knowledge."

Tool libraries provide a solution to excessive consumption and waste, and these solutions do start at the household and local level. The global machine will not make these changes on its own without being forced. To scale and make a fundamental difference, though, local actions need to be bolstered by strong public policy. What starts locally needs systemic support to make it come to fruition, and to ensure that solutions are not built only on the gracious time of volunteers, but rather embedded in every community.

"We are a not-for-profit volunteer-run organization. Most of the volunteers come in at the end of their work day for three hours, and having financial support and a paid staff person would make a world of difference, meaning we could be open all day and make the tools and services more accessible," Bettina tells me. "I would love to see more policies and funding for that from governments at the municipal, regional and national level for the true circular economy. I would like to see the support of the government to make this go global. You need lobbying and a critical mass to get systemic change."

As people push for policy change and government support, tool libraries forge ahead on account of the passion of volunteers and the growth in members who are hungry for sharing instead of ownership.

"The majority of our members tell us they like the tool library because it is a great place to learn, it has environmental benefits, it's great for their pocketbooks, and they come for the community," said Bettina, visibly proud of what she created. "There are great synergies and connections happening, where people start talking about projects they are doing, share stories and swap phone numbers to help each other out. There is this connection happening. To see that growth of community spirit, to witness it, and know it is happening because we are here — that is what feeds me and keeps me going."

This spirit fuels Bettina, and the many volunteers worldwide that are creating and sustaining tool libraries. "Financially, we can cover our bills, but it's tight," Bettina admits. "We are always looking for other revenue streams. Our demo nights, like one on plumbing, are a great draw, as are our workshops on mending and darning. These have been a great source of revenue for us. Another one is the repair café."

With three-year-old Owl and eighteen-month-old Wren in tow, plus my wee one growing quietly in my womb, I trekked nauseously through the snow to visit a repair café organized by Bettina and her team. Set up in a back room of a large garden and tool store, the café happened to be near a cluster of big box stores by a highway. A handmade sign pointed me in the right direction, as did the people walking in with old broken lamps in their arms. A duo of friendly women in green T-shirts greeted us, and pointed us towards the free cookies and coffee.

Around the expansive room, a series of workbenches formed a circle on a functional concrete floor. Behind each workbench sat a volunteer tinkering, wiring, or soldering. A bright lamp curved over each fixer, as they curved over a lightless lamp or a defunct toaster. Apparently one person earlier in the day brought in a pair of unicorn ears complete with magical horn and headphones, which pleased Owl. Fixers welcomed any and all appliances at the repair café. Usually when you see a broken appliance it is in the back of a cupboard or on the side of the curb, waiting to be thrown "away" into some unseen corner of our planet. At the repair café, these belongings received a new life. The skilled volunteers behind the workbenches used the old mentality of repair on new technology, so that appliances get used and reused rather than lying in a landfill simply because of a loose wire or a missing part. Instead of wandering down the miserable aisles of a fluorescent-lit store searching for their next disposable toaster, people laughed and learned together, and left with a functioning, free appliance on the other end. "We brought repair cafés to Ottawa," Bettina told me. "We wanted to bring these to every neighbourhood, they should be in *every* neighbourhood. Not just downtown. They need to reach every demographic. We went to some neighbourhoods where there was a lot of affordable housing, and those were the most rewarding cafés. There is this one woman I'll never forget. She brought in her toaster oven, and said, 'It hasn't worked, and I haven't been able to eat warm food in three months.' To be able to fix that and really make a difference in someone's life is very rewarding. She was crying when she left."

The first repair café happened at the Fijnhout Theatre in Amsterdam on October 18, 2009, started by Martine Postma. The goals to reduce waste and maintain repair skills while strengthening social ties caught on globally, and the movement continued to grow because of local leadership. As with the closely-related tool libraries, repair cafés held fast to accessibility as a core value.

"You can never charge for a repair café," Bettina told me. "The philosophy is that everyone should be able to access it. It's always free to attend, it's always free to have something fixed."

Generations come together at repair cafés. Bettina described this to me, saying, "We're seeing the younger crowd embrace sharing, fixing, and repairing. It is a lot of work, but it is worth it. Everyone loves it. Fixers range in age from sixteen to seventy-five, and they are so happy to be able to make a difference in someone's life."

These gatherings brought people together and supported them in becoming more circular in their homes, by reusing belongings and restoring junk to a useful life. By helping people repair what they already owned, we cut down on the resources we pull from the Earth and reduce the waste that goes to the overflowing landfills of our planet.

Unfortunately some items cannot be repaired, not even by expert volunteer fixers. Planned obsolescence means our electronics fail after a short time, because of their design by companies that are married to exponential growth. Often, spare parts become unavailable, or companies construct products such that you cannot even open them. To protest this planned obsolescence and inability to make repairs, the right to repair movement formed.

Janet Gunter, the co-founder of The Restart Project and a driver of the right to repair movement in the UK, met me in 2019 via Skype after an exciting and busy week interviewing with outlets like the BBC and *The Guardian*. An American–British activist and anthropologist, Janet lived and worked in Brazil, East Timor, Portugal, and Mozambique before returning to Britain. Living in countries around the world first inspired her passion for repair. She saw how many communities continued to nurture the art of fixing, which had been mostly lost in countries throughout Europe and North America. We bonded over this, as I talked about similar observations from my time in countries like Kenya, Cameroon, Ghana, Bénin, and Tanzania, where people repaired electronics, clothing, footwear, and vehicles to extend their life. This contrasted with the prevalent habits in my home country, where we often threw out objects that were not broken, particularly electronics.

"The problem is that we are increasingly shut out of stuff, and the stuff that we think we own," Janet told me. "We aren't able to fix it because of the lack of access to spare parts, repair information, and poor design. That has economic effects, so people end up spending more, while also accelerating their consumption of electronics, which have a huge environmental footprint. And then of course, we are losing our repair muscle, and becoming passive and useless in our repair of technology."

The solutions started locally, as with the repair café I visited in Canada's capital, and they took on varied approaches in different countries.

"The right to repair movement looks different everywhere. In the US, it is [composed of] a lot of DIY-ers and small businesses. In Europe, it has a completely different flavour, fuelled more by environmental concerns," Janet explained.

Like Bettina, she emphasized how important community-building and intergenerational learning featured in the Right to Repair movement.

"What makes our events fun is that we link up different generations. So you have people who are really good with computers and who understand the ins and outs of software. And then you have the older crowd who can troubleshoot any electric appliance. It's interesting seeing those two generations coming together," she said from across the Atlantic Ocean, pausing to reflect. "I also think it is important that part of nature is thinking of ourselves as social animals. It is really important for us to get together and fix, and connect with strangers. It is ultimately a very human–animal scenario. We crave human contact."

The hunger for community in an increasingly isolated world grew as strong as the desire to reduce our environmental impact, and fortunately the satiation for both could go hand in hand.

Janet spoke adamantly that the right to repair movement must not restrict itself to the local level.

"The trap with these grassroots and individual-based approaches is that they can get stuck at the local level. The work of the right to repair movement at the community level is to connect people, but it needs to be bigger and greater to create system change." She explained to me that in Europe, residents pushed for a diverse set of policies, from a focus on eco-design, which has been used for energy efficiency over the past couple of decades, to newer standards like repairability ratings that could inform consumers how possible it would be to make a repair to their new purchase. We needed policies that help us understand how much energy gets used in the manufacture and shipping of products across their life cycle.

In Europe, Janet saw a broad willingness to use these policies, fuelled by environmental and consumer rights concerns. In the United States, the strategy looked different, with a focus on seeing right to repair legislation introduced into as many states as possible. Dedicated individuals moved from the home to the state, and worked to get legislation into major states and markets.

"We need to do things that make us feel better, and things that are going to save the situation. But where possible, we need to keep our eyes on the prize of that high-level change that has to happen."

Not everyone showed enthusiasm for the growing right to repair movement. "Some companies are pushing back, claiming that any DIY is inherently dangerous, coming up with spurious and bogus excuses related to risk and liability," Janet told me, without mincing words. "Their claims have definitely impacted the results of legislation. That is one big backlash we are facing. There is also backlash from the media, saying, 'Aren't you encouraging people to do dangerous things?' We get that quite a lot. Actually we do quite a lot to inform people about the risks and get them started safely." She also talked about the important need to address security risks.

As we talked, it seemed fitting that I used my old faithful 2013 laptop to speak with Janet. "Laptops that are a few years old are actually still quite useful for most of the things we need them to do. They can actually have second and third lives," Janet reflected after telling me that laptops and cell phones show up as the items most commonly needing repair. "That is what we are trying to do, is help people keep a laptop longer. We are teaching people not to believe what they are told. You may not have a really fashionable and trendy machine, but you can do almost anything on an older machine. And I think this changes peoples' relationships with consumption, with things."

Within the entrenched structure of a consumerist and wasteful society, many of us awoke to our impact as individuals but this came with self-blame. While individuals in their homes hold a role to play through consumer choices and pushing for policy change, we need to reject a culture of guilt. "It is important that people get the message that it is not all on them. It's not enough for you to be a better recycler without some change at a higher level," Janet said unwaveringly, and I felt chills go up my arms at what she said next.

"We want to feel the inevitability of the system change that we need. We want this to be a beacon for the people who are upset. We want for people to have enough disquiet with the ways things are, and for them to have the imagination to see that this is not an end-of-history moment, and that everything is going to be completely different by the time we die."

We can start to see our homes and technology as extensions of nature, too. "What we are interested in are regenerative systems," Janet told me. "In learning from nature, and seeing technology as a continuation of nature. It is not a different thing. All of the elements in our devices, all of the materials in them, came from the Earth."

My conversations with Bettina and Janet both emphasized the importance of refusing products we don't need. They talked about community building, local action, intergenerational cooperation, and how shifts start in our homes. They both said adamantly that the responsibility cannot rest entirely on the shoulders of the individual. Policy and system change remain essential, to take this from our homes and communities to deep-rooted shifts.

⸻

Ravens are like us. Unusually intelligent, omnivores, defenders of territory. From the Arctic to deserts to ocean islands, they thrive in varied climates, and typically prefer to stay in one home rather than migrating. Brilliant, they learn quickly and adapt to new circumstances, and communicate effectively through a series of varied sounds. They mate for life, most of the time. In addition to showing cooperation and apparent altruism, ravens can be strategic and ruthless, waiting in trees above a pregnant ewe, preparing to eat her newborn lambs. Neither humans nor ravens have many natural predators, but when the environment changes by vast degrees, as it is doing now, we both respond with a stress response. While ravens can be vicious with others, they show devotion to their families. (Despite this, it is the mothers who receive judgement, with female ravens notoriously considered to be heartless mothers. The derogatory

German word *rabenmutter*, or "raven mother," refers to a bad human mother, primarily because she works outside the home.) However, ravens often show themselves to be very good caregivers, with both parents taking care of their fledglings, even counting on other community members to help care for their young. They return to last year's nest, repairing it every year. Once ready, young ravens wander off, though their elders remain together. In myths and stories throughout history and across cultures, ravens can be depicted as either sinister or as creators of life — perhaps because we ourselves possess both qualities, and see ourselves in them. According to *Birds of the Northern Forest*, ravens are "the very embodiment not of evil but wilderness."

In our early months at Birdsong Cabin, we borrowed and lent frequently with people in our community, and shared a second-hand tractor with our new neighbours down the road. We rented tools from the tool library, and repaired lamps, furniture, toys, and dishes in our small attempts to embrace sharing and repairing. These individual, home-based actions bolstered my confidence as an environmentalist and helped us reconnect with a connected way of living, even if they did not solve all the world's problems. I mulled over where the environmental movement sometimes went astray: laying the weight on the shoulders of the individual, leading us to guilt, shame, and sometimes inaction. While we hold a responsibility and need to be stewards, none of us chose to live with the climate, biodiversity, and waste crises, and the responsibility to fix this trio of complex problems individually is too much to bear. None of us can do this alone. On my quest to discover new ways of living, I found it freeing to slowly let go of the guilt and know myself, like that raven, as an animal who is a part of nature.

7

MY HAND-STITCHED WINGS

Fashion

"The thing about climate is that you can either be over-whelmed by the complexity of the problem or fall in love with the creativity of the solutions." **MARY ANNAÏSE HEGLAR**

We awoke to Owl's voice in the dark, the time somewhere north of two a.m. "My feet are wet!"

The possibility of sleeping through the night disappeared with the arrival of my first baby, yet to return. Every night I stayed up too late, luxuriating in the quietness and ability to govern my own minutes, eating up the hours before the first child woke. The precise times at which I was woken throughout the wakeful night — 12:14 a.m., 2:23 a.m., 3:09 a.m., 4:40 a.m. — made me an audience to the march of nighttime towards dawn. Whether Owl or Wren woke first changed, but the disrupted sleep remained reliable.

Nightmares, accidents, cold feet, hot foreheads, throw ups, visits to the bathroom, the need for back scratches, simply wanting to know where I am. "Mama!" If they didn't wake, then I did, wondering where they were and whether they were safe. When they appeared at my bedside, on the edges of my dark dreams, I could order them back to bed, insisting they stay in their own bunks until the light blinked sleepily over the forest out their bedroom window. But as much as I despised being roused, I secretly hoped they would wake up. I missed them from the minute they fell asleep, and awaited their tiptoes into our bed. Snuggling together under the covers, with someone's onesie-covered feet pressing uncomfortably into my belly, our limbs tangled like raspberry vines, resembled the days when my body made their home. Baby birds in a nest, still needing me all through the day and night, still attached, still nestled under my wing for a little bit longer. Owl! Wren! Mama's here.

"My feet are really wet!" Owl repeated, after barely waking me the first time. She stood at the edge of my bedside, wide awake, staring at me while I blinked and peeled myself away from the streaked clouds of a stormy dream. I looked at her feet, to find them standing in two inches of icy water. Our bedroom floor formed the bottom of a shallow, unwelcome lake.

"Nik, our bedroom is flooded!" We clambered out of bed, both squeezing through the narrow space between the bed and the walls, mine on the other side of the kitchen and his on the side of the woods, still dark in that desert expanse between midnight and dawn. This was the time for owls and coyotes, not us.

"Water is flooding in through this wall," he said, and we watched snowmelt trickle into our bedroom.

"The water flooded under us while we slept," I said, nauseous and grumpy on account of the first trimester, my feet now wet too.

We turned on the bedroom lights, their false brightness falling on a scene of a flooded bedroom, a wakeful toddler, and two bedraggled parents acclimatizing themselves to the chore of cleaning up. We rooted through cupboards to find every towel in the house, and when those soaked up as much water as they could muster, we dragged out blankets and bedding to lie across the sopping floor. Exhausted, I knelt and pushed the waterlogged linens back and forth, then loaded them into a laundry basket. Nik picked it up, and the handles broke off with the weight of water. The weight of snow. The weight of months of snowfall, which mounted high on the hillsides, now melting to flood our canyon of a valley. Nik fired up the tractor and carved a pathway in the snowbanks to grant the free-flowing meltwater a path, not through our bedroom, but rather through the meadow to the awakened creek. After four a.m., with the flooding solved, we considered the floor dry *enough*. We pointed rotating fans at the glistening moisture that would eventually cause a layer of mold to grow on the bottom of our mattress, which rested directly on the floor, a work in progress like the boxes still waiting to be unpacked. We crawled into bed where Owl was finally asleep, as though she were the parent and we were the toddlers finding our way to a warm cuddly body in a big bed. *Sleep.*

In the daytime, the restless creek roared. You could hear crashing water while washing dishes with the kitchen windows closed, seventy metres away to the closest point of the water's edge. Snow melted up on the hills, soaking into the forest earth until the overflow streamed its way around tree trunks and down the hill to the creek. Every hill acted like a tributary, filling the creek from every direction, until water rolled over logs and rocks with great splashes, joyful collisions of water crashing upwards, and then falling back into the current to move along the creek bed. Water made shapes: semicircles around the curves of the bank, triangles between the bark and a branch of an old snag tree lying across the creek. "Never, ever, ever, ever go to the creek without us," I told my children daily, my voice too intense, on account of my fear. Fear of fast-moving water, fear of the road where cars sped down the hill, fear of rare illnesses, fear of every unpredictable and uncontrollable calamity that might find us. *Keep us safe*. A mother's blessing. A prayer, a plea.

Coltsfoot began to grow along the sopping clay of the creek's banks, and then grew everywhere. I knew so little about the plant that I thought they were dandelions. Their yellow flowers extended outward, more flat than a dandelion, the petals more spiky. I learned that the plant was good for respiratory health. Little did I know I would soon be fixated on anything that can help a person breathe.

As immense volumes of water melted, we started preparing our garden. I felt the call to grow food, that itch in the hands to shepherd seeds into nourishment. An eager amateur, my gardening experience remained limited to cheap seeds and haphazard planting practices, which unsurprisingly led to mixed results, and mostly failure. Ever stubborn in the face of defeat and obsessed with nature's cycles, I wanted to learn about planting as part of an ecosystem. More comfortable in the pages of a book than out in the world, I learned about permaculture, a method of growing food that takes inspiration from nature's cycles and the garden is modelled on a flourishing natural ecosystem. Together, Nik and I decided to try hügelkultur, a centuries-old permaculture approach where biological materials like rotting logs form a mound, continually composting for years and enriching the soil for growing food.

Nik whirred up the tractor we shared with our neighbours. He carved six trenches in the back of the meadow, a line of ominous-looking oblong holes, curving in a slight fan with the bend of the creek. Large trunks of trees made the first layer of the hügel beds, covered over in branches and brush, progressively smaller and faster to decompose. Soil filled in between the branches like water around ice cubes in a glass. The twelve-foot long garden beds made long mounds, both an untouched canvas for growing, and a disruption on the meadow landscape. These naked piles of soil — good idea, good intentions, daunting prospect.

We prepared other beds outside of the garden, too. As my baby grew, I burrowed through the house looking for newborn clothing and supplies, finding none. We had expected Wren to be our last baby, and gave away our baby items in the move to the woods. Now we faced reentering the newborn stage unprepared, but with a nonplussed third-time parent comfort that we would figure it out. With each pregnancy, I felt determined to use second-hand materials and make motherhood as environmentally-conscious as possible. I decided with pregnant-woman-conviction that I needed a bassinet immediately. I searched online for the right one second-hand and found it. I drove too far, to a suburb on the other side of the city, after my day of work, and went up to the suburban door to collect the bassinet, made of rattan fibers. An officious porch pick up, one of a dozen I made, to find reusable diapers and newborn clothing that could have come to our door from Amazon for the same money and far less effort. I sat with the weight of the tradeoffs, driving alone with my bassinet in the back seat, spending precious evening time away from my children, burning fossil fuels, in an attempt to cut down on waste and emissions from shipping goods all over the world. I drove home and kissed my older two on their foreheads, finding them at the dinner table, halfway done with their meals and on the fleeting path to bedtime.

Other newborn supplies found me more easefully. A new friend who was a mother of three children brought me a large cardboard box full of maternity clothes, providing great relief, as I did not know how I would afford new clothing to see me through months of a dramatically changing body. Opening the flaps of the box, I found carefully folded pants with stretchy tummies and maternity shirts. Dense elastic bands from the box helped hold together my painful pelvis, which suggested it might disperse into several pieces if I stood up too quickly, like bone continents drifting apart. Somehow this new friend, who I barely knew, managed to help take care of me on my pregnancy journey, when she had three young children under her care. I'd experienced this before in my previous pregnancies, when loose acquaintances, prenatal-course classmates, neighbours, and strangers gave me boxes of baby supplies, onesies, glass bottles, and maternity wear. Some donations overwhelmed me, with boxes filled with large clothing and intimidating plastic toys for a much older child, alluding to my own far-off future. *How could my baby possibly grow that big?* The second-hand gifts mixed functional necessities I did not know I needed, like a breast pump, with sentimental treasures such as hand-knit sweaters and a baby's first outfit. Women upkept intricate or haphazard organizational systems, organizing clothing by age and child and type, in large containers in crawl spaces, garages, attics, and closets, and bins under the beds. Boxes labelled 0–3, 3–6, 6–12, and 12–24 months. Organizing the nonstandard small 4–6 year clothing with the large-fitting 2–4 year clothing, lest the child grow quickly before the articles could be worn. Winter sweaters in one place, gloves and hats in another. Shoes and boots split out, by season and by size. A way to save money and reduce waste, two necessary skills of most mothers. I filed away my own boxes of clothing, and we called them The Future Boxes, and to me they spoke wistfully to the passing of time and the changing of seasons.

Young mothers overloaded with responsibility and disgracefully short on personal time found a way to look out for me, and I gratefully received their generosity. A private network exists of mothers extending care to one another, confiding in one another about impossible challenges, laughing about preposterous situations, commiserating about peeing their pants when they jump on a trampoline, weeping with a mutually understood exhaustion, and offering support even when there is little left to give. Against a context of dismal societal support for modern parents, this net of care extended by fellow mothers often begins with pregnancy, as it did with me. The first of my close friends to have a baby, I found my way through a mix of intuition and copious reading, holding some parenting tenets deeply important. I knew I wanted to cultivate a positive mindset about childbirth, equipped with both information and choice, and that I would go with the flow of the birth experience instead of holding fast to a certain vision. I suppose I felt the same about all parenthood. I knew that

I wanted to embrace a gentle parenting philosophy, guided by relationship instead of obedience, and loving boundaries instead of the longtime mainstream approach of physical dominance, power imbalance, and shame. Maybe revolutionary, radical, gentle parenting can heal the world's ills.

I knew I wanted to be thoughtful about the Earth, and teach my children about reciprocity and care, and diminish the waste and energy that can go into bearing and raising children. In this spirit, I committed to second-hand clothing and toys for my babies, following them through childhood. Clothing shared quietly between an informal, robust network of mothers helped form bonds, strengthened a new mother's support system, and showered us with care when we found ourselves at a vulnerable and transformative time.

With the garden beds dug and bare, and the newborn clothing and bassinet gathered, I again packed my bags, and kissed my children's foreheads as my tears wove their way down my cheeks to soak their hair. I left in the night and flew to the Pacific Coast.

⸻

Cherry blossoms lined the streets on the outskirts of Portland, Oregon. They grew beside wisteria vines and lush, fuchsia gardens. Inside, dried craspedia and thistle hung in hip bistros. Outside, big, old trees dripped with moss — the romantic result of the damp, mild, West Coast climate. The large cotton-candy blooms and the towering mossy trees were novel and delightful, having flown from my Québec winter. At Birdsong Cabin, snow still cuddled our cabin.

I had travelled to Portland to immerse myself in the Sustainable Fashion Forum. Hundreds of sustainable fashion designers, journalists, experts and influencers gathered to go deep on the issues and trends influencing sustainable fashion. A group of women in tailored linen rompers and flowing dresses walked down the sidewalk together as I shyly walked up to the chic Hotel Lucia for the opening reception. I was an introverted bookworm who didn't know a soul at the event — and four months pregnant at a VIP reception with bespoke cocktails containing such ingredients as rose-infused tonic, rhubarb, orange oil, and cardamom — and I found myself uncomfortable and a long way from my cabin in the woods.

It was also a long way from the relationship I had formed with fashion in the past. As a teenager and young adult, my drawers and closet overflowed. Disposable clothing comprised my excessive collection: cheap fabric not intended to last more than a few wears, and fickle trends not meant to last more than a few months. A gnawing guilt grew when I learned that the people who made these garments suffered brutally long hours, unsafe conditions, and unjust labour practices. The unfathomable environmental impact of the resource extraction, greenhouse gas emissions, toxic chemical dyes, and ever-growing waste that marked the fast fashion industry from beginning to end made me ashamed. The reason my clothing cost so little was not because it was inherently inexpensive, but rather because other people and places absorbed the cost, out of my sight. I started to choose clothing from a mix of thrift shops and clothing swaps when I could, though at the time, I felt the stigma of not being able to afford new clothes. I could not buy new ethical clothing, though, because like many my budget was tight and I lived frighteningly close to not having enough to pay rent. So, despite my knowledge and associated guilt about the environmentally destructive and unethical practices that produced my cheap garments, I continued to supplement my second-hand wardrobe with clothing from fast fashion stores, because I could afford it. It was a many-year process to become comfortable with having fewer clothes in the first place, proudly wearing second-hand pieces, selecting high-quality used ethical fashion when I could, and letting go of guilt on the odd occasion when I needed to resort to fast fashion.

As a parent, I experimented with how to embrace circular fashion for children. For us, this looked like swapping or buying second-hand for my family, as well as receiving from the Buy Nothing community. Particularly with the high-value, long-lasting pieces needed for outdoors, like snowsuits, we bought new clothes when we could not find them second-hand, and passed them down through our children. I tried to reduce how much we washed clothing, knowing that avoiding unnecessary laundry loads extends the life of garments, and I became an expert at stain removal after losing a few sweet onesies to a perilous blueberry end. My aspirations to mend torn garments usually went unfulfilled, and instead sweaters and leggings piled up in a wicker basket beside my bed for some eventual day when I might patch the ripped knees or learn how to make the scraps into a quilt.

Despite my efforts to reduce textile waste, I shuddered to imagine every clothing item I ever owned. Each garment still existed, long after I dropped them at the thrift store, brought them to a clothing swap, or tossed them in the garbage. Where were they now? Would they fill a room? A whole house? All the uniforms I'd donned and discarded. The provocative clothing of a shy, anxious teenager trying to misportray herself as normal. The dancer's uniform of tights, leotards, knit overall warmups, torn leg warmers, and an eclectic set of costumes, on top of a bounty of old ballet slippers and pointe shoes. In my late teens and early twenties, the fast fashion black pants and button-up shirts of a restaurant server, followed in my mid-twenties by the obligatory blazers and pumps of a new professional who'd never worked in an office before, like a child mimicking an adult in a play. Over the coming years, my career ensembles gradually evolved to a more authentic-to-me style: straight-legged pants, loafers, a turtleneck or linen shirt, and lipstick, a rejection of the younger professional who tried too hard. I sometimes wore the regalia of a mother of young children, with leggings, a clean-ish shirt, and that messy bun, barely covering a nest of knots. My gardening uniform included a faded green tank top emblazoned with the logo of a local regenerative farm, worn braless, on top of old denim shorts, all accessorized by bare feet and a tattered wicker basket. Clothing that told a story, worn and shed like so many identities.

In other words, I arrived at the sustainable fashion show in Portland as a mere mortal, trying my best. In a narrow stall in a marble hotel bathroom, I zipped myself awkwardly into the only fancy outfit that still barely fit around my growing belly, a basic black romper from a generic mall maternity store. I self-consciously put on lipstick, and walked nervously into the reception, though I needn't have worried about my social anxiety in this crowd. Everyone breezed past small talk, ready to discuss a shared passion: how to transform the fashion industry into one that is sustainable, circular, ethical, and inclusive.

Over the next couple of days, I immersed myself in panel discussions that centred on the many complex facets of sustainable fashion. Material use and reuse. Circular fashion, where today's clothing can be tomorrow's fabrics and resources. Inclusivity of all people and bodies. Justice and rights for workers. Changing ownership structures, including rentals, subscriptions, and resale. Sustainable business models and transparent supply chains. My pen flew, taking notes about the in-depth, frank conversations that took place on the forum stage, and in the one-on-one conversations that followed on the sidelines of the runway. Through conversations and subsequent research, a few learnings stood out about how we need to design the world of sustainable fashion.

Each of us interacts with textiles every day, from the clothing that we put on in the morning to the sheets that we wrap ourselves in at night. Our clothing is protective and a basic human need. It is also an expression of our personal and cultural identities. Whether or not a person has an explicit interest in fashion, our clothing is inextricably woven through our lives. When we interact with clothing, outerwear, bedding, towels, and other textiles, we connect to the land or animal that grew the material, the people who made the clothing, the rivers where the contaminated wastewater from the factory flowed, the places the textile travelled, and wherever on our planet it ends up — usually a Global South country deemed to be a dumping ground for the unwanted clothing of wealthy countries. A single textile connects people and places like a thread, even though most of a textile's environmental and social impact occurs out of our sight in our current globalized system. How we make textiles is intimately related to agriculture, workers' rights, climate change, and resilient regional economies.

Our clothing forms an intimate relationship with the health of our soil, ecosystems, and bodies. Natural, locally sourced textiles are as important environmentally and health-wise as organic, local food, even though we don't always think of it that way. The clothing we wear can be compared with the food we ingest: both start by growing on the Earth, cultivated by farmers, processed by workers, transported some distance, and then our bodies interact with them daily. We don't know what chemicals hide in fabrics, what ecosystems suffered damage, or what injustices workers faced. Our skin, our largest organ, is very porous, meaning that any chemicals in the fabrics we wear can travel easily from the material into our bodies, affecting our health. What goes into our crops and our textiles also goes into us, and into our waterways.

Sustainable fashion is a broad, catch-all term that includes a diversity of actions meant to ensure that all our textiles can be created without harming nature and people. In practice, it can refer to the use of natural fibers instead of synthetics, recycling waste products into new garments, or the reduction of water and greenhouse gas emissions used in production. It also serves as an umbrella for a gamut of alternative approaches to mass consumption, such as rentals, subscriptions, thrifting, thoughtful purchases from local designers, or mending to extend the life of a garment.

Sometimes, particularly when used by large companies, sustainable fashion might mean *more* sustainable than the current wasteful, extractive, emissions-intensive fashion system, which does not necessarily mean it is as ambitious as it needs to be for meaningful change. Other times, the term might describe regenerative, inclusive, and ethical fashion, reaching its highest environmental and social potential. Sustainable fashion is a helpful term but one to think critically about, because its definitions are loose and it can be used by anyone for either genuine or marketing purposes, and it is susceptible to greenwashing or dramatically varied interpretations. Sustainable fashion also sometimes focuses only narrowly on bettering environmental impact, without also working to include improved social justice.

Circular fashion is a regenerative fashion system that is meant to continue in a closed loop indefinitely. This emerging solution reduces the extraction of virgin materials, reduces textile waste and pollution, and regenerates nature. The Sustainable Fashion Forum, founded by Brittany Sierra, defines it like this: "Circular fashion is a holistic design approach rooted in Indigenous ancestry that aims to 'design out waste' by reducing the number of natural resources used to make our clothing and diverting products from landfills. In short, circular fashion (a closed-loop system) is making new materials out of old materials." When we make fashion circular, garments circulate for as long as possible, using a variety of practices like mending and reuse to extend their life, and recycling as a last resort. From the very design of circular clothing, the whole life of the garment is considered, and at the end of its useful life it can finally safely return to nature. Common circular fashion practices include eliminating waste from the design stage, upcycling, mending, swapping, thrifting, selecting fabrics that can be composted, or recycling waste into new materials.

To be meaningful, though, sustainable and circular fashion start with reduction of consumption in the first place and a redefinition of value. We need to consume less clothing, and the most effective action we can take is to buy less and wear what we already own. But too often, companies sell us the idea that we can continue to consume fashion at a great rate, if only it is organic cotton or if it is made out of old water bottles (though those efforts can be helpful and have their place in a set of many solutions). In reality, the best and most effective way to lighten our environmental footprint remains to buy less. To wear clothing longer. To mend ripped garments. To make do and experiment with an outfit we already have, rather than buying something new. In Portland, during a panel called *Repair, Repurpose, Reinvent: Extending the Life of Our Clothes*, Erin Wallace from ThredUp said, "There is an overproduction problem. Only ten to twenty percent of what we give away can be absorbed by thrift stores." As Nicole Bassett from the Renewal Workshop said, "We need to consume less. We need to think before we buy something." Good questions to ask ourselves: Do I need this? How many times will I wear this? Where did this item of clothing come from, and when I am done with it, where will it go?

For those items we *do* need to buy, we can change our definition of value. Fast fashion defines itself by its low cost, though fast fashion brings with it extraordinary environmental and human costs, but they are not shouldered by the person purchasing a garment. Our capitalist system's preoccupation with profit has led us to a troubling situation: immense waste, polluted water, climbing greenhouse gas emissions, poor working conditions, factory disasters, habitat loss, clutter, the lie of shopping therapy as medicine for our wounds, cheap quality, and the stealing of creative designs by big companies. It is time to shift the conversation from cost to value — and our values — while also making sure that costs are not prohibitively high and that they are not excluding traditionally marginalized communities.

As Eden Dawn, the Style Editor at *Portland Monthly*, said, "We need to be changing the conversation of value from cost to one of importance." When possible, we need to shift from having a lot of disposable clothes to having a few, carefully selected, high-quality items we treasure for their inherent value: creativity, inclusivity, and sustainability.

To do that, fashion needs to go circular from the design stage. Trying to fix the problem after disposability is already designed into our clothing and the fashion industry is insufficient, like aloe after a sunburn instead of proper coverage before exposure to the sun. Clothing should be designed with its whole life cycle in mind. There needs to be a creative plan for how each and every garment is going to biodegrade, or be dismantled, recycled, or resold. The fabrics, the zippers, the stitches, the timelessness of the design: all of these need to be considered with a lens of environmental care and protection. What happens to this specific fabric once it has a hole in it? Will this style still be desirable in two years? Can this zipper be easily removed to be reused in another garment? Does a designer's company build sustainability into its business model? Who makes this clothing, and how are they treated? Designers need to ask these questions from ideation.

While design comes before we wear clothes, most of the focus is on what to do after we are done with our clothing. Clothing companies often promote the recycling of textiles as the solution, and the idea resonates with people. Not all recycling is created equal, though. What we think is recycling often actually ends up as waste. Sometimes this is because facilities are ill-equipped to process the amount of waste that is produced, or because materials lack characteristics of recyclability. Textile recycling, however, has been around for centuries. Nicole Bassett from Renewal Workshop talked about watching the process of a sweater rebecoming yarn in Italy. We should return to true textile recycling as the gold standard in how fashion can become circular. For textile recycling, the best candidates are wool, one hundred percent cotton, one hundred percent polyester or sometimes a cotton/polyester blend. New innovations for recycling textiles exist — for example, recycling that extracts cellulose from textile waste and uses the fibers for new clothing — but we need to remain wary of relying too heavily on these technological approaches to recycling, because they take time to scale, and refusing, reducing, reusing, and manual recycling clothing should come first. Also, by purchasing high-quality items that retain resale value, clothing can be reused many times before recycling is on the table. Recycling in isolation of other circular practices risks justifying continued excess consumption, which does not solve the waste problem of the current fashion system. Recycling can provide a useful tool in a circular fashion system, but only as part of a larger whole that emphasizes reduction, redesign, and repair first, with recycling as the final tactic after exploring more meaningful options.

Sitting on the side of the runway, I scrawled in my notes that we find ourselves at a moment of needing to solve many problems at once. "Just" focusing on sustainable materials and practices falls short. As we reinvent an industry that became one of the top-polluting and wasteful in the world, we also must recognize that fashion contributed to poor working conditions and exclusivity to people based on race or size. We enjoy an opportunity to redesign fashion to be environmentally-friendly *and* inclusive — *and* supportive of workers' rights. We can look at the connections between harmful environmental pollutants and poor air quality from factories located near marginalized communities, or people in Global South countries being displaced from their homes by literal mounds of textile waste. Good initiatives confront many problems at once. Robin Allen shares an example of a project outside of Portland called Helping Hands, where women donate clothes, and a week later return to "shop" the donated items. The money raised supports women who face domestic violence, who are provided with a VIP shopping experience to help them select clothing for their size and style, while at the same time helping to reduce shame and restore dignity.

We can build relationships with the people designing and making our clothing. Not only is the anonymous fast fashion approach environmentally destructive and the driver of a huge, insurmountable waste problem, but it also hides the supply chain from us so that we don't know where our clothing comes from, who made it, or what conditions workers endured. By buying high-quality clothing in less quantity from small companies, if financially possible, we can support creativity, sustainability and good jobs. The #WhoMadeMyClothes campaign from Fashion Revolution sheds light on workers' rights, for example. And many companies take their products back when customers are done with them, to repurpose them in one circular, closed loop. Jessica Schreiber, the founder of FABSCRAP, said, "We are at a moment in time where donating has been the only option, but now we have companies who want to create a relationship and take a garment back and be responsible for it." FABSCRAP takes materials in New York — for example, from Broadway shows — and creates a marketplace for them, engaging the local creative community in the fabric's reuse.

There are options for businesses that want to build this kind of relationship, and likewise when we are buying new, we can connect with designers, makers, and menders.

I heard a theme that traditionally marginalized communities need to be seen, heard, and included as fashion becomes more sustainable. People in BIPOC (Black, Indigenous, and People of Colour) communities have been talking about more sustainable, inclusive fashion for years, and their voices need to be centred in the conversations around sustainable fashion. For example, as second-hand shopping gentrifies and becomes more mainstream, it is important that marginalized and low-income people who rely on thrift stores continue to have access instead of being sidelined. We need a democratization of sustainable fashion so that it belongs to all people, and not to only a privileged few in a way that mimics the elitism and inequality of the fashion world we wish to leave behind. This will be one of the defining differences between the new, circular fashion world and the old one. Fashion stands at the crossroads of many socioeconomic injustices and we need to look at them all honestly and creatively. Women, for example, continue to be most affected by climate change while also showing up as a disproportionate force in the fashion world. How then can we make sure that women are involved both as leaders and as communities affected by fashion and climate? Slow, circular fashion companies need to make sure that their collections represent all sizes. We need to think about race, gender, and size in how we design and market sustainable fashion. As Cassie Ridgeway from Altar PDX said, "We are working together to create a movement." The folks at Mara Hoffman agreed, saying we need to share resources and, "We can only advance collectively." I started to think of fashion as an ecosystem of justice, climate, soil, labour, gender, creativity, expression, and culture, made up of people each with their own offering and niche, intricate in its diversity and interconnections.

━━━━

The fleeting trip to Portland came to a close, and I ached to draw it out longer while also wishing time would speed up so I could go home to the woods. I sat in a public park, barefoot in a field of wildflowers under soaring West Coast cedars, savouring the illusionary spring before returning to the lingering snow in Québec.

On my last day, I stepped up the metal stairs on a bus to explore beyond Portland. Sitting quietly, surrounded by the noisy din of people, I approached Multnomah Falls, Oregon's tallest waterfall, where water cascades down basalt cliffs and over a technicolour tangle of moss, plants, and trees. Rainfall, an underground spring, and snowmelt feed the waterfall that spills for hundreds of feet, creating mist and spray along its downward journey. The gorge began to form between forty and sixty million years ago, when molten lava pressure mounted until it pushed up mass amounts of granite to frame the Columbia Basin. More recently, a mere six to seventeen million years ago, ancient volcanoes erupted, irreparably changing the landscape as more than twenty massive basalt flows streamed into the gorge. Somewhere in these untold millions of years and uncountable volumes of granite and basalt, a hanging valley formed in the rock, carving out a shallow canyon suspended high above the bottom of the soaring rock structures. At the end of the last Ice Age, glacial lake outbursts called the Missoula Floods periodically swept down the Columbia River Gorge, flooding much of Western Oregon — and forming a tall waterfall that now runs through the hanging valley before tumbling over the granite, creating an omnipresent mist that dampens the hair and camera lenses of people seeking escape from modern life. Millions of years of geology and cataclysmic events ranging from lava to ice created a majestic accident that humbled me, one tiny sensitive organism missing her children.

Two million other human beings also visited the falls that year, with that irresistible homo sapiens' draw to spend time with water and trees. The place felt like an ancient and powerful site, as well as a well-run and noisy tourist destination, with a gift shop built in 1925 and throngs of people walking in both directions along the trail. Remembering I would travel home the next day, I stopped in the gift shop and bought two wooden whistles for my toddlers: one in the shape of an owl, and the other a wolf. I opted not to buy one for my third baby nestled inside me to save money, justifying the decision with the reminder that he came with me on the trip. A map of the Multnomah-Wahkeena Trail Loop in the gift shop identified where to find footbridges and viewpoints, and a dotted line ran off the bottom of the left-hand side of the map, indicating that only 1.2 miles would take you to Angel's Rest, and slightly to the east, Devil's Rest. Names of places stood absolute on the map in old-fashioned font: *Fairy Falls, Benson Bridge, Wiesendanger Falls, Dutchman Falls, Wahkeena Spring*. Wahkeena, I learned, means *most beautiful*, a word of the Yakama, or the self-named Waptailmim, People of the Narrow River. The names on the map spoke of the history of the people who lived here since the beginning of time, mixed in with the names of settlers — like Benson, a highway builder, and Wiesendanger, a Forest Service Ranger and "Mr. Keep Oregon Green." The names — all unfamiliar to me — provided clues to places with meaning, stolen land claimed and renamed.

I walked quietly uphill along the switchback trail, mist droplets gathering in my hair, as families ran loudly around me and friends stopped to take group photos with the falls behind them. I offered to take a snapshot of people awkwardly trying to squeeze into a selfie, and they smiled kindly as I handed their phones back and we parted ways. I walked slowly, to catch my breath and give my pelvis moments to rest. I looked at the soaring geology, biology, and mystery that surrounded me, gifts offered to all of this humanity.

"What would it be like, I wondered, to live with that heightened sensitivity to the lives given for ours?" wrote Robin Wall Kimmer in her inimitable gift to the world, *Braiding Sweetgrass*. "To consider the tree in the Kleenex, the algae in the toothpaste, the oaks in the floor, the grapes in the wine; to follow back the thread of life in everything and pay it respect? Once you start, it's hard to stop, and you begin to feel yourself awash in gifts."

Heightened sensitivity came naturally to me. Walking along the path and through my life, I felt the personhood of every creature, saw it intermingling with my self, sensed our shared experiences of pain and breath and life. I remember finding my way into heated debates in high school, as we all formed our strongest opinions and navigated questions of religion and ethics, where I argued that all people and animals could be me, and I them — I considered them so close that I lost myself, or found myself in creaturehood. I never forgot suffering: I easily called up grief at remembering the injured bird named Diana that died after being rescued at my dad's farm thirty years ago, or a tragic news story I read a decade ago. Sometimes the sensitivity threatened to consume me, where my porous boundary let in all the pain of the world and my shoulders held themselves stiff for years, tired of carrying burdens. Here I advocated for care, and secretly wondered if maybe you can care too much. Or maybe that heightened sensitivity, that connection to suffering at seeing the dead body of a raccoon on a highway or a bird struggling to fly, is natural and good. I did not know.

I continued to walk uphill, considering my sensitivity and the trees and the rocks, and I fell. I crashed to my knees and then my side along the trail. I clutched my belly. Two people gasped, and stopped to help lift me up to my feet.

"I'm okay," I quavered, scared. My camera lay broken on the dirt, and I dragged it towards myself, before sitting on a bench at the side of the pathway. Fellow tourists walked past, looking sideways at me, pregnant and shaken, breathing deeply, blood dripping from both knees through my pants, and tracks of dust along my body. I gathered my breath, and tears streamed from my eyes, making my worry known. I retreated down the pathway, slowly and with fear. I held my stomach the whole time, willing my unborn baby to move within me, assuring me of his safety.

Once, the lush leaves, limbs, and lichen of a rainforest changed the direction of my life, though I didn't realize it until later. I travelled alone to Gombe — the jungle-forest in Tanzania where Jane Goodall observed chimpanzees and forced the world to re-evaluate the definition of humanity. I made that journey when I was twenty-two years old, the same age as Jane when she first went to Tanzania, alone, in the 1950s.

The year before, I volunteered at an orphanage in Kenya, with good intentions and white saviourism in my tightly packed backpack. On a foundation of Christian missionary stories, charity porn commercials, and a heartfelt, deeply experienced compassion for stories of suffering, I wanted to turn my values into action. I went to Kenya, with most of the trip subsidized by a small grant. I arrived at the airport in the middle of the night with no one to greet me. My expected host, arranged through an American company online, did not show up. I took a taxi to a derelict hotel, where I tucked my mosquito net too tightly into the edges of my bed and fell asleep, worried about how I would find my way the next day. Fearful and lost, I wanted to hide in this one room and dreaded leaving. In the morning, I trepidatiously walked the metropolis, searching marked and unmarked streets for an address I had scrawled on a piece of paper. Once I found my homestay host and started volunteering as a teacher in the orphanage, I grew disillusioned. I felt like a tourist in a theme park, and the children there were treated like props rather than human beings. I asked for a lesson plan from the previous teacher or for guidance on what to teach, and the headmaster encouraged me to do whatever I wanted. Young, alone, and untrained as a teacher, I desperately wanted to do a good job, be helpful, and prove to everyone that I was capable and confident on this solo trip to Kenya. I made lesson plans and bought chalk and notebooks, and mimicked the teaching style of educators I knew growing up. On the weekends, I travelled to Mombasa and the Maasai Mara on a shoestring budget, seeing places that the kids I taught had never visited. At the orphanage, the photo ops with Kenyan children as a backdrop for life-changing experiences of young Western travellers seemed prioritized over the childhoods of the young people in this dim, transitory place.

Having learned from that dismal and eye-opening experience, the next year I sought out work with a small, locally led charity, which I found in a community that supported Congolese refugees in building their new lives in Uganda. In contrast to my work at the orphanage the year before, when working with the Congolese–Ugandan organization, I was a valuable contributor. The experience of the women and men leading and participating in the programs were centred, rather than my travel experience. After those meaningful weeks in Uganda, I embarked on my journey to Gombe.

My voyage was intentional — Gombe drew me in — but also haphazard and underfunded: I barely earned enough money to make rent for my shared basement bedroom in a dingy apartment and then pay my bills, let alone travel internationally. I had experienced enough misadventure and malaria in Kenya the year before to believe that I could disregard the guidebook's clear recommendation to *never travel by bus along the border of the Democratic Republic of Congo.*

I left Kampala, Uganda on a bus with an overstuffed backpack, a guidebook, my journal, a copy of Dr. Goodall's *In the Shadow of Man*, and a few oranges in a plastic bag. I subsisted on oranges purchased out of the bus window for the next few days. Using guidebooks and internet cafés, I had carefully plotted out my bus route, in a naive waste of time, I soon learned. According to my self-made itinerary, the journey to Kigoma, Tanzania should have taken two buses and about as many days, but my careful plans unravelled, and I soon found myself on a bewildering route.

The bus broke down in the middle of the desert. Once repaired, it chugged along to a different town than the one

I had expected to arrive in. We drove through places that certainly didn't make the index of Lonely Planet. We rattled into busy town squares as night was falling — *never be outside after dusk!* declared the guidebook — and people informed me the next bus would arrive at some point, and at some place, that remained undetermined. The route I expected to take no longer existed, and I needed to find another way, with no stations, schedules, internet access, or maps. I had no cell phone, and no travel companion to commiserate with or to consult for advice. The bus was full of live chickens and bags of dead fish, with every seat filled with a person who seemed to calmly know where they were going, as I wondered anxiously what would happen next.

This meandering, unpredictable journey was not in my nature. As a child, I alphabetized my books along with a careful system of colour-coded stickers. As a teenager, the back of my bedroom door disappeared under a six-foot-long to-do list. The list grew ever-longer, with new tasks and goals added more quickly than checkboxes could be ticked — a practice I carried into adulthood and never stopped. In a lifetime of trying to gain control, I held none.

I trekked deeper into Tanzania. The journey to Kigoma took four long days and nights. I accessed very little food and had nowhere to pee. Every time I took my malaria pill, I developed a temporary fever and the shakes, and sweated profusely as we sat stalled on a dirt path in the middle of Tanzania under the beating sun. At one point, we stopped at the side of the road in the middle of the night. The doors opened, and men with guns walked onto the bus, chatted kindly with my fellow passengers, and then disappeared into the pitch black.

From Kigoma, I hoped to somehow take a boat to the

Gombe rainforest, though I had no idea how. I flew off the bus, grateful to be on solid, albeit unknown, ground. A town with a name I knew. Someone gathered my backpack, now caked with orange dust from rattling around in the bottom of the bus, and threw it and me into a taxi. I asked the driver to take me to a hostel, and while not a single room remained available, the staff took pity on me, this shaking, ill-equipped traveller, and they found a peculiar bedroom-slash-closet for me to sleep in, to my immense gratitude. I washed my hair in the cold bucket shower, and thick, sludgy water ran in rivulets down the drain, a dark red-orange from the dust that collected in my hair through the open bus windows.

The next morning, I attempted to take $200 cash from the ATM to book a return flight to Dar es Salaam, hoping to avoid a repeat of the bus experience in a few days when I needed to travel across Tanzania before going home. The machine beeped at me accusingly. Declined. Out of money, I decided I would figure out my return journey later. First, I would travel further away.

After finding my way to the shore of Lake Tanganyika, I looked up at a massive wooden boat, which I had heard could take about a hundred people down the western coast of Tanzania, passing Gombe on the way. While I could not afford the charter boat that travellers normally take to Gombe, for a couple of dollars I negotiated a spot perched on the wooden gunnels of the cargo boat. The boat left the shore, fully loaded with passengers, cargo, and bags marked UNHCR. The boat pitched and tilted down to the surface of the water. I held on, inwardly terrified I would fall in, while outwardly pretending that I routinely made this passage. The boat pulled up on a small beach and I crawled my way down to the beach, dragging my fetid backpack behind me.

I found the small cabin where I would spend the next few days, at the Gombe Stream Research Centre where Jane Goodall undertook her research. There appeared to be about four people in the area, including me. On one side stretched the wide watery expanse of Lake Tanganyika, which flows between the Democratic Republic of Congo and Tanzania. On the other side waxed the lush, leafy edge of Gombe rainforest.

As the copper circle of the sun set over the lake that night, I breathed with relief to be at the end of my humbling journey to get here. The natural beauty of the dark forest landscape existed as a cohesive whole ecosystem, unaltered by billboards, housing developments, or electrical wires, and the dark and deep lake rippled quietly under the cycles of the setting and rising sun, and the waxing and waning moon. I reflected on the circuitous journey, which had brought me to this wild and beautiful place.

My body had grown accustomed to living in artificial light and built cities, misbelieving them to be a kind of truth, far away and disconnected from the enduring cycles of this black lake and green forest. At that time, I saw myself and urban areas as divorced from nature. Reconnecting with nature's cycles, if only briefly, felt freeing. I realized that throughout my whole life, I suppressed my own cycles, resulting in a lost connection to my own humanity and my place in nature. Being raised in a society that regulates almost every aspect of life severs a connection between humans and nature that is essential to our being. We plant our crops in perfectly straight lines. We mass-produce things to be uniform, without distinction from each other. We decide exactly where our trees should go in our cities and fence them in accordingly. To see nature — *as she is* —

revealed how unnatural my world had become. Our world was not a factory, but rather a whole wild place. We were not consumers and clients, but rather citizen creatures who formed part of a cyclical planet. Why then had we forced fake linear structures on top of them, expecting them to succeed against the laws of nature? Our bodies, our land, our seasons all embodied cycles. Like the rings of a tree, these cycles were not perfect circles, but rather showed experiences of weathering. We, too, embodied cycles, and they would not be perfectly circular.

Watching the glowing sunset over Lake Tanganyika, something inside me let go. Cracked open. My body connected to the land around me, and it hit me how hard I was trying to force a linear life in a world governed by cycles. I had repressed nature's circles and instead, fixated on lines: deadlines, bottom lines, finish lines. The sharp lines of my clavicle as I jutted my shoulders forward in a desperate attempt to look skinnier and worthier. The lines of A pluses, and checkmarks on overly ambitious to-do lists. Sitting alone, watching the round, setting sun and the curving surface of the still lake, a deep wisdom in me gently encouraged me to live with, and not against, my own nature.

The next day, these revelations deepened as I observed a family of chimpanzees forging a path through the decidedly non-linear tangled vines, criss-crossing trunks, and cascading waterfalls of Gombe. Witnessing our closest living ancestors in their natural forest home became one of the most beautiful and transformative experiences of my life. It showed me how we — humans — are as much a part of planet Earth as every other species, and her sovereign cycles affect us equally. I watched a mother chimpanzee as her young son raced ahead of her, twirling playfully around trees, and her adolescent daughter trailed dreamily behind her. Years later, I would have my own cheerful toddler son and pensive elder daughter. Their deeply familiar dynamics clarified for me that we humans exist as much a part of nature as a lush patch of moss or a wildebeest foraging for grass. Reading In the Shadow of Man by candlelight at night in her research cabin, Dr. Goodall's words struck me then as they've struck me every day since. It is the peace of the forest that I carry inside.

I repeated that phrase over and over to myself in the years that followed, the words smoothing like a well-worn stone in a stream. But they became harder to believe the further I travelled away from the forest. I felt anything but peaceful back home.

Back in Portland on the bus back from Multnomah Falls, both knees bled through my torn maternity jeans on account of the fall, and my pelvis ached more than usual. My camera groaned uselessly when I tried to turn it on, and I knew I didn't have the funds to replace either the jeans or the camera. None of that mattered. My baby moved within me. Limbs stretched in slow luxurious motion, the underwater roll of a spine against the walls of my belly, and I hesitantly relaxed into knowing he was safe. Keep us safe. The worry about harming him in the fall dissipated, very slowly, without fully lifting, without a clear moment of relief he would survive this pregnancy. That moment would not come until he entered the world through birth, and then a new set of worries would begin.

The bus delivered me back to the city, passing the lush flowering trees cloaked in craggy moss. Beautiful pink cherry blossoms laid the picturesque backdrop for my time in Portland: warm West Coast air, time to quietly enjoy pregnancy (a luxury usually afforded only in a first pregnancy), gathering with groups of like-minded people, and another solo trip with my paper and pen. Cherry blossoms also popped from the page in *Cradle to Cradle* by Michael Braungart and William McDonough. As they explain, cherry trees exist not just for themselves. They create this incredible beauty, and only a small minority of the blossoms and fruits fall to the ground to germinate and grow into a new cherry tree. These trees also create habitat for many creatures, provide beauty for passersby, and feed organisms and microorganisms. When their breathtaking blossoms do fall to the ground, they nourish the soil, their home. We can be inspired by the cherry blossom and follow nature's lead in disrupting and reinventing the fashion industry. We need to create a world of fashion that brings joy to people, flourishes within nature's cycles, contributes to collective equality, and nourishes the soil we walk on.

I made my way to the airport for a series of red-eye flights. Over a decade after Gombe, I still seemed to take the hardest, cheapest routes to go on my meandering solo migrations from home. I arrived bleary-eyed in the morning and started a day of work in the office before hazily finding my way back to the mercy of the woods. *Thank god*, I thought as I always did when I rounded the bend into the hidden valley. A race to greet me at the door and shower me with love commenced, with Owl and Wren jumping up on me, our bodies joyful to be reunited. We kissed and hugged, energetic like puppies. Bear greeted me at the door with his steady love, pushing his head through the fray of children, nudging me for affection. Nik waited his turn, and came in for a deep kiss. All of us, reunited. One safe unborn baby, sleeping through it all, a centrepoint in the middle of my body, a nexus in a cluster of creatures happy to be home together. Many individuals once again made up one complete whole.

Life bloomed around the cabin, a northern sort of spring compared to Portland's West Coast botanical abundance. Moss, coltsfoot, chicory, clover, and wild strawberries appeared, impossibly alive after the brutal winter. The rushing creek filled with melted snow, racing freely over sopping earth. A woodpecker worked diligently on the trees and a heron fished in the creek, sharing their land with us as we contemplated planting the hügels to cultivate food. We added rich mushroom compost to the garden beds, and red worms came with the complex mixture, their segmented bodies decorated with cakey black stuff. We continued to build up the hügel beds, using essentially waste materials from around our land, laying rotting wood in the soil to embrace circular living in our home. *What a privilege to be a part of this circle.*

We walked outside as a family, embarking in stops and starts on the uphill path that loops through the forest. We crossed the narrow plank of wood that crosses the creek, Bear leading without fear, me following with my hand holding my round stomach protectively, fearful of another fall. We curved around the basin of trees, and out of breath, I paused and looked around. With hands on my hips and taking shallow inward breaths, I glanced down at the forest floor flourishing prolifically with mushrooms. These expressions of the Earth's magic, mystery, and diversity sprung up on moss, soil, and bark. Lacy gills, spongy bulbs, undulating frills, smooth stems, and terracotta umbrellas provided fleshy reminders of our planet's ability to digest, rot, and cycle again and again. My eyes rested on a flash of colour. I reached to the ground awkwardly over my fast-growing belly and lifted up one delicate yellow feather. The sign that a Yellow-Shafted Flicker flew through here, travelling through this same forest, home to many creatures I know mostly by what they leave behind: hoof prints, scat, scratches on bark, sawdust at the bottom of a tree trunk. And feathers, those fashionable and functional adornments that provide safety, warmth, survival, the perpetuation of future generations, and free flight.

8

THE 37-DEGREE ISOTHERM

Economy

"(T)here burns throughout the line of words, the cultivated act, a fierce brief fusion which dreamers call real, and realists, illusion: an insight like the flight of birds." **SYLVIA PLATH**

Coltsfoot flourished, a ubiquitous plant, roaming confidently around our cabin. Akin to the other hearty species that flourished here for months on end — dandelion, chicory — coltsfoot fed our depleted clay soil. A robin appeared in the strident coltsfoot of our shared home, watching me as I watched him. With a worm in his beak he hopped away, keeping one eye trained on me. He reminded me of the robin's nest inside my bedroom, at the highest reaches of my bookshelf, far from the wingspan of curious children. I carried that nest with me in cardboard boxes for many years — travelling across geography, bringing some mother's home with me from house to house.

Robins know when to move as daylight patterns change. At the end of their wintering period, robins, like many birds, experience *zugunruhe*, a period of migratory restlessness. As day lengthens or contracts, an internal, anxious cue tells them it is time to fly. Beating their wings for many hours, they cover 200 miles on a good day, though many die on the journey. Russet chests rise and fall repeatedly as they cover great distances. They travel alone or in loose flocks, sometimes with other fruit-eating cousins like mockingbirds, waxwings, and pine grosbeaks, and they form roosts of thousands in swamps. Though perceived as a domestic and familiar species, robins are grand adventurers. They wander widely and unpredictably, finding their way in loose flocks to northern Great Plains, high Rocky Mountains, and western deserts. They roam to varied places in winter but then wayfind to the exact same backyard in spring, including mine, returning to human homes across continents.

Robins, like me, are nomadic in some seasons and homebodies in others. When migrating, they follow the 37-degree isotherm, the geographic line connecting different places with the same temperature. At 37 degrees Fahrenheit, the soil thaws just enough for earthworms to come out of hibernation, during which they have formed a ball of a hundred bodies below the frostline. As ice becomes water, the worms undertake their own vertical migration to the surface of the Earth, towards sunlight and birdish danger. At the same time, robins move ahead of warm fronts and time their arrivals around the rain to meet the earthworms with predatory precision. With this expert timing, they also find the fresh mud required for building nests. They use the angle of the sun to know where they are on the planet, and if blown off course, they reorient themselves by seeking out the sun's angle again.

I continued to be birdlike in my own pregnant migrations, though instead of following the sun like the robin, I followed the night's stars across continents, or perhaps the artificial sun of airport terminals. I travelled pregnant with all three of my babies. With Owl, I journeyed with her in my belly to the United Nations General Assembly in New York City, and again at thirty-two weeks she came with me to lead a menstrual health program with girls and women in rural Cameroon. At eight weeks in utero, Wren had to be one of the youngest boys at the Women's March in Washington in 2017, and nine weeks later he accompanied me to document stories of adolescent mothers in Ghana. My third child wandered with me to Colorado in the heart of winter and Portland during that big melt. Every time I fretted and grappled with a pull to stay home, but listened to my own *zugunruhe* and a strong impulse to continue my calling. Once again, I kissed my sleeping toddlers in their beds, questioning why on Earth I was leaving. I needed to stay and needed to go in equal measure — both choices at once wrong and right. I tore myself away from their warm, softly breathing bodies, which invited me to crawl maternally back to bed, and again cried quietly in the back seat of a dark taxi that took me from the sleeping woods to the sleepless glow of the airport. My unknown baby accompanied me for his third time on an international trip, and together we flew to Helsinki.

I travelled to the 2019 World Circular Economy Forum in Finland, a global gathering of people who spent their days trying to transform economies so that they operated waste-free and powered by renewable energy, rather than continuing with extractive economic systems harming us all. After my work in environmental economics and after my kids' bedtime, I stayed up reading about alternative economic models to the one I knew. Now I would be surrounded by the people who researched those reports and wrote those books.

The circular economy had been gaining in popularity for a few years in Western countries, especially in Europe. In our current economy, we design things to be disposable, and in a circular economy — as I learned from the sustainable fashion scene — every object would be made with a plan for the end of its life from the design stage. A circular economy, like nature, could cycle indefinitely, and through redesign, reduction, repair, reuse, and other practices, waste could be designed out of our lives. Many communities and cultures around the world embrace circular practices like repair and reuse every day. Indigenous peoples for millennia lived — and often continue to live — in a circular way, one that respects seasons and maintains balance through reciprocity with the natural world. This thinking is not always acknowledged in mainstream discussions about the circular economy, but it certainly informs those discussions and offers much to learn.

Founders of the Western concept of the circular economy included Walter Stahel, a Swiss architect, who had been working on the concept for decades. Ellen MacArthur, a yachtswoman who sailed around the world, saw the ravages of plastic waste in the oceans, inspiring her to create the Ellen MacArthur Foundation, a leading organization which advances the circular economy as a global movement dedicated to creating a world without waste. People like Michael Braungart and William McDonough advanced *cradle to cradle*, a method for reimagining the way we make things, so that they have no end of life and rather they can be perpetually reused, repurposed, or remanufactured into something new. Janine Benyus, a biologist and innovator, developed the idea of *biomimicry*, in which nature's design could be a model for human design, like learning from turtle shells about packaging design, or about desert living from a barrel cactus. Biomimicry embraced key principles from nature such as resource sharing, collaboration, and decentralized networked structures, such as those demonstrated by mycelial networks under our feet. The concept also learned from nature about adaptability, resilience, knowledge sharing, open source principles, and creating localized, community-based economies.

Even as I joined the forum, cities and countries announced commitments to address throwaway culture by embracing the circular economy, creating roadmaps and passing legislation. Businesses and citizens used the term more and more until it began to flirt with the fringes of mainstream conversation, with articles, Instagram posts, and businesses calling on people to close the loop.

I soaked up other alternative models, too. I discovered earlier the value of the *sharing economy* in my explorations of tool libraries, and now understood it did not aim to redesign the economy but opted instead to function within capitalism, through the sharing of resources like a car, house, or workspace. I now learned about economic models that strived further, seeking to redesign the structure and ethos of the whole economy. The economist Kate Raworth developed *doughnut economics*, an economic model that rejected the idea of endless growth and instead focused on operating within nature's boundaries (like biodiversity, land, water, and climate), but above the social foundation that would provide the needs of humanity (such as food, water, energy, equality, and political voice). Within those two rings of social and ecological needs, shaped like a doughnut, lay the space where humanity could live safely and justly, if a regenerative and distributive economy were put in place. Carol Anne Hilton put forward *Indigenomics*, a framework for rebuilding and supporting Indigenous economies around the world, and pulling down the systemic barriers that prevented those economies from flourishing. In addition to strengthening the Indigenous economies, Hilton showed that strong Indigenous economies were good for everyone. I also heard about the *regenerative* or *living economy*, in which humans would regenerate land, water, ecosystems, and biodiversity instead of building our lives on an economy that extracted and depleted the Earth. A *well-being economy* recognized that the current linear economy destroyed life and eroded justice, and laid out an economic vision that prioritized human and planetary well-being.

Another concept, *degrowth*, emerged in France in the early 2000s. Degrowth proposed we abandon neverending, exponential growth as a goal, and instead put forward a model of ecological and human well-being where growth may stall or even decline. (Kate Raworth in Doughnut Economics proposes being growth agnostic, and that focusing on meeting humanity's needs while staying within nature's limits may mean economic growth, decline, or stasis at different times and in different places.) Degrowth would happen through changes like reducing production and consumption, establishing alternative ways of living, and implementing policies like a universal basic income. The progress and the health of society would be measured not by Gross Domestic Product (GDP) or exponential economic growth that benefitted a minority, but rather by life expectancy, housing affordability, fulfilling work, quality of healthcare and education, and other social metrics that improve life for the vast majority of people. Degrowth could also mean that unpaid care work, which is devalued in modern capitalism, could be treated as meaningful and valuable work. The term *degrowth* originates from Latin languages, referring to a river returning to its regular flow after a disastrous flood.

How much do we love the current economic system, the status quo, the flood? Enough to face hazy skies, empty of birds? Enough to let our forests empty of our fellow species? Enough to see our wetlands, forests, and meadows razed and replaced with pavement? Enough to live lonely on this planet, without the species and ecosystems that have evolved alongside us? Certainly we don't love the current linear system — the convenience, the status quo — that much. Besides, the trappings of that system lay increasingly out of reach for most people, with the majority of people struggling.

While intrigued by possible alternative models, the word *economy* caused me to freeze: I found it intimidating, the realm of serious men. My body responded with imposter syndrome to the world of economics, an unexpected reaction when I took the job in environmental economics at the same time as I moved to the woods. Never a nervous public speaker before, now before presentations my hands turned icy cold, and an unpleasant full body sensation of both sleepiness and fear took over my body. My voice quivered and my legs went numb under the boardroom table. We worked towards admirable ends for the environment, but the vernacular of economic credibility made my palms sweat. *"Where does this sense of inadequacy come from?"* I asked myself, frustrated after I spoke to a board of directors, so nervous that a glass of water beside me shattered in the middle of my presentation. I hadn't touched it, but it seemed to break on account of being so close to my anxiety. I carried on, meek and childlike with a shaky voice, fighting the urge to be sick from nerves.

As I delved uncomfortably into jargon and frameworks and my physical reaction to them, I asked myself questions about my own relationship to the economy. The word *economy* held its origins in the Greek word *oikonomia*, meaning household management. The term referred to how society managed its limited resources. In other words, *economy* should connote how we steward our home. When I thought about the word that way, as caring management of our home, it felt like the word might not just be for the suit-clad investors and economists, but it might be for me, too. Perhaps it was for all of us, and benefitted us all if only we understood it better. *Economy* does not necessarily mean unfettered economic growth at all costs, and it needs to be understood and meaningfully redesigned in order to address climate change, protect biodiversity, and ensure fair and equitable livelihoods.

In the conversations in Finland, some people, me included, worried that the term circular economy risked being co-opted or absorbed into the lexicon as a new buzzword that did not mean enough. In the design and scaling of a circular economy, it would also be important that we let go of the celebration of a solitary saviour. We like having innovators — be they people or companies — that we adore. We heap praise on them and expect them to bring us to safety. Headlines about the circular economy often focus on the biggest companies and the novel, innovative material they are using or their new commitment in the next decade. While those important commitments should be recognized, one company's actions cannot get us out of this mess, and we need collaboration and global solutions. Business as usual — but with recycled materials — falls short. The relentless pursuit of sales and consumption — but with more conscious products — won't solve our problems.

So what might be enough? As I learned from people gathered in Finland and along my journey, building corporate strategies for degrowth, where perhaps companies make and sell fewer items, employ more people, and the folks at the top live within more moderate means.

What might be enough? Consumers remembering they are citizens of the Earth first, and saying no to purchases they don't need. Living more simply and buying high-quality, circular, and second-hand items only when needed.

What might be enough? Communities strengthening bonds and sharing resources and services amongst one another.

What might be enough? A circular economy that models itself not off the old linear economy, but rather truly looks to nature for inspiration. Nature refined this blueprint over billions of years: using only what she needs, building resilience through diversity, cooperating among individuals and species, rotting waste into food, and reusing and repurposing materials in an endless cycle.

For the circular economy, or any alternative model, to be meaningful, it needed to recognize Indigenous worldviews and pay reparations to the people who had been exploited, traumatized, and marginalized in the centuries-long project of the linear, patriarchal, colonial, capitalist economy. An alternate model needed to look not just at reducing physical waste, but also at what and who powered the new economy, including renewable energy even with its various pitfalls, as well as with just labour practices. We would need to stop treating workers in the same linear fashion that we treat our trees, minerals, soil, and water, extracting as much as possible for as little money as possible, meaning many people face long hours, burnout, stress, unsafe working conditions, low pay, and lack of humanity. It means many people struggle, overworked, while others face underemployment. Humans, as an integral part of nature, function not in lines but in cycles. This means time for productivity as well as time for rest and recuperation. Promising work models experiment with allowing for the full expression of a person, through flexibility, shorter work weeks, sabbaticals, seventh years for creativity, and more workers for less time and more money so we can tackle unemployment and burnout concurrently. When fulfilled, people don't need to fill their emptiness and treat their exhaustion with consumption. In the inimitable words of Tricia Hersey in *Rest is Resistance*, "We are socialized into systems that cause us to conform and believe our worth is connected to how much we can produce. Our constant labour becomes a prison that allows us to be disembodied. We become easy for the systems to manipulate, disconnected from our power as divine beings and hopeless. We forget how to dream. This is how grind culture continues. We internalize the lies and in turn become agents of an unsustainable way of living." She articulates how the capitalist system and current economy are built on slave labour, and how rest can powerfully advance justice and dismantle oppression.

A truly transformative circular economy needed to grow justice from the very seeds of the new model. People, land, water, and animals would have to be seen, not as resources, but as beings worthy of respect. This required much more than changing economic processes and how we deal with stuff. It required a whole shift in mindset, culture, stories, and relationships to each other and nature. The economy is worthless if it is not designed to be in service to life: the lives of animals and ecosystems. Yellow cypress trees, estuaries, mosses, herons.

Learning about the emerging models to reshape the economy, I realized that along my quest I had moved away from prioritizing individual actions and incremental improvements to the current system, and towards radical, whole-of-society changes. Radical, according to Angela Davis, "simply means grasping things at the root."

The time for incremental change is behind us, if ever it existed. We have been told we can make easy, simple changes. Turn off lights. Reuse containers. Recycle better. Click and sign here to save the world. But the reality is we do not need easy, simple changes. We need the big and difficult ones. Transforming our politics, our economy, our businesses. Reconnecting with our natural selves and our relationship to nature. Redesigning our products, our homes, our cities. The smaller, personal actions empower us and help build collective momentum, but they alone are insufficient. We live in a time that requires leaping towards uncomfortable change. A time for being courageous. A time for saying no and going without things we are accustomed to. A time for a whole-of-self transformation, one that is messy and imperfect and wholehearted.

I did not yet feel confident enough to fully embrace this radical self-transformation. I felt childish, timid, and naively earnest. Afraid to get it wrong. Afraid to waste precious time on actions that others would criticize because they were insufficient, or harmful despite my good intentions.

I explored environmental action within the frame of normal trends and my research, but I remained unclear on *my* role. Protest and grassroots action? Letters to politicians? Consumer decisions, like supporting my local farmers' markets when I could? Daily actions like cycling and composting? Teaching my children to love nature? Internal work, deconstructing capitalist stories about my productivity as worth, so that I could learn first how to stop extracting from myself so I could eventually help us stop extracting from a hurting Earth? Simply doing and buying less, focusing on what I could do in my home? Trying to help redesign the economy, with big work changing systems? Art that moved people? Stretched across my many responsibilities, these actions felt like far too much — and facing the immensity of the quickly accelerating climate, biodiversity, and waste crises, they also seemed deeply insufficient.

The Whittakers took a long walk on my aunt and uncle's ninety acres of forest, meadow, field, and pond. We trekked through the long grass and around the old barn, filled with a decades-old Mercedes-Benz, piles of cut wood, grain milling equipment, and mysterious shrines my uncle built. Burrs stuck to our pant legs, shoelaces, and the ankles of our socks as we walked over a hidden population of earthworms under our feet. Golden light crossed the serpentine path, and the nostalgic sound of geese flying overhead called out against the sunset. Two-month-old Wren slept against my chest in a carrier, and two-year-old Owl walked beside me in her rubber boots. Three dogs forked off into the long grass to chase private scents, and our extended family grouped into duos and trios. Conversations that had stayed polite and contained indoors now flowed freely outdoors.

Small toads leapt out of the way of our giant feet, and I made a mental note to ask my dad to catch one to show to Owl. He used to do that for me when my sister and I were girls. As I drifted to the childhood memory of a small, watchful toad in his hands, my dad walked up to my children and me. He cupped his two hands around a frightened, staring toad. *You can count on Wade Whittaker to catch a toad and quietly show it to a child*, I thought. Just as you can rely on him to give a robin's egg in a nest for a graduation gift, after saving it for over a decade.

Later, as we drove home in the dark, Owl and I talked sleepily about our gratitude for the day in our nightly ritual. Bedtime had always been the time, the only time, when she showed vulnerability, when I learned how she experienced her life and what made an impression on her. As tires crunched on country gravel roads, and with her strapped into her car seat in her pajamas, she shared gratitude for the toad we saw hours before.

"He had a sad face," she added.

"Oh, really? Why do you say that?" I asked, curious to understand. Usually so closed, so brave, Owl felt frequently overwhelmed by emotions and sensations that often left her in attack mode, a way to cope with being a sensitive creature in an abrasive world.

"He was away from his family."

"Oh, that would make him sad. Do you think he is back with them now in the grass?"

"I think so." She sounded unconvinced and her face wilted, and I sensed that she was trying to make me feel better.

"Being a toad must be fun," she said, and then, sadly, "except you live a lot shorter." She paused. "Maybe a day seems longer to them."

It has always been hard to know how much fairy tale to offer her, or how much to allow sorrow to exist.

At night in Helsinki, I disappeared whenever I could to wander the cobblestone streets, away from the overwhelm of socializing at the conference. Walking anonymously and alone, I could be myself, finding the perfect restaurant and writing for hours. In midsummer, the sun set around eleven p.m., enabling my night owl habits despite the forum starting early the next day with its attendant badges, coffee urns, and freshly showered participants. On my last night, I slowly enjoyed my meal surrounded by the din of humanity that fills a restaurant, the noise touching every wall like water in a glass. Worries crept in that I'd spent too much money or stayed up too late, but I knew that I would soon reenter childbirth, newborn care, and the full-time parenting of three children four years old and under, and I needed to take this pleasure where I could.

Walking through narrow streets on an indirect path back to my hotel, I questioned the sessions in which I spent my last few days. Supply chains, incentives, material flows. Important conversations about how to end waste and create an economy that worked in a closed loop — topics I cared about. So why did I see myself as too earnest, too emotional, too led by the heart? Other sensitive people like me had to be out there, I believed, feeling deeply under the demands of extroversion and ambition, under the outward polish. Humanity exists in all of us — the mammal part, made of water and carbon and oxygen. The part that reacts with the wind, turns our faces to the sun and rain, finds belonging in towering forests, brings ocean air into our lungs. We hurt that mammal self as much as we hurt the other mammals, our kin. Endangering our own species as we do the others. Addicted to a progress, growth, and consumption machine that engines against our well-being, our home. What do you do when you walk around in the world as sad as a girl who is crying for a toad that is separated from his family? What do you do when you have a mammal body with a human mind, made of earth and water, grieving human suffering and the disappearance of nature and creatures so deeply that the despair threatens to suffocate you?

I thought darkly of my own questions as I walked in a faraway cobblestone city. Despite my fervent desire to understand, I didn't have answers. I suppose you do everything that you can. You storm with the energy of a wild horse, to not drown in the despair of doing nothing. You remind yourself you are one of the deeply sensitive ones for a reason. You remind yourself that many more exist out there, a community grieving this great loss of life and land, and who are desperate to be a part of a revolution of regeneration that gives back to the Earth with creaturely imperfection.

When I returned home from Helsinki, I took a taxi back from the airport, filled with excitement as the car's nose dipped down the curving road over the creek and towards our cabin. *Home.* I ran in the front door and covered my children with kisses, my tears running into their hair as they hugged me tightly. They cried, too, and from Wren's cheek I wiped a rolling tear on my pinky finger and placed the liquid on my tongue, tasting its saltiness. Motherhood is physical, and the distance from children painful. I dug through my suitcase, which started its day somewhere between Scandinavia and Russia, and pulled out gifts of Moomintroll books, a small Marimekko change purse, branded conference memorabilia, and packages of free treats from the airplane. We sat on my bed, exploring the new treasures, and my eyes drifted to the top of my bookshelf, to where the decades-old robin's nest lay.

My dad found the nest when I was six years old. He saved the fragile thing for twelve years before giving it to me when I graduated from high school. An organized tangle of faded brown twigs and soft grey feathers, the shallow cup held together with archaic mud. The mother crafted the nest after she coordinated with the sun's angle and made the perilous journey along the 37-degree isotherm, staying ahead of warm fronts in pursuit of home. Her mate found nest materials and protected their territory as she built and weaved, as she managed their household. Oikonomia. Nested in the middle lay a single light blue egg, now preserved for three decades. How many robin generations pass in thirty years? Surely this mother's once-tiny babies are now ancestors many times over. The bottom side of the egg was cracked open, from where Wren grabbed at it while we moved into the cabin. Rage swelled in my throat when he dropped the fragile thing on the cement floors of our new home, after I'd carefully moved it across six apartments, an island home, a country home and then, to the woods. An ancient nest and egg are not easy objects to transport. Thin walls, easily hurt. I held my anger in messily, vibrating with the irreplaceability of the nest and egg, and then laid the nest and egg on the furthest reaches of my bookshelf to protect them from further damage. Even the intact side of the egg showed a pencil-line crack running down its length. Between my thumb and forefinger, I could hold the delicate, dusty egg, which over time faded closer to the grey of its feathered home, or of the dust that collected in the nest. If I was very careful, I could turn it around to peek into its yellowed inside, and see where a crackling, amber layer peeled away from a snow-white wall. The messy inner work required of birth and transformation. The nest and egg documented life and care, a legacy of some robin mother's life's work. Hopefully her children experienced her as a nest-builder, provider, nurturer, and teacher, when she herself was wayfinding.

9

WHEN ROTTEN GRASS BECOMES FIREFLIES

Growing Food

"And yet, that gentle turr-turr-ing tugging at the heartstrings is also a signal of repair, recovery and rebirth, the rebraiding of unravellings." **ISABELLA TREE**

I planted the seeds late, on the summer solstice, after returning from Helsinki. I gathered the supplies and the wherewithal to go down to the garden and do the thing for which there never seemed to be enough time: plant seeds in soil. On top of an over-accumulation of school drop-offs and Zoom meetings, a conveyor belt of urgent deadlines, and halfway keeping a house tidy, when would a person possibly plant seeds? And lovingly? After their children's bedtime, of course, and before the next work day of overlapping screens and tabs. In the sacred space that falls after kids' bedtime, a magical catchment in which I imagine I can do a thousand things. "Carving" out time? Is that the right way to describe time stolen from responsibilities for other important needs? As if all available time is already filled, completely?

I tucked shovels and trowels under one arm, and on the other I carried a wicker basket. In the basket was a bottle of rosé and a copper mug, snuggled securely beside half-opened packets of seeds, with their remaining pearls of life safely secured by squares of clay-coloured masking tape. The small collection of seeds had remained relegated to the barn workshop, still taped shut, after moving around with us to our numerous homes.

I walked down to the meadow, basket in tow, waist-high wildflowers arcing towards me from both sides, with mutual adoration. Every time I walked down through those flowers into the meadow, I took a deep breath to finally slow myself. Every time, I greeted the flowers and the soil and the garden beds. Out loud. "Hello, Milkweed. Hello, Chicory." Every time, they welcomed me in the dusk as they sleepily closed their petals.

From under my foot, a Northern Red-bellied Snake darted away, startling me the same way I startled him. Panicked, scared for his life, he slithered into the thick growth at the edges of the meadow.

"You are safe," I crooned, wishing I could take away his worry.

I spoke to him the way I wanted to speak to myself. *You are safe.* I spoke to nature the way I wanted to speak to myself. *You are beautiful. You are loved.*

"I love you," I said out loud, to the trees with their tops blurring into the darkening sky. It dawned on me: these trees, birds, and wildflowers loved me every day, even as they watched me rush and flurry. Like I did as a mother to my children, they said I *love you* a hundred times daily, often not heard but hopefully felt. I hurried and fretted too much to hear it. Finally I said the words in return, and it must have meant the world to the Earth, like when my daughter and son lay sleepily on their pillows and surprised me with I *love you* back.

Thousands of fireflies greeted me with joy and light, twinkles of gold flashing across the meadow. I had never seen such a congregation of these luminescent creatures, not here in the woods or anywhere, sparkling around me in every direction, at every level of the sky below the tops of the trees. In that Japanese calendar of microseasons, the time before the solstice is when rotten grass turns into fireflies.

Planting the garden was not a chore. I was not one person plodding along, planting alone, but rather part of an earthly festival, in the good company of fireflies, soil, and worms, accompanied by the instrumental score of the rushing creek, lit by the setting solstice sun and the rising moon. I got into the celebratory mood, opening the wine and pouring a splash with words of thanks at the base of each of the six hügel garden beds, and then I poured a taste for myself. I shared sweet sips with the other party guests: an assembly of bugs in my copper cup. Joyously, I planted, an earnest amateur in the soil. I sowed seeds lovingly, at first. Intentionally, sweetly, without knowing what I was doing. My past attempts at growing food had been scrappy and largely unsuccessful, with old damp seeds and poor clay-heavy soil. Distracted and inconsistent planning, and neglectful weeding. Cheap old seeds poked into an untended lawn outside a rental apartment. That first bathtub-and-steamer-trunk garden of carrots and nasturtiums on Ward's Island.

Early attempts in the backyard of the rural house, alongside baby-having, child-rearing, and a demanding career. This was my most wholehearted attempt at growing food. My mind sought answers for how to plant *right* — what depth, what spacing, how many seeds? Who grew pleasantly with radishes? I tried in the dark to read the small print on the back of the seed packets, straining by the light of the headlamp, the black print inking into the black air. I followed the instructions dutifully, to the best of my ability, but no matter how hard I tried, a strong sense of apology rose up, and I berated myself for planting wrong.

Though the longest day of the year, night still fell. Somewhere in the evening, a madwoman — me — known to rush and overproduce, decided she must plant all six beds at once, tonight. Maybe not a decision, but rather a well-practiced pattern of pushing and perfection. After thoughtfully planting the first three beds, I moved more quickly. I started shoving two — or three, or eight — seeds in one hole, plunging seeds into the soil at varying, erratic depths. Spaghetti at a wall, seeds in the soil. Hours passed and my urgency grew, unchecked. I became haphazard. Rushed. Frantic. Mosquitos swarmed my headlamp. They bit my arms, face, and neck, and I scratched at their bites with dirty nails, between hastily popping more seeds into the Earth. I planted wildly.

With two beds left to plant, several packets of seeds remained in the wicker basket. My mind blamed myself for my shortcomings, my wrongness, my chaos. I berated myself for not being done already, for not having done this sooner, for not knowing how to grow. Above all, I felt guilty for not planting with enough care. I told myself that I should be both faster, to get the job done, and slower, to cultivate loving seedlings. Either way, I knew I was wrong.

Even the fireflies and mosquitoes disappeared, wisely choosing bed. The fruit flies drowned in my cup. Only my lone headlamp flickered in the meadow, a solitary beam where before thousands of lights lit the land. The celebration was decidedly over, but I kept planting.

Watching me unravel, the garden smiled wryly. "You care so much! You're frantic! Why don't you come back tomorrow?" she thought quietly.

I have never known when to leave a party. I stay too long, because of guilt and awkwardness, or I fear offending the hosts. I have also never known when to quit something. *Why didn't I quit? Why did I keep pushing?* I asked too late, and I let go slowly. My ardent persistence confused me — is it admirable commitment or utter madness? There are shades of both. *Perhaps I should stop halfway through and seek some balance,* I thought, knowing myself. Knowing I would not stop until it was done. With my all-or-nothing focus, balance is elusive.

The garden planted, I went to bed, itchy and embarrassed, but satisfied that I had completed planting the garden. *I have a lifetime of work to do before I am balanced and calm,* I thought. Before I sorted myself out, and learned how to take care of myself. *Isn't that why I moved here, to the woods?*

For days, I searched her soil for sprouts. Signs of life. It was too soon, but my eagerness refused to wait. Finally, I spotted green spots smaller than a mouse's ear. These might be shoots from the seeds that I planted. Days and nights passed, and the sprouts grew taller, encased by the split-open carcass of seed that once held their baby bodies. I imagined the drama of breaking open that must happen for roots and shoots to grow. I knew what that felt like: the cracking open of birth. The bewildered, deeply moving afterbirth and aftermath, where identity is broken like those seed casings and remade. Breaking open, down, and through is part of the process of new life, and the attendant life-altering change of becoming a mother. That radical change is necessary for all of us, the carers, the cultivators of seeds. Bigness and softness are good, and require courage. Luckily Mother Nature showed me, with her seeds opening, that shattering can provide fertile ground for growth.

The passing of weeks saw the seedlings mature. They begin to differentiate from one another more clearly. My beginner's eyes watched in wonder as celery, radish, cucumber, Swiss chard, and rapini announced themselves. When I walked down through that alley of adoring wildflowers, I greeted the meadow and the hügels. Every single time, I thought of the solstice, with its wine poured gratefully into soil, its fireflies, its mosquitoes smothering my headlamp, my slow unravelling. I was amazed that vegetables grew steadily, in spite of the disorder with which I planted the seeds. Even though I barely knew what I was doing, and oscillated between joy and resentment, trying to get it just right but doing a slap-dash job, she gave generously. She offered me radishes, tomatoes, leeks, celery, beans, cucumbers, lettuce, cabbages, and one pumpkin-y gourd. She gave me rich Swiss chard as long as my arm. She offered my daughter six sunflowers ringed with nasturtiums — one for each garden bed — and even the one that was later unearthed (twice) by my son flourished.

When I pulled the first radishes, garlic, and beans from the garden, I shook clumps of soil back onto the beds. Taking bites of food that I grew in collaboration with the sun and soil, I gratefully received the nourishment offered by the Earth, even in all my wayward imperfection.

I still pushed myself too hard at work, after a million promises to slow down. I said that others made me do it, but I silently wondered if I fell into old patterns and forced myself too much. I made impossible feats possible, and earned headaches and dizziness from too much glare and achievement. Motion sickness from too many Zooms in which my eyes darted ceaselessly from place to place. Dart, dart, dart. Frantic, productive, distracted. I accomplished so much and received praise. Meanwhile, from the window beside my desk, beside that old feathered pine with its neighbourhood of birds, I averted my eyes from the endless glow of busyness. I saw the meadow. There, beyond the waving walls of wildflowers inviting me to visit, lay the six hügels where, at the pace of life, food grew. I unravelled and respooled daily, while she grew gently. I looked at the soil, where I was a clumsy and content amateur. There is where I remembered that I lived on a planet of nightingales and willow warblers. Little wolverine moss and great blue whales. Meadow, creek, jungle, mountain, grassland, desert, tundra, and woodland. There is where I remembered that I live on a planet of glittering fireflies.

In the garden is where I let myself stand, unknowing of answers. Relieved of the responsibility of a world on fire. Noticing that the peas all died while the beans thrived, and I had no idea why. I did not need to know, and *the result was not my fault.* The peas' failure to thrive was not a measure of my worth. I was not to be blamed for the peas, nor praised for the beans. I planted seeds and cultivated the garden wholeheartedly,

10

CREEK AND HERON

Birth

"The change will come from those who know they do not exist separately but as part of the river." **v**

The resilient coltsfoot shed delicate flowers with their manes of narrow yellow petals, though their hardy green bodies continued to grow. Wide leaves expanded slowly, roots creeping downwards, unseen by me. As above, so below. Goldenrod burgeoned everywhere. The stalks grew tall, with the golden florets waving gently at shoulder height. The goldenrod sipped summery rainwater and signalled that autumn whispered close by again.

Motherhood made herself known as many conflicting things at once. I experienced darkness, in a way I hadn't for a very long time — breathless with anxiety, small, ruinous, teary. Like I broke things that I touched. No matter how much I did, I fell sadly short of *enough*. There rushed a current, but somehow every time I tried to find it, I found myself struggling against its patient flow. My anger and grief about the disappearance of landscapes and creatures continued to plague me, amidst a tangle of pregnancy anxiety. I felt simultaneously grateful and exhausted, visited by vivid dreams and an aching pelvis. Despite my mood and pelvis, I felt at ease with my third pregnancy in five years. It was familiar. My sweet creature stirred within me, moving often, calm and reassuring. He hummed of mystery, as close as a person can be while also living in a far-off universe. I held my belly with adoration, trying to be as close to him as possible, daydreaming about his name and birth date, and what he would look like. Overwhelming pangs of sadness lived separately from the all-encompassing love that grew steadily for him.

During this pregnancy, I migrated to Boulder, Portland, and Helsinki. It was now time to stay in one geography to nest. I travelled slowly between work in the city and family in the woods each day. In the lunchroom one day, a colleague who was a mother of three shared her experience of *not* pushing during childbirth. She let the baby arrive in its own good time, letting go of control and allowing her body to guide the process without any active pushing. This shocked me — *was that possible?* I'd read countless books on positive birth, and the concept of *not* pushing was new to me. I thought back to my childbirth experiences, largely positive if intense. Birthing Owl, I roared her into the world with a ferocity I had never experienced in my life. Feral, powerful roars, and a forcefulness that led to a major and rare tear that took time to heal. With Wren, I endeavoured to roar less wildly, and his arrival, while somewhat gentler in a birth tub at home in the minutes before two a.m., still required intense active pushing. Thinking of my colleague's experience, I left work early and walked slowly in the mid-September heat to the library, where I returned a quarter-finished copy of Ina May Gaskin's *Spiritual Midwifery*, a book I'd read in previous pregnancies. I didn't need it. Slowly walking up the cement stairs, I walked to the library door and slid the book in the return slot. Each time before I gave birth, time slowed down, and I slowed down too, in the hours leading up to labour. I ambled late to commitments, unwilling to rush, trusting my natural pace.

That evening at home, once my children slept, instead of giving in to sleep I started working with my hands on the projects that drew my interest during pregnancy: macrame and drying flowers. I knotted white rope, formed the triangle of the number four, pulled the end of the rope around and through, tugged the knot up to the top with satisfaction, and started again. I took dainty white wildflowers from the side of the ditch and taped the stems together with flower tape, wrapped them in ribbon, and hung them from the wooden beam in the kitchen. Never before or after that pregnancy had I been called to pick wildflowers and lovingly tie them with plump cream string, or to knot the macrame string to create wall hangings, but when my third child lived inside me, I felt an inexplicable draw to these handcrafts. I stayed up late, drying my flowers, as the hours before the awakening of children and the beginning of the next work day shortened.

Friday the thirteenth started at dawn, after a night of contractions. I tiptoed out of bed to make a mug of tea, which I cupped in my hands as I walked out of the sleeping cabin into the early morning light. That night a full moon would appear. I walked rhythmically alongside the forest, and walked onto the large rock in the middle of the creek. We called this rock the splash pad, because the kids stomped in the shallow water around it in their rubber boots. The creek's current also splashed over those rocky surfaces, particularly in the springtime as the snow melted down from the hills. As my contractions kept coming, I pictured all the seasons, those of both nature and my own life, playing out in relationship to this flowing creek.

The most cyclical of things, pregnancy and birth and caring for babies, can be treated with impossible linearity in our mainstream culture: you should conceive in this way between certain ages, and by this or that week, you should feel a hiccup or a kick. You should time the spacing of your children in a particular way. Your contractions will be this long, labour will last that long, pushing will be less than two hours, and the umbilical cord will be cut at this time. Your baby will sleep by so many months, stop nursing at a certain time, and reach monthly milestones. Timelines. Time. Lines. My experience proved different. Becoming pregnant and welcoming my first child somehow freed me to listen to my intuition over other voices and follow my own rhythm rather than external timelines.

I saw the moon in the morning sky, as I walked and walked and walked. I could not stop walking. I walked back down the road as the sun rose higher, away from the splash pad and towards the cabin. I walked around the kitchen island, the one that the kids ran around before bedtime, moving continually with calm, knowing obsession. Around and around, moving to absorb the immensity of every infinite, intensifying contraction. When contractions begin, you feel like your normal human self, and as they become faster and more intense, you enter an otherworldly darkness.

Eventually, I woke Nik and called the midwife, Gabrielle. Nik inflated the birth tub in the living room, on the red and blue patterned rug, between the fireplace and the sliding-door window looking west onto the cars and the woods. We planned to give birth at home in a tub, as with Wren. Owl and Wren ran around as Nik pushed on an air pump, slowly inflating the tub.

"With the full moon and Friday the thirteenth, many women are ready to give birth," Gabrielle explained over the phone. "Can you come to the birth centre?"

"Nik," I breathed inwards in the middle of a contraction. He continued to pump. "Stop. No tub," I explained, curving my back to absorb the pain of the contraction. "We can't stay here, let's go to the birth centre." We left the tub half-inflated, and I kept walking around the kitchen island wordlessly when the neighbours came to take Owl and Wren. They performed the mundane routine of velcroing shoes and grabbing hats from the overfull drawers in the front hall, while I walked.

Nik and I piled into the car, and as the station wagon curved away from Birdsong Cabin and out of the quiet safety of our valley, I thought of the birth story my colleague told me the day before. *How could I possibly not push?* I'd spent my life forcing things to happen.

A decade before I stood in the creek on the crest of childbirth, I became unnerved when my surgery was scheduled for a Friday the thirteenth. I was uneasy with how that famously superstitious date collided with my personal emergency. Near the end of my dance training, I suffered a traumatic accident in class. During a sequence travelling across the floor, I rehearsed a movement where I kicked as high as I could with one leg, while tilting as far as I could to the ground with my torso on the other side. I performed the movement aggressively, and without having enough time to register what happened, I fell to the ground hard, hitting my head, thigh, and left elbow. In the habit of pushing myself to the limit, I pushed myself too far. I fell unconscious.

After coming to on the studio floor, paramedics rushed me in an ambulance to the hospital, where I received a make-shift cast on my arm. The doctors explained that the cast would see me through to surgery. They gave me morphine and I suffered a disorienting reaction to the drug, because I had lied about what I'd eaten for breakfast that day. I'd eaten next to nothing, but my anorexia was my secret and I wasn't going to spill it to some strangers from the naked vulnerability of my medical gown. They told me it would take months for my elbow to heal, and though I should be able to use it for daily tasks in time, my arm may never work normally, and I would never dance properly again. Instead of feeling devastated, I dug into disbelief and denial.

"I have tickets to go to New York City this weekend, and I have performances and auditions coming up," I protested to the doctor, refusing to believe I faced multiple surgeries and a long recovery with no guarantee of a functioning arm at the end. I could not move my fingers, but still I insisted from my stretcher in the fluorescent hospital hallway that I would be dancing at the barre the next day. The doctors patiently explained that this was not a straightforward broken arm and that I had suffered permanent damage, but I refused to listen. I refused to accept boundaries. If I were going to succeed in a competitive field, I needed to train, audition, and perform. Our final performances and auditions were lined up to launch our careers, the pinnacle of our conservatory program. But my denial was futile, and I soon found myself in surgery to rebuild my broken wing.

The operation went well. The surgeon pieced my arm back together with a collection of metal plates and screws, and a line of staples bridged a raw, four-inch scar. I spent the night in hospital awake and in pain, thinking about a future for which I'd sacrificed so much, but which nevertheless disappeared in front of me. I could barely sit up or move my fingers, let alone dance, and my dreams of performing around the world and choreographing moving dance works evaporated. I lost my restaurant server job immediately as I couldn't carry anything, and I relied on a line of credit to pay my bills. My identity as a dancer, developed since I was three years old, crumbled, and I did not know who I was without it. Twenty years of rigorous training, dreaming, and dedication ended in a hospital bed, where I lay unsure about what came next.

Over the next eighteen months, two more surgeries addressed various complications and rebuilt my arm, and I went to the physiotherapy trauma unit five days a week to relearn how to use my arm for simple daily actions like holding a spoon and washing my hair. For weeks after each surgery, my elbow was locked at a ninety-degree angle, and I attempted to straighten it with excruciating exercises. The nurses tied my arm to the bed, as straight as it would go for as long as I could tolerate. I continued to train in the studio, alarming my fellow dancers and teachers as my heavy cast threw me off balance in messy pirouettes. Even in crisis and pain, I refused to stop striving. After the cast came off, I performed on stage with every movement adapted to my signature crooked left arm. I couldn't yet see how pushing too hard and the obsession with perfection landed me here.

Staring ahead at an uncertain future and the possibility of failure, I kept pushing. As my ballet teacher once said to our whole class during a barre exercise, "Everyone try harder — except Alice Irene." I always tried too hard and pushed too far. I went into frightening debt financing my own dance works and continued choreographing to accommodate my crooked left arm, even as close dancer allies told me that I was no longer a real dancer because I'd taken a nine-to-five job. I still resolved to keep trying.

During my final performance in an artist residency, six-week-old Owl waited in her heavy baby seat in the theatre dressing room, part of the hushed magic of backstage. Under the hyperactive glow of makeup lights, her perfect newborn face reflected in the spotted, blurry backstage mirror. After the performance, I stood outside the stage door, crestfallen and in tears: all my hard work left me unfulfilled. Empty. The sacrifices no longer felt worthwhile.

After a decade of successes, failures, injuries, hunger, and heartbreaks, I summoned the courage to let go. I quit dancing. Quitting seems shameful when, for years, you build your worth around the conviction that you will do anything to succeed. My self-worth hinged on my unwavering dedication to professional dance. Over time, though, I learned how to be at peace with the words, "I used to be a dancer." The words evolved from shameful to liberating. Since girlhood, my identity, my days, and my dreams of my future devoted themselves to dance. Now, I needed to imagine other futures for myself, not out of choice but out of grief and heartbreak, in a tiny microcosm of the work we need to do to reimagine our society. By letting go of the childhood dream, I became beautifully unmoored. Free to rebuild a new version of myself in an unknowable future.

Arriving at the birth centre before nine a.m. on that Friday the thirteenth, I heaved myself out of the car and placed my half-eaten banana on the dashboard to roast in the sun. I concentrated on the fruit and thought, *when I see this banana again, I will have my baby with me.* The midwives greeted us and set us up in a birth room. Young and outdoorsy, my midwife Gabrielle wore brown corduroy overalls and smiled often.

"I'm going to go help a woman down the hall who has been with us for a few hours," she let us know, leaving Nik and I to the clean, bright room.

I kept walking, leaving Nik mid-sentence whenever a new contraction approached from far off in the distance, and I readied myself for it to swallow me completely. Doubts and fear flickered — *could I really do this?* — and I repeated mantras. *I can do this. My body is made to bring my baby into the world.* Nik offered me a massage, like the ones I needed when birthing Wren, but I refused. I walked non-stop.

When it came time, I knew my son approached, ready to be born.

"Nik, go get the midwife."

"Are you sure?"

"The baby is ready."

He ran down the hall, leaving me certain our son would arrive before they returned, though I did not care much. I always craved privacy in childbirth. A whole-body impulse came over me, similar to reaching the top of a rollercoaster, with only one way to go, and I held back the urge to push and roar mightily like I had before. I rejected the stories and film scenes I absorbed over decades that told me I needed to push hard and mightily. I thought of the creek, and of the wise words, *this is the way the river is flowing.*

Nik and the midwife arrived, and she followed me as I walked to the corner of the room with the next contraction.

"I can do this," I told her, holding onto the wall.

"You *are* doing it," she laughed kindly.

I walked to the middle of the room and gave in to the greatest intensity I ever experienced. I stood up, partway between the bath and the bed and the door to the hallway, my feet planted on the floor. I opened my mouth wide, silent, in an expression of awe rather than fear. Instead of pushing or doing anything other than accepting everything, I let birth happen to me. The room expanded, and power surged through me, through my son. Infinite stars, all-consuming ocean waves. I gave in and let birth unfold, in its own time, outside of my control. I was the whole world.

The midwife caught the perfect creature and passed him to me, the most energized and powerful person in the world. *I love you I love you I love you I love you I love you* I whispered, pushing my face into his.

Birth unfolds, long or slow — long *and* slow — teaching us hard lessons along the way. Sometimes the experience hits us with such strength that we believe we cannot tolerate another minute. The only way for birth to unfold is to experience it, gently or with great force, calmly or with fear. *Through.* Childbirth taught me so much, every time — the time I pushed with all my might until I held my firstborn, overcome with shock, pride and relief; the time with my second born when I pushed with more restraint surrounded by water in the middle of the night; and the time I let go of control and listened to my wisdom and third baby as he led. Three homes with Nik, and a baby in each. The bigness of the experience pushed me to the brink of what I could withstand, and to the expansive greatness of my love, strength, and wholeness. Birth showed me that great tenderness and great power can coexist.

My own birth into being an imperfect mother, learning to care for the Earth, my children, and myself with deep love, acceptance, and power unfolds, with stops and starts, long and slow and not quite how I expected. The indescribable power of birth is transformative and healing, and needed for life on this planet.

The regenerative, resilient world we are ready to usher in will be like childbirth. The only way to bring it to fruition will be *through*. It will take every fiber of our being to bring it to life. There will be moments when it looms bigger than us. Too daunting, too insurmountable. It will take surrender. It will not be tidy, controlled, well-timed, or predictable. It will not acquiesce to our longing for an easeful transition. We will have to call up the natural wisdom embedded in our genetic material, and it will take the vast amounts of strength that we have in our bellies.

After birth, I held my beautiful third child in my grateful arms, lying dazed and blissful in the comfortable bed with my placenta on a tray on one side of me, and the world's most delicious breakfast of orange juice and muffin on a tray on the other. My energy plummeted, and I could barely sit up, other than to coo over his perfect face, his perfect body, the smallest of my babies. We phoned loved ones on FaceTime to introduce our treasured son, and my first worry about his screen time flashed amidst the timeless beauty.

Ciarán Keith Heron. Ciarán means little dark one. Keith, the name of my father and grandfather, means wood. And Heron, after the bird who lives in our creek and whom we saw often, gliding elegantly over the splash pad where my children played and where I later stood, holding a mug of tea in my hands as I worked to bring a new creature to the banks of this flowing water. The bird's namesake enjoyed the auspicious birthday of Friday the thirteenth.

There are as many different birth stories as there are humans in the world, and every childbirth experience is valid, in all its joy, trauma, fear, transformation, and complexity. Sometimes birth calls on us to learn the lessons that come hardest for us. How to push harder, or how to embrace the unexpected, or how to surrender, or how to abandon plans. How to establish boundaries, how to collaborate with our new child, or how to survive through hardship and pain. Birth stretches us to the limits of ourselves. For me, this experience of letting go transformed me completely. I understood that my ongoing struggle to listen to my own inner voice was unfolding as a gradual and imperfect process, like the healing of my wounded left wing, which remained crooked and still complained when it rained. I faced more work when it came to dismantling tired, old stories that did not serve me anymore. After that birth experience, I suspected that, despite my impatience, I could not learn these lessons quickly. Perhaps I needed to remember that this is the way the river was flowing.

Back home, I joyfully laid Heron in the second-hand bassinet, and introduced him to Owl, Wren, and Bear. The dog sniffed Heron protectively, and welcomed him into his watchful care. Owl and Wren cooed and kissed Heron, while inside their worlds altered irreversibly and I imagine they grappled with scary questions about losing love and attention.

"Did Wren always look this big?" I asked Nik. In the morning, Wren graduated from the baby to big brother, and he looked impossibly grown up.

I gazed at Heron's wise, old face and saw what many people experience at the birth of a child: a whole-body knowledge that every human being enters this world full of love, wisdom, and potential. Wholeness. Over the coming days, sleep-deprivation and Heron's constant needs tested me. Taking care of a newborn as well as two other young children demanded that once again I dig very deep into my well of patience, energy, and self-sacrifice. Taking care of a newborn as well as two other young children demanded that once again I dig very deep into my well of patience, energy, and self-sacrifice, and I dug deeper into that well than I thought was possible. Human beings are full of resilience, compassion, and hard work when they love someone with their whole heart.

It is good and necessary that we enter the Earth equipped with the innate traits of the newborn — love, wisdom, and potential. It is also good and necessary that when we love someone as deeply as a mother loves her new baby, we deepen these traits with practice. We turn them into resilience, compassion, and hard work. The love is worth the work.

Lying in bed, breastfeeding for hours while reading stories to my older children, I savoured time to think, if only in those stray sacred seconds of quiet, which are promptly punctuated by laughs, demands, and tears. Giving so much of myself, I felt needed not just by my newborn infant, but by the moment of crisis in which I found myself. So much suffering, so much fear, so much breakdown expected ahead. So much I needed to give. Nik gave deeply, too. Late at night, after putting the children to bed and bringing me food, he put on his headlamp and walked out to the barn to fix up the apartment. He readied the barn for short-term rental so we could hopefully make ends meet and allow me a nine-month maternity leave, something I had been denied with Owl, though I would still need to work one day a week. The same week as Heron's birth, Nik launched a handyman business with a post on our community group page, and, exhausted, travelled to clients' houses to install dishwashers and fix roofs. Our capacities to give deepened again.

We are being called upon right now, I reflected as I held my new son. The planet that we love deeply and rely on for survival needs all of us to recognize that we have taken more than our fair share, especially those of us in wealthier countries, and in doing so we have created a great imbalance. We are being summoned to love and care for the planet as deeply as we do our own children, even as we raise them to do the same.

The stories we hear daily tell us that we are not good enough to rise to our environmental moment. For a long time, our cultural myths told us that we were superior to nature to justify our domination of land and animals. Now, we hear that we kill our planet through our every action, and that this Earth would be better off without people. Human beings, our cultural myths tell us, are self-interested above all else. And even if we want to protect the ecology of this planet, we waited until it was too late. In all these stories, we hear that humans are not a part of nature; we are *apart* from her. Naomi Klein writes that blaming the climate crisis on "human nature" and our supposed inherent greed allows us to ignore that the crisis is caused by harmful, powerful systems like capitalism, colonialism, and patriarchy, and also allows us to justify the need for sacrifice zones and sacrificial people in a fossil-fueled system. Throwing up our hands and saying environmental crises are humanity's inevitable outcome also "erase the very existence of human systems that organized life differently, systems that insist that humans must think seven generations in the future; must be not only good citizens but also good ancestors; must take no more than they need and give back to the land in order to protect and augment the cycles of regeneration."

Lying in bed, gazing at new life, I tended a newfound belief that people can indeed be good, and that cultivating a life of care and regeneration is our calling. Belief in our goodness doesn't absolve us from responsibility, but relieves us of our rottenness and our inaction because of fear of doing the wrong thing. Fear of failure and addiction to perfection uphold white supremacy, patriarchy, and environmental domination, all interconnected harmful systems built on control and oppression. Believing in myself as beneficial rather than harmful provided a deep and unfamiliar freedom.

I am good. I *am good.* I looked at baby Heron. *You are good.*

That summer, more than any other, I saw the heron, perched on the scraggly, reaching branches of the white pine that arched over the creek. He watched for fish for hours, eyes searching the creek's bed. When I drove around the bend, up out of our valley, with my two toddlers and newborn loaded in the back seat, he watched me until I drove out of sight. From time to time, I saw him abandon his post. He flew majestically from his large branch — head pulled back, feet tucked in — and with slow wingbeats he followed the precise curve of the creek's flow.

11

COYOTE AND WREN

Breath

"Once again for you I fall / Underneath the tree so tall / Upon the limbs and nest and dirt / Does a bird here question love?" **DANIEL RODRIGUEZ**

Snow fell on the coltsfoot, hiding it handily. For the first time in months the landscape breathed without one iteration or another of that stubborn, oxygen-giving plant. My productivity-focused mind wrestled with the coltsfoots' hard work, searching for the purpose in all that growing and surviving and adapting, only to decompose and rest in the soil. With the snow falling outside my cabin window, I read that coyote mothers pull back their lips and bare their teeth to pull the cinnamon fur from their own bellies. With the clumps of fur firmly and painfully extracted, they line the mud-baked walls of their dens to keep their babies warm.

Wren flitted and sang like a bird, young and joyful as I imagined wrens to be. When he ate something delicious, he closed his eyes to savour the taste. *Mmmmm, Mama. That is delicious.* His eyes stayed tightly closed while he took joy in the food, in the act of being alive. Zany and wry at home, he appeared reserved to the outside world. He sang beautifully and often, and intently focused on one toy for hours. It could take a long and patient search to find him, folded in a corner somewhere, quietly packing a backpack overflowing with puzzles and games. Perhaps he is like a canyon wren. "[O]ften when one can plainly hear its musical song reverberating from the walls of a canyon," the 1977 *The Field Guide to North American Birds* explains, "it takes a long and patient search to spot the singer, perched high up on the ledge or quietly picking its way through a clump of brush." Wren looked up at me and asked if I would go to the desert with him, and I enthusiastically agreed. My adult mind — repeatedly tracing over those worn grooves between worries stretching into both the obsolete past and the unknowable future — learned from watching him. He gently and persistently taught me about the joy of today.

That winter, as always, he acted more thoughtfully than a two-year-old toddler ought to be. "Thank you for changing my diaper, Mama. Thank you for putting me to bed, Mama." I never trained him to say these things or mandated that he be kinder than his years, as our relationship is a parenting experiment of partnership rather than obedience. But still he thanked me for my daily, loving drudgery. "Thank you for being my mama, Mama."

Mischievous like a wren, he frequently found himself in trouble in an innocent way, out of a curiosity to see what would happen. When he drew on the walls with a marker,

I swallowed hard and summoned my patience to ask him, "Why, my love?" He cried, "Look, I drew on the wall!" proud of his artistry and oblivious to my irritation. I, the mother bird, wet a cloth and together we washed the colour from the wall. Marker diluted and turned to water, running down his little arms, painting his wings Inchworm Green. My frustration cooled, and I resigned myself to his playfulness. "Well, we're having an adventure, aren't we?" I asked him, green Crayola water covering our similar hands. With my Wren, these little moments were delicious enough that I closed my eyes to savour them.

One morning, he woke up rasping, after being his usual joyful birdish self the night before. He had gleefully piled his stuffies into his crib, adding elephants to puppies to rabbits to lions, and then snuggled sweetly into the rainbow collective of their fuzzy bodies. When he woke up in this messy stuffed menagerie the next morning, he struggled to sip oxygen into his small lungs.

We drove through the falling snow to the clinic, with a sick two-year-old Wren and two-month-old Heron in the back seat. At the clinic, the expedient doctor seemed unconcerned with Wren's rasping. She told me flatly, "Give him the medicine and wait half an hour," as I struggled to avoid acting the over-worried mother. "Go to the hospital if it gets any worse," she added as a formality, handing me a prescription slip. Wren lay joyless on the floor. Listless and slow. His chest sucked into his lungs with ragged breaths, as if each inhale struggled to force its way in through his small ribs.

I lifted him from the floor and draped his hot body over my chest to carry him out of the medical room. He seeped sickness, the type you would try to avoid out of self-preservation, if you hadn't grown him painstakingly and with devotion in your own body. If you didn't see his body was an extension of your own. I carried my newborn in his cumbersome car seat over one arm. My arm went numb under the weight of it, as I struggled to carry them both out of the clinic. Wren's breaths sounded horrible, as though they were being grated on their way into his body.

"How are you doing, my Wren?" I asked when we arrived home, and he barely seemed to register the familiar sound of my voice. I laid him on the couch, and his breathing quickly worsened. An instinct in my stomach kicked in and insisted I listen to what I'd been ignoring all day, since those first surprising ragged breaths. *Wren isn't safe. He cannot breathe.*

His breath became shallower and he slumped, non-responsive. Everything in his young body seemed passive, except his eyes. His eyes panicked. I poured him back into the snowsuit, moving so quickly I forgot to bring his winter boots. I hastily packed up the baby, turning our usual agonizingly slow exit from the house into an abrupt, one-minute affair.

"Bring the keys, bring the health card, bring your driver's license," I said out loud, worried if I didn't narrate my motions I would drive to the wrong place or crash. My measured actions struggled to control the uncontrollable, and we again drove through the snow, up the winding road that traces the hill leading out of the safe world of our secluded valley.

Fear is a physical experience. Fast, loud, breathless. All-consuming. It lives in the mind, blood, and bones all at once. It is shaking hands clipping a rasping child into a car seat. Fear is a calm voice that reassures a child struggling to breathe, while blood beats in your ears.

The traffic over the bridge moved slowly, with red brake lights bleeding out in front of me. "Wren, you're safe. Mama is going to make sure you are safe," I assured him through the rear-view mirror, my shaking measured voice sounding calm to no one as I broke my pledge to never make promises to my children that I couldn't keep.

His breathing nearly stopped, and fear flashed in his eyes. He sipped for air and could not find it, and I felt my blood hot in my veins. My alert mind sped through my options. One. Pull over to the shoulder and breathe into his small mouth, holding him while I hopefully bring breath back to him. Two. Call an ambulance and wait. Three. Run through the stalled traffic with him and his newborn brother heaped in my arms, along the long, snowy road that yawned towards the emergency room.

Instead I drove onwards, the car behaving as it should. Straight and slow and normal. As if we were going to get groceries, four wheels tracked in a straight line, one anonymous family vehicle in a row of traffic. We arrived at the emergency door and, after struggling to find a spot in the busy parking lot, I parked frantically on a slant, far from the entrance. Wren's breath stopped. I ran from the front seat, unclipped his buckles, and held him like a baby as he started throwing up over us both. Snow fell. His socked feet dangled, this tiny bird in my arms. My everything, dependent on oxygen like the rest of us. Vulnerable and mortal. His life, like all of ours, an uncertainty. *He is my everything and I need him to breathe.*

We moved from the island to the 130-year-old house in a rural town with our infant Owl in tow. The town lay at the furthest possible reaches from the city, while still at commuting distance, at least on paper. On our first day there, with our belongings surrounding us in boxes and our friends eating gratitude pizza, a heaviness sunk deep in my stomach. *This is not my home.* Our intention had been to find a place in our budget and have the best of both worlds, but the reality sank in that what we entered was the worst of both worlds. Busyness, cars, costs, worry, isolation. Too tired to connect with communities on either end. Construction crews quickly turned the land around the town into developments, with streets being named after the trees cut down to make space for new houses.

In the country, the chaotic pace continued unabated. The overwork and my unreasonable expectations for myself changed, but they didn't lessen. Pregnant, I commuted four hours a day to and from a rewarding but grueling job downtown. I moved up the ladder at a large charity and took great pride in my work, but beat myself up for having to leave important meetings early so I could make the two-hour drive home, and then chastised myself for being two minutes late for daycare pick-up. My boss expressed frustration with me for leaving early and my childcare provider showed anger at me for arriving late. After worrying about the needs of my work and my daughter, there was nothing left for me or my second child, Wren, who grew inside me.

My body told me I did too much. I developed a strange illness throughout that pregnancy that left me gasping for breath. I slipped bashfully out of important meetings to suck medicine from a puffer. Constant infections made me sick, and I lost my voice for weeks. I struggled to breathe. Neither my midwife nor my doctor could diagnose the mysterious respiratory illness. Contractions and the possibility of early labour threatened me for most of my pregnancy, while I prayed to hold the baby inside so that I could meet my responsibilities in a new leadership role as well as being the maid of honour at my sister's wedding, which I deeply wanted to attend. One evening that looked like every other one, I slumped down on the floor against the wall, exhaustedly playing blocks with my toddler with one hand, while answering urgent emails with the other. I could barely hold myself up. After Owl's bedtime, I worked at a rapid-fire pace until I tumbled into bed, directly from the screen to the sheets, dreading the fast-approaching alarm at five a.m. that would demand I get back in the beastly car again. The punishing commute exhausted me and I rarely enjoyed my pregnancy with Wren. When I did enjoy our pregnancy, I did so privately in stolen moments, like in the thirty-second elevator ride between the parking garage and my desk.

But the peace of the forest again found me. Or, at least, the peace of one tree found me. I found solace in the old maple outside our rural home. Every morning before I braved the two-hour morning commute, I greeted the tree. A few deep breaths in the dim dawn light kept me earthbound, as I stared at the maple tree cloaked in her autumn, winter, spring, or summer dress. Returning to her at the end of the day, adrenaline raced in my blood from the aggressive traffic and the race on country roads to reunite with my Owl. I greeted the tree with relief, finally exhaling deeply for the first time in twelve hours. Through every season over several years, the connection with that tree gave me the resolve to face the grinding days ahead.

In the middle of one night in August, Julian Ross Wren was born in that old rural house. He looked like me, and he seemed musical and gentle from the first. Holding his ancient but brand-new body to mine, I looked down at the wide maple floorboards from the 1800s and wondered who else had been born in this home over the decades, and what that maple tree looked like over the decades. When was she born? When did a maple key fall to Earth beside a beautiful farmhouse, the seed floating downwards before shattering open like I did to create new life? The beautiful immensity of shepherding a creature from my body into complete individuality overcame me, and birth again proved to be the most difficult and exhilarating moment of my life. From his first day Earthside, Wren taught me about lightness and joy.

I ran into the fluorescent emergency room, leaving two-month-old Heron in the cold car alone. I raced as my Wren threw up on me again and then gasped for air. People stared at us. I transferred Wren to a nurse and they rushed him in, no triage or paperwork or waiting rooms or vending machine snacks while we waited to be seen.

They gave him oxygen.

"Do you want me to sing you a song?" I asked when I returned with his new baby brother, my voice shaking despite my long-held belief that I can be calm in an emergency like this.

"Blackbird," he whispers. His favourite song.

My voice quivered as I whisper-sang familiar lyrics about broken wings and learning to fly. Wren looked scared, despite my soft singing. Usually he sang along. Usually he sang along so loudly that my nighttime lullaby turned into a rousing concert with laughter and clapping, and I tried to hide the smile at the corners of my lips while I half-heartedly asked him to settle down. But on the stretcher, his clothes covered in vomit, with sweaty hair plastered to his forehead, he just listened solemnly. He looked older than usual, yet also more like a baby than usual. Old and young. Frail and vulnerable and sick.

But he breathed.

Wren spent the next several hours getting tests, taking temperatures, and receiving rounds of oxygen and steroids through a mask. Doctors and nurses visited us, and revisited us. Nik and Owl visited us too, the five of us together in the hospital room before the two of them went home for dinner and to restore some small, if tenuous, sense of safety. Wren finally managed to fall asleep, and I felt deep relief, as if oxygen could finally enter my own lungs, too. I watched through his child-sized green hospital gown as his chest heaved in and out, finding the breath that he struggled for. The air came into his body in little swallows, but they were enough. I couldn't eat. I nursed Heron whom I held in one arm, as I held Wren's hand with the other across the metal edges of the hospital gurney. I kissed him and fed him and changed his diaper and brought him sips of water. I answered questions, sang songs, read books, and mopped his sweaty brow.

The doctor released us from the hospital hours past bedtime. Wren and I held hands on one side, and I carried the heavy baby car seat with Heron on the other arm. The three of us walked out into the snow, under the starry sky. Airy snowflakes fell fast enough to fill our footprints behind us, making the ground white again.

"Mama, thanks for being here with me today," he whispered thoughtfully. His breath inhaled shallow and strained, but the cold air was meant to be good for his breathing. My Wren looked up at me and repeated the phrase I often said to him in tricky moments. "We're having an adventure, aren't we?"

"Yes, my love, we are having an adventure."

That night, I lay on the bedroom floor beside my sick boy's crib, sleeplessly listening to his rasping breath and watching his trembling ribs. *Is this an emergency?* I questioned with each ragged breath. *Should I go back to the hospital?* Every hour, I wrapped him in blankets and, despite his sleepy protestations, dutifully carried him outside into the winter air, following the doctor's orders. Held tightly to my warm body and swaddled in a blanket, in the midnight midwinter air Wren could breathe.

"I love being here with you," I whispered to him, sounding like I meant *here* our house, but really I meant *here* on this planet.

Holding him bundled in the blanket in the cold, dark air, something caught my eye at the edge of the forest. A coyote trotted swiftly through the trees, her grand bushy tail pointed downwards as she wove a thread of oval tracks towards the forest, snow filling the prints behind her, too. She vanished darkly into the woods. Recognition stirred in me. Today, I pulled my lips back and bared my teeth, and pulled the cinnamon fur from my own belly. I lined the mud-baked walls of our den and kept my babies warm.

12

THE PEAR TREE AND THE SHREW

Seeds

"Everything and everyone that I love is a carbon-based life form connected inextricably by cords of flowing energy and matter to oceans, tundra, coral reefs, and prairie soils."
ELIZABETH SAWIN

I slowly started to trust in Wren's safety, that we could rely on his breath. "Can you breathe okay?" I'd ask, worried but trying not to sound worried, asking a two-year-old to measure his breath and reduce my fear. I spent many nights not sleeping on his floor, surrounded by a shroud of mist from the humidifier turned to maximum, listening to the in-and-out of his breath that sometimes sounded ragged from the croup and asthma, our very survival and happiness depending on his inhalations and exhalations. As his breathing slowly improved, I considered my worries about breathing finished.

As the year turned over from 2019 to 2020, Nik and I argued in our minivan at exactly midnight, driving down a rural road in a mundane disagreement about when we left our friends' party. Exhausted from their latest-ever night and the gregarious-but-boring energy of adults at a party, the children slept in their car seats in the nondescript grey family vehicle. We bought the van after insisting we would never buy one. After two months squishing into the station wagon with the three car seats in the back seat and Bear in the hatchback, we bought a used Dodge Caravan. We decided that to make the most of the new minivan — that universal symbol of banality — we would rent out our home in March 2020 and drive across America. With the three kids under four and Bear, we planned to sleep in motels in Michigan, Illinois, and Iowa, and then camp along the way in Nebraska, Colorado, Utah, and Nevada until we reached the West Coast's redwood forests.

Our argument would have been forgettable, other than its auspicious timing at midnight of a new year. Could this be a portent of a turbulent year? When we arrived back at our cabin, Nik carried the toddlers and baby to their beds in the small room they all shared, and I angrily walked out into the cold night and the first minutes of 2020, with Bear by my side. The frozen air, quiet stars, and tall embrace of the surrounding forest chilled my frustration, and Bear and I walked beside the sleeping creek. Back in our cabin, Nik and I made up and decided we would open a bottle of champagne and stay up late, waiting until midnight on California time, to start the year off with a celebration of our upcoming road trip across America. The children slept in their beds and cribs, Bear curled up like a baby puppy on his pillow, and the creek lay frozen under the stars of a newborn year. Nik and I, though, stayed awake dreaming of our family adventure with our argument long forgotten, and at three a.m. we said *santé* as we clinked glasses at California's midnight.

On a Tuesday morning in March, I changed children's diapers and packed a bag with backup kid underwear, pants, and snack pouches. I bundled up the three children into one-piece snowsuits and buckled everyone into their car seats, in the complex process of taking three small children out into the world. Rehearsing our slow exit from the domestic space into public overwhelmed me, and I allowed myself a sigh of relief when each child sat buckled in their chairs, life controlled for a merciful moment. We drove to a passport office, where I grabbed a ticket and waited for an hour in a waiting room lined with plastic chairs, one of which I jumped up from countless times, entertaining four-year-old Owl, safeguarding two-year-old Wren as he toddled around oblivious to the boring norms of society, and breastfeeding Heron, holding his head in one strong arm while reaching into my backpack for snacks with the other. Our number came up on the digital screen, and I herded the four of us up to a kiosk, where they let me know another passport office across town would better serve us. I piled the children back into the minivan, through a parking garage, and repeated the whole scattered process in another, larger fluorescent office. We left the office hours later with the paperwork and comical baby passport photos submitted, the last step in our process before the cross-continent road trip.

Back in our gracious mess of a home, Nik and I fed the children dinner and distractedly led the bedtime routine, while we snuck glances at our phones to watch the unfolding global pandemic as it neared our patch of Earth. A global virus, rolling unchecked from human to human, place to place, until it reached everyone. That night, we received strict orders to stay at home, as hospitals filled and we learned that public space endangered us. I thought back to the busy passport offices, and my two toddlers walking unchecked with a carefree freedom that soon would be considered a relic from the old days. I recalled their hands touching elevator buttons, the backs of chairs, the floor, the water fountain. Their bodies inches from others, their mouths and lungs within dangerous distance of presumed Covid hosts. The day began with a denial that life would change and an insistence that our California plans would continue, and ended with grave promises that our lives would change irrevocably. We went to bed with a deep fear about an illness that threatened our ability to breathe. Like everyone, we cancelled our plans, as well as the routines of daily life. We lived in isolation, and worked and schooled online, with screens as a weak replacement for real life. We wiped down our groceries with bleach, and attended weddings, birthdays, and funerals on Zoom. I returned to work with Heron on my breast below the screen, as Owl and Wren leapt through the frame. I clicked mute to spare colleagues from Bear's bark punctuating their presentations. Our monotonous daily routine became a mix of occupying children while working, and stealing attention from both. At night, we rewatched *The Office* and read news about death counts and overflow hospital wings set up in parking lots. Crippling fear made itself at home amidst a parade of identical days, without any relief from the monotonous and exhausting business of pandemic parenting.

With our cross-America trip canceled, our only excursions amounted to Nik lining up to scour the half-empty shelves at Costco for food. After one of his first trips into the massive, undersupplied warehouse of goods, Nik came home visibly shaken. Like everywhere else, supply chain disruptions meant the normally grossly abundant grocery store lacked even basic items, with shelves mostly cleared and people nervously stockpiling food. Only days into the pandemic, the instability and fragility of our industrial, global food system showed, eroding the lie that copious, always-available food would be normal forever. Seeing that we were unsafe, we shared with many people a collective urge to feed ourselves and to support local farmers, with less reliance on fragile supply chains that threaten our survival when they waver. We desired to eat nutritious food grown in concert with nature's cycles, rather than chemical-laden food that eroded the balanced systems of our planet. We shared the human desire to sink our hands into soil, and the wonder of seeing seeds turn into sprouts, and sprouts into food. We decided to turn to the garden, aiming to better feed ourselves more self-sufficiently and to gradually increase our food resiliency in this second year of gardening at Birdsong Cabin.

The springthaw creek rushed behind the garden, keeping us company in our work. A neighbour offered unideal soil that needed a home, and when we accepted, they reversed a truck into the meadow, pulling up to the garden with a trailer full of earth. Our dinner half-eaten, the kids watched the excitement of the truck through the window, until we eventually abandoned the table and ran down to the garden. The bigger kids climbed in the trailer and helped shovel, with Heron contentedly curled on my chest in the baby carrier. We scooped the clay-like dirt onto the beds, with Nik taking on most of the work when I convinced the resistant children to go back to the cabin for bedtime. Over a period of weeks, in the cracks of the day between work, Zoom calls with friends and family, and parenting, we returned to the garden. After unwillingly donating much of our garden harvest to the deer the previous year, we started to build a fence surrounding the six hügel beds. Nik dragged a tangle of chain-link fence from some bushes where a previous owner left it, and where over the course of a few years, impressive fast-growing plants attempted to swallow it entirely. We disentangled the chain link from itself, pulling out metal posts that then formed the structure of the new-to-us fence. The kids helped us tie the fencing material to the posts until it encircled the garden, coming together in a rickety gate door that read *Pet Safe: Happy Pets, Happy Owners*. "Hello, garden," I whispered whenever I opened the gate, after some wrestling with the old metal latch. With our burgeoning food safe from the deer, if not the mice and the birds, we began to plant.

Kale. Arugula. Tomatoes and peppers. Basil, parsley, cilantro, and mint. Cucumber. Garlic, onions, radishes, potatoes. Swiss chard, several varieties of lettuce. Strawberries. A feast for our family. We planted the old seeds from the workshop, unsure if they would even germinate, and purchased seedlings from a local farm, which soon put our scrappy beginner plants to shame. The weeds — or *wildpretties* as Owl called them — threatened to take over the food plants, but we did our best to remove the dominant plants and save our growing food. Unable to dedicate much time to caring for the garden, it became an experiment in survival and growth, with a result of some plant death as well as considerable abundance of food in a feral garden.

The kids and I walked down to the creek, where I leaned against my favourite tree, a soaring curved cedar that splits from the base into two distinct trunks, both blanketed with thick moss up to four or five feet high. I relaxed into the more southerly trunk, and she received me like a pillow receives a sleepy cheek. I never knew this tree existed until Covid told me I had nowhere to go. I spent eighteen months ignorant of her, due to the abundance of the forest and the busyness of life, and only the pandemic sent me down there, with crayons and a pile of papers tied with string onto make-shift clipboards made from cereal boxes. With the children, I discovered the tree that resonated with me more than any other on Earth. While I breastfed Heron against her moss-covered body, Owl and Wren stomped in the edge of the creek, scooping water with pails or trying to catch creatures with plastic pink nets. I called out to them never to come to the water alone and watched, worried, ready to jump up if anyone strayed too far. Years later, maybe I would remember those days as the happiest of our lives, selectively ignoring the illness and fear. One day, as pandemic spring bled into pandemic early summer, we gathered our buckets, papers, and crayons, and walked away from the creek and the cedar, through the ferns, and up towards the garden.

"What's that?" asked Owl, excited.

I leaned down, looking in the grass. "It's a watermelon!"

Growing in the middle of the grass, where some of the clay-like soil still lay after being transported by the truck in the meadow, grew a watermelon that could fit in your palm. Pleasingly round and sweet, the fruit lay somehow untouched by the animals who use the meadow as a pas-sageway between the forest and the creek. The kids mused excitedly about how the watermelon seed found its way here, the same way an errant Scrabble tile marked Q showed up in the soil. "A mystery!" shouted Owl. We picked the fruit and brought it home, where we cut it into two halves, revealing a ripe, pink middle. Biting into the sweet flesh, we marvelled at how similar the watermelon looked and tasted to its big cousins, just in perfect miniature. The surprise watermelon delighted the children, and me too, a gift made particularly generous because times felt both boring and terrifying.

What a bewildering blessing that seeds — small, unassuming packages — can travel and hide, finding their ways to new places, waiting for the right conditions and environment to burst into life, somehow translating water, soil, and sunlight into many types of plant and fruit. In a phenomenon called seed dormancy, seeds can shelter in the soil for months or even years, showing patience that I do not possess. They do this either because of an inherent quality of the individual seed, or because their environment is less than ideal and they likely won't survive — so they wait. Many of the plants in my amateur garden lacked seed dormancy because of generations of selection and cultivation, and they germinate as soon as they are touched by water and warmth. These plants' wild ancestors, however, knew how to be dormant. How to wait. How to rest. Seed dormancy adapts particularly well in places of fire, something which should be of interest to us, on our ever-hotter home with wildfires in unprecedented places. The appearance of the surprise watermelon offered me delight, and learning of seed dormancy offered me some sad hope for the future of food and seeds, suggesting to me that a diversity of foods might find a way to persist, through the flames and the drought and the floods.

In the bathroom after the children went to sleep, I ran the clippers over the back of Nik's head, and watched the brown and silver hairs fall around my bare feet. I found my glass of red wine on the bathroom counter and took a slow sip, while scrolling through a playlist to find a song fit for the moment. Leaning in nervously, I tentatively glided the clippers around Nik's ear. I couldn't remember the last time I'd looked at my husband this thoughtfully, this closely. Maybe it was when we were first dating. He had asked me to cut his hair for years but, nervous, I kept brushing it off and encouraging him to go to the professionals. It just took a pandemic lockdown for me to try my hand at this homegrown haircut. In the before times, I never possessed the energy to cut his hair. Ten p.m. stayed reserved for collapsing in front of the TV, after the kids slept in bed and the kitchen stood clean, or clean enough. Without the pandemic, we would have been on the open road in California, making our New Year's fight and three a.m. celebration a prophecy of some sort, and instead we stood housebound in our bathroom. I cut his hair, hesitantly at first, but my confidence grew as I managed to take hair off while keeping some on. I trimmed the sweet nape of his neck and the graceful curve of his crown. When I finished, I proudly observed the unexpectedly good haircut. My husband looked handsome and new.

Figuring out what to do with our hair seemed frivolous as sirens called out in panic across the world, as people struggled to breathe alone in hospital rooms and living rooms, and while helpless families said goodbye by video call. Yet, while fearing all that tragedy, my family's hair kept on growing and our ever-scragglier locks called out for some attention. In those early upside-down days of the pandemic, I wondered what other people were doing. As weeks rolled into months, I didn't need to use my imagination any more. Online, my aunt posted a proud photo of my uncle's new short crop. My best friends exchanged photos of the haircuts we'd experimented with on our partners and children. A former neighbour posted about how her eyes welled with tears when she turned to see that her husband had cut off her young son's curls too enthusiastically. A dear old friend bravely gave herself a pixie cut and then a close-cropped buzz in preparation for her first day of chemo, to fight off the ovarian cancer that found her in the midst of a pandemic. My sister showed off her fresh haircut, courtesy of my brother-in-law, as we chatted on a video call, trying to cross the distance between us.

Encouraged by my tentative trim of Nik's hair, I turned next to Owl's long curly hair, taking off quite a few inches despite — or perhaps because of — her turning her head around every few seconds to look at me. With her new cut I saw the teenager she would become in a decade. When it was Wren's turn, he lay back in the bath, eyes closed and chin upturned, and I gently washed his hair, singing Fleetwood Mac's "Landslide." As he heard my muffled voice through the water and my hands held him aloft, I hoped silently that he felt safe in this era of pandemic and environmental crisis, even though I did not. At least for a few more years, until he found out what he'd inherited, what all the grown-ups knew and kept secret from him for as long as they could. When I swept up their honey-brown and blonde trimmings from the bathroom floor, I kept the curls on the kitchen counter all day in the dustpan. I couldn't bring myself to toss out these pieces of their childhood and these traces of my motherhood.

In addition to planting our victory garden and cutting our own hair, we filled the early pandemic by paying closer attention to the birds around our cabin. I ordered a bird-watching book and a laminated bird guide, *Québec Birds: A Bilingual Folding Pocket Guide to Familiar Species*. After dinner, Owl would sit on my lap and Wren would sit beside me, or vice versa, and Heron watched from his highchair. We laid the fold-out guide across the table between our uncleared dishes, and beside every bird we spotted in our valley, we made a circle with the dim goldenrod yellow ink of an old dry erase marker. Blue Jay. Wild Turkey. Red-tailed Hawk. Ruffed Grouse. Mourning Dove. Turkey Vulture. Grey Jay. Common Raven. Red-winged Blackbird. Mallard. Canada Goose. Downy Woodpecker. Pileated Woodpecker. American Crow. European Starling. Red-breasted Nuthatch. Black-capped Chickadee. Carolina Wren. American Robin. Northern Mockingbird. Common Yellowthroat. Brown Creeper. White-throated Sparrow. House Sparrow. Northern Cardinal. Great Blue Heron. Ruby-throated Hummingbird. Song Sparrow. Twenty-eight species, familiar to us. With nowhere to go, we paid closer attention to our neighbours — free birds who had liberty to travel and congregate in a way that we did not, and they brought with them a reminder of far-off places in a wild world.

Poet and ornithologist J. Drew Lanham, after studying birds in many places in his career, discovered the abundance of bird life in his South Carolina backyard, which he saw as a pandemic refuge:

> "Most would define wildness as places unreachable without extraordinary effort; places far off the beaten path — places removed from our conveniences and

our contrivances. Names like "Denali" or "River of No Return" or "Bitterroot" or "Katahdin" evoke the perception, reinforced by legal definition, that the extreme state of wildness known as "wilderness" is determined by a lack of access — roadlessness — and the absence of any apparent signs of human impact. But then if we loosen the bounds a bit, let the leash on "wild" drop, perhaps we'll find it's closer by. What would happen if we became aware of how wildness thrives on occasion under our noses in vacant urban lots, discernible by the unbinoculared, high-def glimpse of a bare-naked, squinted eye? If we listen on moonlit autumn nights with open minds and hopeful hearts, we can behold it flying over us where we are: journeying birds blessing us with the distant unimaginable in moments of nearby."

We revelled in our nearby. I unearthed a 1977 edition of *The Audubon Society Field Guide to North American Birds*, which I started to read as poetry about birds, searching through the more mundane passages for sentences that surprised or moved me. The pages showed me robins as harbingers of spring that sing with rich caroling notes, the cactus wren with a most evocative sound to those who love the desert, a barred owl seen only by those who seek it out in dark retreat, and a downy woodpecker who benefits the forest.

Despite his name plastered proudly on flocks of bird books, and his stature as America's father of birds, I soon learned about Audubon's dark side, and the vast number of birds he killed from tree branches and in flight. The towering figure considered to be the most prominent bird artist in America shot the birds he chronicled, ending the lives of thousands of individual creatures representing nearly four hundred species. Horrifically, he repeatedly bought and sold enslaved people, and held racist views towards Black and Indigenous people, harbouring beliefs about white superiority. The Audubon Society wrote, "[H]e was a complex and troubling character who did despicable things even by the standards of his day." Despite this, the organization decided after much debate not to drop the man's name from their name.

He threaded wires through birds' heads, tails, and wings, manipulating them and pinning their bodies in active positions, creating dead facsimiles of what he observed in the wild, before he painted their portraits, capturing them indefinitely. One of those birds, the golden eagle, he bought from a Museum Proprietor in Boston in 1833, and the animal affected him deeply. He felt compelled to release the eagle into the wild. "But then, reader, some one seemed to whisper that I ought to take the portrait of the magnificent bird," he wrote, "and I abandoned the more generous design of setting him at liberty, for the express purpose of [showing] you his semblance." He killed the bird, with much inner turmoil, and he experienced a mental breakdown after the two weeks it took to paint the bird's portrait. He experienced enormous grief and guilt at having killed the majestic creature, along with thousands of other birds. In a rare occurrence, he also included himself in the painting, a small figure in the distance in the bottom left hand corner, where he hangs over a gorge, balanced precariously on a tree that spans from one side of the cliff to the other. A dead eagle — presumably the mate to the one Audubon agonized over liberating or killing — drapes limply, strapped to the man's back. This older version of the painting still exists, but in the final published illustration of the golden eagle, looking at the bottom left-hand corner you only see an empty tree trunk across the gorge, with the depiction of Audubon vanished. The reason why he is missing from the final painting is a mystery.

I spoke with J. Drew Lanham about his work revisiting the history of famed conservationists.

"It's about challenging some people who I hold in high regard, from a thinking standpoint, and others who we've always held in high regard, but then we understand as we revisit history — not rewrite it, but revisit history — that they talked a good game, but they didn't intend for everybody to play in that game," Drew told me. "You know, battling with the legacy of someone like John Muir, for example, who is everywhere in the conservation and environmentalist movement, including on T-shirts with sayings and maxims. But he was a person who seemed intent on discovering wildness where Indigenous people already existed. And seeing that wilderness is a better place cleared of Indigenous people, it was then made better for whiteness to discover it. In his travels through the south, seeing Black people and sort of lampooning them in his way to dominate who they were as human beings and to not understand the struggle here. And then we celebrate him and hold him up as the father of wildness. It's not that I want to erase who he was, but I want us to understand fully who these people were."

The men we praise as individual saviours often reveal their shadowy truths, giving lie to our myths of heroes that prop up hierarchies: some human beings who stand above other humans, and then human beings who stand above earthly creation. At times, we kill like a bird of prey eating the young of their brethren, and at others, we resemble a murmuration of starlings, coming together in awe-inspiring unison. Like starlings, we can form an intricate community of safety, warmth, information sharing, and survival — an invitation to gather and sing — but only when we resist myths that preach individualism and hero worship.

We dug a deep hole in the thawed soil in the meadow, twenty paces from the garden gates, and I walked up to the cabin to retrieve something from the freezer. I returned to the meadow, where Nik and the children waited, and I unwrapped a precious item from inside a Ziploc bag. I slipped the contents into a large bowl, and looked with amazement at the placenta which nourished Heron inside of me while he transformed from nothingness to life. The placenta spent a winter in the freezer, like a dead pet bird stored in the recesses of the family freezer waiting for the backyard to thaw. I expected the organ to look dormant, but a few minutes of warmth seemed to wake it quickly. Biological ruby red and traced with branches of blue river blood vessels, the few-pound object — a former part of my body — began to bleed in the bowl. Heron and I created the thing together, with his side smooth and glistening, and mine bumpy and rough, a motherly gesture on my part to take life's storms for him, as much as I could. The transient, mysterious organ allowed my son to breathe, eat, and protect himself from disease while preparing me to one day nourish him with milk, and handled a complex exchange so that his blood and mine never met, even while sharing one body. Maybe 100 or 200 million years ago the placenta formed in humans, as well as independently in other creatures, in a winding evolution from laying eggs to the unbelievable phenomenon of live birth, allowing each of us to be here at all. My and Heron's placenta looked like a human heart. We slid the dark organ into the hole in the meadow, and I held Heron close to me, saying a blessing of thanks for him, for us, for the improbability of life and the near-impossibility of this safe and happy life. *Keep us safe.* We lifted a pear tree sapling into the earth, its small roots quietly starting to braid with the root-like vessels of the placenta, in what I hoped would become a years-long process of a pear tree swallowing up our tree of life.

Later in the first pandemic summer, I found a curious creature outside our front door, a dead little animal that resembled a mouse with a long snout. A shrew. With the kids, I carried the weightless individual down to the meadow, laid it under the fledgling branches of the pear tree, and we decorated the animal with flowers. She might be taken by a fox, or maybe, like the placenta, she might decompose into the soil, becoming water, soil, and pear.

I pulled frozen jars of breastmilk from the freezer and unscrewed the lids, leaving them on the counter to thaw. I had saved it in the freezer without knowing what I would do with it all. Yellowish-white jars started to frost, thaw, and sweat. Countless hours of love, hormones, and toil, squeezed with discomfort through a plastic funnel into a waiting bottle. Hundreds of ounces pumped in the front seat of a car in a parking garage, glancing furtively around to make sure no one watched me, or pumped in a washroom stall outside a conference session while I sat teary-eyed over a photo of my baby to help the milk flow. I remembered the story a taxi driver once told me on a late night drive: she saw a deer dying, and as the doe's last act, she lay on her side and nursed her baby. I stared at the milky jar. Unable to bear pouring all that hard work and unconditional love down the kitchen sink, I stood above a garden bed and poured the creamy liquid into the soil around the growing vegetables, to mark the end of the baby years and the start of something else.

———

I kept cutting Nik's and the children's hair, and over months of practice, I looked with sweet pride at my family's haircuts. Even this recovering perfectionist did not mind the small mistakes of one curl that hung too long or one ear that looked ever-so-slightly higher than the other. As my nervousness diminished, I slowly saw cutting my family's hair as an act of care. Caretaking is a combination of vulnerability, love, and closeness. It takes all three to cut a family member's hair. In a time when we distanced ourselves from our communities, friends, family and the public sphere, we needed closeness most. Being close to somebody — to my husband, as I traced the razor over the hills and valleys of his head with my other hand on his familiar shoulder — felt more special than it did before. Humans are naturally caretakers for that which we love. I saw it in countless daily acts as people helped one another muddle through. Small and large acts of care happened everywhere, as communities, neighbours and strangers helped one another out in ways that previously seemed unimaginable.

I did not know if I would continue to cut my family's hair after this pandemic. Like all of us, I did not know what the world would look like. I did not know what we would keep, what we would lose, what we would shed, or what we would find. Staring down the barrel of a pandemic winter, I knew that caretaking would serve as a powerful survival strategy for our families and our communities. I also intended to always look at my husband as intentionally as that night when I first cut his hair. Close enough that I saw every strand that fell over his forehead, and that I knew precisely where his neck started to curve. I intended to remember to be present with my children as I washed their ever-growing hair, and to be grateful for the intimacy of that act rather than resentful of yet another task in a long day. I intended to remember that our home is with each other, and that there was that one year in 2020 when we spent months together without leaving our cabin, and we never lost love for one another.

Naturally, months into my pandemic haircutting career, my own locks began to tangle at the bottoms as the roots grew and grew. Too long, too dishevelled, too much like I hadn't left the woods in ages. Knots developed at the back under my ponytail, like they had in the old rural house. I could use some care. When closed businesses started to hesitantly open their doors, I donned my mask and went into the local hair salon. As the hairdresser cut off twelve inches of neglected ponytail, "Landslide" sang out from the speakers mounted on the wall, asking me if I could handle the seasons of my life. I believed that I could — that we could — but not without caring for each other.

13

LION'S TOOTH

Ancestors

"We are surrounded both by our ancestors whispering that
we can do what our moment demands just as they did, and by
future generations shouting that they deserve nothing less."

NAOMI KLEIN

Seasons pass even during a pandemic, and after our first full
lockdown winter, the children and I paid closer attention
to the vast diversity of mushrooms emerging unpredictably throughout the forest, collecting the ones we knew
we could safely eat. I again experienced discomfort with
my great privilege, watching colleagues on Zoom unable
to leave their apartments, their children restricted to a
few hundred square feet, while we enjoyed the freedom
of the forest. Dandelions grew through the snow melt and
we turned their sunlight blooms and saw-edged greens
into foraged luxuries like pesto, shortbread cookies, and
summery wine. A sign of hope and healing, the yellow

flowers seemed especially auspicious during unsure times, or maybe I simply watched them more closely when I had nowhere to go. Owl and I soaked linen and cotton garments in milk overnight, then dyed clothing in a hot bath of dandelion blooms with a fun process and lackluster results. She wrote about the natural dyeing process in her school newspaper, complete with a photo of her in a pale yellow tank top, already a kindergartner with a byline and a life of her own.

My body felt healthier than it had in years, on the crest of a new phase as my youngest baby entered toddlerhood, enjoying his own liberation that took him further from me and deeper into his selfhood. I grieved the inevitable distance between us as he left his newborn days behind him, and with them, he ended my identity of new motherhood. Society celebrates a new mother with a first infant and then slowly disregards a mother of multiple and older children, and I resisted my coming graduation to mother of three big kids, worrying that my struggles and realities would somehow mean less now. Besides, I loved the baby years more than anything. The natural and necessary progression to secondary character in another person's story felt complicated, yet also freeing to become part of a wider reality than myself, a side part of their constellation while still at the centre of my own. I knew no greater bliss than birth and motherhood of my babies, and even as I celebrated their growth, I mourned the packing away of baby wraps, onesies, and miniature reusable diapers into boxes I wedged in the far corners of the storage cupboard, no longer Future Boxes but rather Past Boxes. I tucked them into the descending corners of the slanted cabin roof, stored in an inconvenient place by design: I no longer needed them.

The five of us drove to collect a brood of baby chicks, the newest creaturely additions to our home. I rested the cardboard carrier on my lap for the drive home, in disbelief that the weightless box held ten beating hearts. We brought them home and introduced the small flock to Bear, who let the birds climb on him as he craned his neck to sniff their feathers. A coop building project began, with the kids picking up their hammers and helmets to join in building a space for the chicks. Heron in particular, at one year old, revelled in donning hearing protection and hammering at the coop framing for hours. Nik repurposed wood from a neighbour's old deck, cobbling together various free supplies and painting the whole thing to make it look new. The safe, warm enclosure contained the nesting boxes, and also included an outdoor run and ramp. As much as possible, we wanted to let the chicks free range around the meadow when they grew big enough, filling their bellies with good food and helping us keep the increasingly prevalent ticks away. We chose Barred Rock chickens, a hearty heritage breed able to withstand both our frigid winters and humid summers. Once the most populous chicken breed in America, Barred Rocks fell in popularity with the rise of industrial chicken farming. Our fluffy chicks lived in our home in a large dog crate, where they soon outgrew my tolerance of their living inside. When they were mature enough, we moved them out to the new coop, and within months they multiplied in size, their bodies barred with characteristic black and white squiggles. I imagined building a unique relationship with each chicken, but in the end I could barely tell them apart, with Virginia, Elizabeth, and Geraldine becoming interchangeable. Unique markings made Butterfly the exception as the only distinguishable chicken, which made sense when we discovered the chicken was in fact a rooster. We fed the whole brood kitchen scraps, including the carrot batons and cucumber discs that went to school in lunchboxes and came home untouched — what the children ignored, the chickens fought over.

Finally employed, Bear loved protecting the chickens, barking at a bear or the rustle of leaves from a squirrel with equal commitment. We later added one more creature, a younger Great Pyrenees needing to be rehomed from a farm. Nik picked her up and brought her home, where the kids and I greeted her as she leapt five feet into the air, straining at the end of her leash, her paws flying higher than my children's heads. *What have we done?* I wondered silently, nervous to approach the leaping beast, imagining adding her to the chaos of our creature-filled cabin. Her white matted fur covered an underweight body, with ribs poking through her sides and knicks on her cheeks and nose. Her jaw opened and closed, hyperventilating with anxiety, and I saw a resemblance between her and I. Later that night, I sat on the living room rug and she curled up in my lap with affection, seeking safety, and I knew we made the right choice. We named her Sparrow. Our cabin now housed five humans, two big dogs, three aging cats, and an assortment of chickens.

"We're not feeling great," my mother told us over video call, sitting beside my stepfather Garry, who we call Gad. Both of them looked visibly unwell. "Probably allergies or a cold, but don't come next weekend just to be safe."

We stayed home. It quickly became clear my parents struggled with Covid, weeks before the first vaccines rolled out. Our family of five had already come down with the illness early in the pandemic and suffered from breathing challenges and unpredictable symptoms, amidst resurfaced worries about Wren's asthma. We came through the other side and healed slowly, with months of lingering symptoms, but my parents' case looked different. They fought to breathe, and I watched my mother's face on FaceTime, that insufficient but essential connector across impossible distances, as the ambulance drove away from the front door and took my stepfather to the ICU. In the following days, my mother lay at home by herself, struggling to breathe and feed herself and even stand up, with no one to care for her. I could not care for her and risk infecting our family again. I called frequently to receive updates about the scary numbers on the oximeter. I encouraged her to go to the hospital, but she worried that if she went, Gad would never come home. I called him in the hospital in the morning after a night in which he nearly did not survive, a near-death experience alone in a room visited only briefly by medical personnel covered in masks, visors, and paper gowns. My mother, ordinarily constantly in motion, lay still, barely eating, telling me she felt peaceful — a word that seemed more perilous than reassuring. Helpless across the miles between us, I watched and hoped for their recovery. My dearest childhood friends and their parents delivered food to my mother's porch, an act of community care that meant survival for so many people trapped alone through the pandemic behind their own front doors. One such friend and her husband delivered a reclining deck chair so that my mother, once able, could lie outside and see the sun. Both she and my stepfather survived, unlike so many millions, and he came home, unwell but alive, and they began to recover slowly.

On a Friday night, after kid bedtime and after my own, I started searching for my ancestors, maybe motivated by the near-loss of my mother. What started as a frivolous procrastination to avoid climbing into bed turned into a discovery mission, as I uncovered names, dates, and grainy scans of photographs of handwritten marriage certificates that somehow weathered boat trips and decades. Mesmerized by the past, I dug deeper, discovering unknown names like Catherine Crawford, Hulda Serafia, Henrietta Edwards, Minnie Brotherton, and Matilda Nilsdotter, with many of the women's names subsuming into their husbands', their maiden names melting into married ones, changing histories and adding mystery. I dug into the meanings of the names I did know, like those of my grandmothers and great-grandmothers. Myrtle: an evergreen shrub that has glossy aromatic foliage and white flowers followed by purple-black oval berries; the lesser periwinkle; Myrtle represents community, thought of as a symbol of peace. Linnea, named for the Linden Tree. Caryl, a free person, or a song. Alice, noble and exalted. Irene, goddess of Peace. Who were these women? How did my foremothers experience childbirth? Did they make people laugh? Which dreams did they realize, which ones did they abandon unfulfilled?

Sleepy, I took Bear outside before bed and looked up at the nighttime sky, where I spotted a first wishing star followed by the rest. In the dark night with my mind lit up by shadowy questions about ancestors, I felt held. How meaningful to be rooted in the endless past, rich with people who came before me and led to my existence. The night sky hanging over 2021 seemed less ominous knowing it stretched back across centuries, the same sky that oversaw the lives of my predecessors.

The next day, while the children watched their shows and I breathed the sigh of guilty relief that comes with screen time, I continued my search instead of cleaning the kitchen. Piecing together clues and adding names to my family tree, it took some time to realize the obvious fact that the tree does not stop with me — my three young children formed the next generation branching into the future. I had looked at the tree from my vantage point, with branches extending far to the right, and now I added three boxes with names to my left: Annaliese Alice Owl, Julian Ross Wren, Ciarán Keith Heron. My name moved into — if not the past — closer to the ancestors. The right-hand side of the tree reflected unearthing facts from the past, but the left-hand side represented an unwritten future. How would the tree grow, beyond me? The family tree on my screen took the shape of lines and boxes, widening on the right and narrowing on the left, but in reality it represented cycles and spirals, with traits and traumas and identities spiralling through generations.

Who came next? And after that? Would I have a grandchild born in 2045, a great grandchild in 2080, and a great-great grandchild at the turn of the next century? What would be left for them then? Would the skies be empty of birds, and would the forest around Birdsong Cabin still stand? How fast would my placenta turn to soil under the young pear sapling, how high would the tree grow, would it bear fruit?

Heron's burgeoning toddlerhood challenged my identity, and so did seeing myself as an interim branch, rather than the end of some line. I felt comfortable with the change, but not with the lack of ceremony around the transition — I deeply missed some ritual to mark the end of my childbirth years and the beginning of whatever came next. While there are baby showers, often focused heavily on gifts and games, the life-altering entrance to motherhood is celebrated only briefly, and then the subsequent stages, like the end of the baby years, are barely marked and left to the woman herself to do, a duty that falls to the side in favour of a multitude of mundane responsibilities. A logistical ship, she passes herself repeatedly, moving in many directions. Perhaps in unearthing the past of my ancestors I attempted to create a makeshift ritual, because I no longer looked forward to pregnancy and birth and first steps, but rather looked forward to my children growing up and being centred in their own stories. Perhaps I explored my ancestry because that's what some people do when they hit a certain age, or maybe it is because women are often the keepers of our families' stories. Perhaps as the oldest child — oldest girl — tracking ancestors' stories, especially women's stories, became my unspoken and welcome duty. I also explored my ancestry for meaning as an antidote to a deep and valid fear about the future. Instead of spending a Friday night doom-scrolling through Twitter, immobilizing myself with fiery information and despair about a rocky future out of my control, I searched for meaning in the vast, deep past. I looked to my ancestors, the lives I imagined for them, and their threads weaving through my own, to guide me into that terrifying future, more rooted and ready to be the old growth tree that I suspected myself to be.

I mentioned my newfound interest in tracing ancestry to a few family members, and parents, in-laws, aunts, and grandparents shared their own much-more-storied experiences digging into our shared pasts. The interconnected family trees lay spread over the proverbial family table in the form of video calls, books filled with record-keeping, and documents sent from my parents-in-law in France, across the lonely miles during a pandemic when we had not seen each other in over a year.

Connecting with my lineage meant a search for *my* place and *a* place. Naomi Klein wrote, "Few of us live where our ancestors are buried. Many of us abandon our homes lightly—for a new job, a new school, a new love. And as we do so, we are severed from whatever knowledge of place we managed to accumulate at the previous stop, and from the knowledge amassed by our ancestors (who, in my case like that of so many others, migrated repeatedly themselves)." My family's migrations to Canada came as part of a large-scale displacement of Indigenous peoples, in a thieving of land that interconnected with genocide and oppression continuing into the present. The reasons for my family's leaving homelands and their stories of their arrival on this continent are lost to me, but result in an uneasy acknowledgement that I live on stolen land, and the place I love is not really mine, and should rightly be stewarded by someone else.

In a conversation with Krista Tippett, J. Drew Lanham said, "[B]roadening the scope of vision so that we see the big picture, we need to understand who birds are to others, what land is to others, that if my ancestors were forced into nature and hung from trees, I might not have the same interest in going out into the forest and naming the trees."

I spoke with Chúk Odenigbo, environmental academic and activist, about ancestors and belonging, and how that impacts people differently. He opened my eyes to the burden first-generation people experience forging connection to, and a belonging in, nature.

"We tend to have to be the ones to form our own bond with the environment in our new country, because this is the land that we know. And the land that our parents know, the land that our ancestors know, is not the same as this land. And so if you're told there are specific ways you can engage with nature, well, then you think, I guess nature is not for me. And you keep your distance. The notion of belonging is incredibly important. It goes back to throwing up barriers to entry and saying you can only participate in this if you follow certain rules, do it a certain way, know the decided way in which you engage with nature or the land — and otherwise you're not welcome."

"How do you think your ancestry influenced the path you are on?" I asked Chúk, curious.

"I'm always trying to change things for the future, and I'm inherently making myself an ancestor to that future generation. I'm inherently saying that I am the ancestor to look over you, even though you're not here yet. And I hope that I'm making things better. So while we recognize that that our ancestors gave us so much strength, so much knowledge, so many teachings, cultures, foods, whatever it is, we also recognize that our ancestors made some mistakes and it is up to us to fix those mistakes, such that the next generation no longer has to deal with the consequences of those mistakes.

"You know, it's not an easy thing to do," he continued thoughtfully. "As a society, we have this habit of attributing things to our grandparents' generation, and saying I have nothing to do with that. But in reality, we all have something to do with that, such as if your great-grandparents owned slaves or your great-grandparents did nothing about the residential school system. You know, it's not your fault.

You can't go back in time, but you still benefit from it in the sense that either you have wealth in your family or it was passed down to you. It doesn't even have to be wealth in the form of money, you can be wealthy in the form of inheriting a house. It could be wealth in the form of, 'Every generation in my family, since whenever, has been fully educated, and so I will not be the first of my generation to go to university.' Wealth shows up in many different ways, but you're benefiting from that, and then you have a responsibility, frankly, to make sure that the people who are harmed by that legacy can also benefit from your wealth in some way, shape, or form. And you know, that can take many different forms: it can be through volunteering, donating money, donating land. It can be through sharing the mic, like really sort of making sure that you understand the privileges and then turning those privileges into responsibilities, but then also don't turn those responsibilities into guilt."

He continued. "Don't put it along the lines of sacrificing yourself, but recognize that our collective liberation is dependent on all of us, because there's very few people in our current society who have perfect power, right? Because every single one of us tends to be marginalized or ostracized for one reason or another. You know, when we do things to undo the mistakes of our ancestors, we're not just doing them for other people. We're doing it for ourselves because upholding the power structures that oppress other people are also upholding the same power structures that oppress us."

Our responsibility becomes investigating our past and deciding which cycles to respect, and which ones to end, before creating new cycles with new generations. Piecing together information, looking backwards and forward,

I played with time; how did my fourth great-grandmother feel holding her son? Who will my daughter one day be the fourth great-grandmother to, and what will the world look like then? How can I best teach my children to challenge oppressive power structures? How can I connect to my deep roots, so that I can unearth my true nature and be rooted for the rocky future?

I asked the dozens of people I interviewed about their ancestry, and whether they thought it impacted their singular path to repairing relationships with nature. Some people knew about their ancestors, and some didn't. People paused as they reflected, and took the question in different directions. One of the responses that struck me came from Cheyenne Sundance, a self-taught farmer and Farm Director of Sundance Harvest, a 1.5-acre ecological farm in Toronto that grows mushrooms, herbs, vegetables and fruit. The urban farm is centred on fair labour, soil health, knowledge sharing, and community building.

Cheyenne talked to me about her vision of being an ancestor by teaching other farmers, so that her success-ful farm business could be replicated. "I would like to be a strawberry mother plant, and all the ideas that come from Cheyenne — myself — are the daughter plants. And you take the daughter plants . . . and those daughter plants create the mother plants." She described how she shares her ideas with other farmers, and they become the mother plants, and as they then share their learnings with others, the cycle continues. "I think I could turn into compost at the end of my life, knowing that it would be super beautiful to have bloomed a whole field of strawberries."

Sitting with my grandfather and father that year at Christmas, I made conversation and brought up our chickens. I pulled up a photo on my phone of the now-bulky birds, and leaned across to show Poppa.

"Barred Rocks," he remarked, always a succinct man.

My interest piqued, I asked questions, and he told me that his mother, my great-grandmother Irene who shares my name, owned Barred Rocks throughout Poppa's childhood. As a child, he helped gather the brown oval eggs, collecting them quickly because of fear of the nearby rooster.

"I was terrified of the rooster when I was a boy, too," added my dad, sharing early childhood memories of the big beast. Keith, the first name of both my father and grandfather, lives on as Heron's middle name, while Wren's middle name, Ross, echoes from my mother's father who died when I was two years old.

"Wren is terrified of our rooster, too," I added, recounting how Butterfly recently took to attacking the children, and how we needed to find him a new home. Poppa told me how, as a boy, he picked mushrooms with his mother. Perhaps Wren too was forming vivid memories of his rooster nemesis or foraging for mushrooms with his mother, which he would recount to his child or grandchild one day.

The time for me to stop birthing babies seemed to come, though I was not ready to be done. Some women said they knew they felt complete, but I ached for one more, despite my great fortune with three children and my overwhelm with too much responsibility. *Maybe this is the way the river is flowing,* I tried to reassure myself, while secretly hoping for one more pregnancy.

The flax seed embryo, the dreaming of names, the elbows and knees stretching outward from inside my belly, the mystery of when they would decide to arrive, the ecstasy of infinite love being born.

My sister and soulmate Imogen shared news: she was expecting a baby. Back home in the woods, I crawled awkwardly into the tight corners of the crawl space storage cupboard and dragged out boxes of too-small baby clothing. The oatmeal-cream knit sweater worn by Owl, Wren, and Heron, when they were the size of kittens. The woolen slippers, the newborn hats, the sweet blanket covered with roses. Mementos of becoming a mother. I gathered clothing for my sister's baby, marking the end of one era and the beginning of another, which included becoming part of the quiet, powerful network of women who care for one another in the most tender and vulnerable of times. My ritual became the careful washing and folding of garments that meant the world to me, treasures leftover from my most sacred days, sharing a body and a home with my children.

14

QUEEN MOUSE AND CEDAR WAXWINGS

Fibersheds

"Find your people.... My people are conjurers. They dream things up, make something where there was nothing, something the world needs." **AYANA ELIZABETH JOHNSON**

Ginger welcomed me from a distance with wise, bright green eyes. Leaving my car parked by an old barn, I walked across the field to meet her for the first time, and she embraced me with the strong comforting arms of a farmer and mother. I planned on talking with her as part of thirteen interviews with farmers, herders, builders, weavers, and makers embracing regeneration in my region. We skipped pleasantries entirely and within minutes talked about our shared love of soil and a desire to connect with our ancestors. I blushed when she shared that she could picture us sitting on rocking chairs on a porch as old ladies, flattered by the immediate kindred connection.

Thirty minutes north of my cabin, Ginger's farm started with a long gravel driveway that ended at an old barn. The structure stood on a foundation of large grey stones, with walls made of weathered wooden boards. Along the left side, I drove past an L-shaped farmhouse whose windows overlooked the surrounding farm. Another barn stood on my right, and beside it Ginger's husband operated a loud chainsaw. Between the home and the grey barn, a trampoline and a tree with sprawling branches occupied the foreground, and behind them, fields of Ginger's and neighbouring farmers fanned away from the road. The shepherdess led me back across the road and through a set of wooden gates to a vast field of wildflowers and clover. I pressed record on my phone, that memorizer and destroyer of moments, to capture the conversation. A flock of eighty sheep surrounded us slowly, walking towards me, the newcomer, with curiosity. Ginger knew them all by name.

"This is Argèntine," she said, introducing me to the eldest sheep in the flock, a matriarch who'd fulfilled her duty bearing lambs, and who would be rewarded with retirement in the barn starting next winter. An Icelandic sheep with downy wool, she looked like a little old lady, affectionate and wise, a creature who had borne babies and seen life. Still nursing Heron, I joked to Ginger that under my shirt I resembled Argèntine, my body worn from years of those generous acts of pregnancy and breastfeeding.

Ginger explained to me how she came to embrace regenerative agriculture on this soil, a transplant from the most populous part of Canada who found her way to a herder's life. She believes this livelihood also sustained her ancestors in Wales, where the English attempted to erase the Welsh language and culture in their first colony.

"I was born to a farming family in Tennessee, and grew up riding on the tractor with my dad while he cultivated our cash crops. We raised animals who provided nourishment for our family, and with whom we spent many hours learning about life and death, gratitude and humility. Family circumstances brought an unforeseen move away from that life immersed in field and forest. When the opportunity arose to purchase this farm with my sister-in-law and her partner, we shifted trajectory in a heartbeat to be here on this land." She paused.

"It felt like returning home from exile. Everything in my being had been longing to be on the land, with wide open sky bordered by forest, nestled in the hills, with sunset-drenched evenings and clear, starry nights. Birdsong of all descriptions greets me in the morning and fresh, cool freedom fills my lungs. Dewy grass marked by bare feet in a trail to the garden. It is paradise on Earth."

When Ginger moved to the farm, she fell in love with three sheep that she brought home in her minivan, an impulsive decision that led eventually to her beloved flock of sheep. She decided to repair her relationship with the land, in the close company of her children and flock.

Sheep, though, were not Ginger's only concern. Her eyes sparkled as she told me how she worked to upend and alter systems: foregoing industrial agriculture to nourish soil and support pollinators. She worked to sidestep capitalism to build a resilient local economy for natural fibers in her own region. I quickly abandoned my pre-planned questions as our conversation unspooled and respooled across geographies and centuries. Our discussion meandered, surrounded by the gentle bleating of sheep in the sun, and the odd nod of a head on our calves, asking for cuddles. A particularly affectionate sheep named Queen Mouse refused to leave my side, and I crouched on the ground stroking her until my legs went numb. Drawn to her gentle spirit, I did not want to stand up and hurt her feelings.

From my spot on the clover, I looked up at Ginger. "You seem deeply connected to this place. Do you think your ancestry affected your moving to this farm and becoming a shepherdess?"

"There's something like knowing where you come from that is so important. A lot of settler people in North America who came a hundred or two hundred years ago don't know where they came from. We just know our families. For me, my sister looked into our ancestry and I was surprised to learn I am Welsh, on both sides. In Wales, there was a cultural genocide, similar to the one that's still ongoing here. With my sister tracing these roots, you know, I just take little snippets of heritage that mean something to me. And those roots help me look at something right now."

Ginger paused and sheep nudged at our legs, interrupting the conversation with the levity brought by animals and children. "Dot doesn't have teeth right now, she is going to get to hang out in the barn next year. She has done her work having babies. Tinder over there is the only pure Icelandic that we have. Downy is a little old lady, a little old lady."

"Oh my gosh, she's beautiful. She gives so much love," I gushed. "Did you find out if any of your ancestors were shepherds?" I asked, petting the sheep.

"It is hard to get any information. My sister didn't connect with individual ancestors, and I learned that the Welsh basically experienced an attempted annihilation of their wealth and culture. This happened under the guise of religion. No more of your Welsh music, no more of your Welsh language.

If you were caught speaking Welsh, you had to wear this wooden yolk around your neck, as a punishment. The only way to get it off your neck was to tell on someone else for speaking their native tongue. How sick. You know, cultural trauma becomes intergenerational trauma, and for us the legacy of this showed up in grandparents who insisted you don't say things, you don't speak out against things. You're meant to suppress everything and get angry, but you never express your anger. In me, this turns up now, during our conversation," she added, gesturing her head towards my outstretched palm holding the intrusive phone. "Why do I feel shy to be recorded? Why do I feel mortified to be seen or heard?"

We said goodbye to the sheep and walked back across the road and entered Ginger's home through the side door, which led to a simple and spacious living-dining room containing a sofa, piano, a round wooden table, and windows looking onto fields and the barn. Across the room, a trio of stairs took us into the kitchen, a space that emanated nurturing care, with mismatched pottery mugs, syrups and eggs from the farm, and the ingredients for school lunches and soups to feed a family. Looking out into another mother's home, I felt a pang of insecurity, worried that my children experienced too many shows, too few nourishing soups, too much chaos. I imagined perfection in her home, easy to do at first glance and when children are out at school, and without being in the personal imperfection of her mind and time.

Ginger poured us hot tea in clay mugs, and we sat at the round table in front of a striking tapestry on the wall, an expanse of cream-coloured wool interrupted by dark grey and brown yarn woven into the landscape.

"I made that," she said proudly when I asked about the piece. "It took me weeks." She reached out her hand and her strong, knobbed fingers gently stroked at a crimped grey brushstroke of wool. "This is from Queen Mouse," she explained, and I remembered the sheep as she sat in the sun surrounded by wildflowers and clover, her long coat soaking in sunlight along the curve of her back. Surely she felt no different than I did standing in the sun, alive in a sacred body that revels in sunlight and summer air.

Looking at her textile art, Ginger sighed and spoke in her playful, delicate voice. "This comes back to the problem of our current capitalist system, built on these long global supply chains. Here I am trying so hard to build a local textile economy here where we live, but to sell this art — or a sweater entirely grown, spun, dyed, and sewed here — would cost $600, inaccessible to everyone. And it is hard for me, making ends meet, as a shepherdess and mother.

"A wise person said to me that money is earthly. It is made of physical material, all of this great, wonderful, beautiful physical material. Money belongs in that realm. And so do products that come from this realm of earthy materials, or even stinging nettle. Trade is the exchange of a product for money, within this earthly rather than spiritual realm, and we've gone off track. We consider human and animal labour a commodity, like what this beautiful animal gives us," Ginger explained, touching the wool from her sheep, displayed on her wall. "I think willing gratitude needs to be there, but at the same time, this is something that's a commodity that can be treated with money. And then you take your money and you get what you need. But this wise person said where we've made an error in our system is that human labour is not meant to be a commodity. You know, we have this earthly body that's material and, depending on your worldview, we come from a spiritual world. Our labour is a gift from that spiritual world. We've kind of gotten ourselves into a tight spot by exchanging money for that labour. And I don't know how else it could be. I don't have an answer to that, but I see how it makes thoughtful objects way too expensive. If we do an exchange for the person's labour and that's what has to provide for their food and shelter and all of those things, how do you afford that?"

She paused. "You know, there's this whole idea of growing flax in this region."

"I'm obsessed with linen," I exclaimed, laughing.

"Flax grows here and we can make linen. But then no one could afford it, because of what it takes to grow, process, and then sew it, not to mention the thirty percent markup to sell it. You know, you can't pay 800 bucks for a pair of pants. So the conundrum is that, had our economy unfolded consciously with intention, we would perhaps not have a post-industrial revolution economy that took away the joy of making things and the joy of wearing a clothing item where you know who made the object."

"We uproot the bad systems we inherited at the same time we work to root new ones," I commented. "I know what you're creating will pass down to your children and other ancestors." I nodded towards the tapestry. "Both the physical work you create, and the ideals and practices around nurturing and disrupting systems."

"That reminds me of something," she said excitedly and left the table to grab a large box. Reaching into the box, she pulled out several quilts, covered in small flowers or checker prints that were in vogue several decades ago. She told me about a quilt that her family passed down, and that travelled across countries. "I knew I was sleeping under quilts that every stitch was made by my mama, with her hands. She made them from shirts that were used and worn out. So then she cut them up into pieces and made them into quilts," she recounted. "And the cotton batting in the quilts was grown on my family's farm. You have a connection to the feel of the quilt, like the connection to this field," she continued, looking around at the landscape that surrounded us and the flock of sheep. "It's grown from the land where we lived, and can return to it again. Though mine won't return to the land — it is now too fragile to use, and I have it upstairs folded and put away."

"A quilt is a story," I said to Ginger. "It is part of your family, and your history."

I pictured the frayed quilt, passed down generations like cedar waxwings pass an apple blossom down a line on a branch. The quilt is an heirloom of this woman, who tried to do justice to her ancestors and remodel the future by subverting the current extractive system, all while herding her sheep, raising four children, and nurturing the early faltering steps of a regenerative textile economy in her own region. Tiring work. Vital work. The quilt stitched stories of her past to the home she nurtured in the present, and it will one day be passed on to her descendants in a volatile future of ecological and societal breakdown. My eyes dimmed with fear of the future, so I returned to the present, to a bucolic scene where two newly acquainted women shared stories of generations past, discussing how to dismantle and recreate systems as they sipped tea, surrounded by fabrics, fields, flowers, and a flock.

We walked out of Ginger's home towards the barn, and her daughter Eleanor ran up to her from the retreating yellow school bus labeled *Écoliers*, and the mother swung her child onto her back. Eleanor's small arms clutched around her mother's chest to hold on, and when they both turned to look at me, their eyes flashed the same bright green. Mother and daughter, a continued thread of generations that stretched on from unknown roots in Wales here to this place, where a mother struggles to take the hard path of recreating systems and starting new cycles, because in an extractive and suffering world, the work is worth the promise of creating something regenerative and even beautiful.

Quilts stayed present in my mind after meeting Ginger and her flock. The image of a quilt began to emerge, with humanity as a collective that is composed of individual patches of fabric that culminate in a greater whole: a collective that is required for a moment of crisis and upheaval. In environmental circles, I bumped up daily against metaphors of battle, wars, and fights as the cure to climate change. While we certainly need to know when to fight, a question began to form: what if we did not need more stories of battle to address ecological breakdown, but rather we needed the metaphor of a quilt?

I began researching the history of quilts as a medium for political messages and radical action. In particular, I discovered a lean, rich zine, *Many Hands Make a Quilt: Short Histories of Radical Quilting* from Common Threads Press that opened my eyes. The publication, written by Dr. Jess Bailey, an art historian teaching at University College London, showed me that quilts were not just antiquated, old ladyish relics. (And who said old ladies can't be radical?) Rather, quilts quietly boasted social justice power and expressions of liberation.

Quilts were not only metaphors for how we can create a more just world — they have in fact been tangible tools of change. As I delved deeper in the history of quilts through Dr. Bailey's work, I found no shortage of literal quilts that sought to create justice at the impassioned hands of their makers. Abolition quilting bees, anti-slavery quilts dating to the 1800s, and police-free future quilts all live as examples of radical quilting. Formerly incarcerated people told the stories of mass incarceration through quilts. The AIDS Memorial quilt, the world's largest community art project, was an act of love and protest. The thin volume by Bailey introduced me to Queen Liliʻuokalani, Hawaiʻi's last reigning monarch, who cared deeply about representation and voting rights, and who, while imprisoned, used her own garments to make a quilt that recorded injustice. I learned about civil rights activist Ruth Clement Bond who, with other Black women, created Black Power, a quilt with a fist at its centre as a symbol of empowerment and a call for coalition building. Artist Susan Hudson, who comes from the Kin Yaaʻaanii clan and lives at the Navajo Reservation in New Mexico, recorded the horrific truths of residential "schools" that inflicted physical, sexual, and emotional violence on Indigenous children, embedding intergenerational trauma for years to come. Hudson's quilt works to record and tell stories of children who were forced to make quilts, which are now lost to history and which she seeks to find. Hudson wants to tell the stories of children who are now grandmothers.

Spurred by Bailey's work, I started to look for examples of climate quilts, like the Climate Action Quilt in British Columbia, and the quilters and knitters who chronicled climate change worldwide, with blue and red textiles representing temperatures climbing ever upwards. The colours in the quilt represented fractions of degrees able to create chaos and end life. In some cases, the materials that formed the quilts were inherently environmental. Bio-quilts used bio-materials like mycelium, seaweed, or naturally dyed materials. Some quilts were stitched from recycled textiles, saving waste from the landfill and giving it a new life.

Whether literal acts of resistance and liberation, artistic expressions of the collective action that we need right now, or physical creations giving waste materials a second life, I became more convinced that quilts offered the right metaphor for our moment of crisis: quilts invoke family and community caretaking, both essential to effective climate action in times of crisis. We will need to mend our environmental action over time, and pass it on to the next generation. We need a coming together of disparate, distinct approaches into one collective whole, with a spirit of repair and intergenerational care. This coming together of distinct, even conflicting, approaches to climate action stands in stark contrast to what we normally hear: a demand that we behave perfectly in our environmentalism, pitting one approach against another, like fighting over whether veganism or regenerative agriculture is better rather than agreeing that we need many imperfect approaches. We need everyone's unique talents, resources, and perspectives — like a square of floral fabric stitched next to a square of tartan textile — so that in the unpredictable years to come, instead of being passive witnesses to a crescendo of crises, every single one of us can contribute to the complex project of repairing our relationship with the natural world and rebuilding our systems to be more just and regenerative.

Inspired by my time with Ginger and her sheep, and informed by my reading about radical quilting, I dug into my own roots to learn more about quilts from someone I knew my whole life: my aunt Millie Cumming, an award-winning quilter and fiber artist.

I read about her before our conversation. It can be strange and revealing to learn how the outside world sees your family. As a child and youth, I knew of her abiding love for loons and her passion for quilts, but her acclaim within the quilt art community remained unknown to me. Millie quilted for over thirty years, with her creations displayed on gallery walls and in the pages of magazines, along with being displayed across the walls of her home and family cottage. We have limited views of the people in our lives, seeing them narrowly in relation to ourselves.

Millie and I met over Zoom, me at my writing desk and she in her quilting studio in an old home on the edges of the Grand River, near Guelph, Ontario, where by happenstance Ginger and her quilt once lived. Millie's eclectic studio housed shelves covered in quilting books, carefully organized, the pages tagged with stickies to remember certain details. Binders full of drawings, swatches, and words captured the processes of quilts already created or to plot out quilts-in-progress, of which she has many. Along one wall quilts are designed, and then redesigned, and then redesigned again, the ideation process taking longer than the making of the quilt itself. Sometimes, in spite of careful planning, a half-finished quilt is taken apart, in pursuit of the right design. Worlds of fabric are organized by many criteria like textile type or geography of origin, and Millie salvages old fabrics from thrift shops and church sales, to be saved from an anonymous end in a landfill and instead be turned into a work of art.

"Can you tell me about your relationship with nature as a child?" I asked my aunt, beginning with the question I always start with during my interviews.

"You won't be surprised," she began. "It was the cottage." It turned out my aunt and I shared the same origin story for our love of nature, which was seeded in the same place: the Lost Channel. "Nearly everything in my memory, up to age ten, was about the cottage and nature. The happiest place."

Millie's parents — my grandparents — built a small wooden cottage in Muskoka on the curve of a bay. Years later, my aunt herself owned a cottage there, a short canoe ride through the lily pads from where her parents' cabin once stood. As a girl, every summer I visited Millie's cottage, the place where I stepped out of my small town and first connected with the natural world as a girl. Her cottage could be reached only by boat, and then a walk from the dock up steep stairs, made steeper by childhood. I was at home there, nestled safely between forest, rock, and lake. Every year, I collected tiny specimens of moss and lovingly kept them in a cardboard box to bring back to my house, but I could not capture what I missed. The mosses never lived away from their home, despite my childhood attempts to water them, and they dried up sadly in a cardboard box by the windowsill.

Perhaps, though, they lived, as Robin Wall Kimmerer writes: "[M]ost mosses are immune to death by drying. For them, desiccation is simply a temporary interruption in life. Mosses may lose up to ninety-eight percent of their moisture, and still survive to restore themselves when water is replenished." She details how mosses revive fully after forty years of dehydration in a musty science lab cupboard. "Mosses have a covenant with change; their destiny is linked in the vagaries of rain," Kimmerer continues. "They shrink and shrivel while carefully laying the groundwork of their own renewal. They give me faith." With no ecological knowledge, I presumed my mosses in their crisp inanimate state to be dead, but perhaps they lived, dry and grey on my windowsill, waiting futilely to return home to the Lost Channel.

Millie told me about her quilting origins. "Auntie Ethel taught me how to sew on her treadle machine, when I was probably nine or ten, and Grandpa Colbourn's sister Aunt Hett made baby doll dresses. So, I had a little bit of that experience, and my mom — your Grandma Alice — taught me a little bit of embroidery, although she didn't do a lot. I made clothes starting in high school, including my prom dress and my wedding dress much later. In high school Home Ec, I made a matching two-piece set for me and five-year-old Anne," she added, and I imagined my mother at age five in the 1960s in an outfit made by her older sister. "I wish I had a picture of that," Millie added wistfully.

"Finding quilting, though, came when my son Andrew was born, without a doubt. One of the earliest quilts I made for Andrew was a big boy wall hanging, which emerged after young Andrew and I were at a garage sale. We found a little cloth book that was five cents, filled with beautiful pictures, much better than you get nowadays. We played around with it for quite a while, and I was already in the process of making a quilt. I cut up the second-hand book and the scraps found their way into the quilt." My aunt was a palliative care doctor at the time, and this early quilt led her on a rapid path from amateur quilter to experimenting as a fiber artist, an art form in which she eventually became renowned. She reflected, "That is one way to become a quilter, by becoming a mother."

Recycled textiles featured centrally in many of her works. "I'm sure a part of being drawn to second-hand fabrics comes from the fact that when we grew up, we weren't rich. We did go to thrift stores and auction sales and clothing didn't come from new places." She continued gathering fabrics from antique shops and second-hand stores over the years, storing them methodically in her studio. "I believe recycled fabrics give you a much more interesting quilt."

She gestured towards her studio. Surrounding her, I saw boxes of all shapes and colours, stacked on shelves in organized chaos. Thousands of books sat in rows, read and indexed, with individual binders for each art project. Her studio held an abundant catalogue of quotes, images, fabric swatches and sketches, all which come together in pieces of art. "I have all these boxes of fabric and I'm well organized. I came across three more antique baby caps, you know, special pieces. One of them I found at a church thrift store, with a little piece of paper. The paper said, 'My great-grandmother made this 150 years ago' in shaky handwriting. I am always planning to put that into a special quilt."

I thought about the quilt in Ginger's home, and said, "We live in a disposable culture, and it seems to me that quilts are like the antithesis of that. You know, holding on to meaningful pieces like those baby caps that someone saved and which is a century and a half old, and creating something new. Is there anything about that that strikes you?"

"I very much want to hang on to memories, so yes, it strikes me deeply," she said, and her face darkened. "But I do worry about what, what comes after me. I treasure every bit of these quilts."

"Quilts are not something that five years ago I would have been interested in, but I am repeatedly drawn to them now," I explained to Millie. "They speak to me as connectors, passed down from generation to generation," I continued, self-conscious that I spoke to an elder about generations. "I'm really interested in care, and at this moment in human history, care is not just a nice, sweet pleasantry, but rather a very transformative force. Caring for each other, caring for the planet, is what we need. I am seeing quilts as an emblem of care for the planet in the same way — a symbol of care, and also an actual act of care."

"Yes," she agreed. "Often people make quilts to celebrate and honour the birth of a new baby, or offer them as a gift for people in palliative care, as they face illness and death."

I nodded. "Ideally, like quilts, we pass down our environmental action and stories about nature from generation to generation, and our care needs to be mended over the span of those generations. Our environmental stewardship is not perfect, but it is this cherished and loved thing. Quilts are an analogy for the way that we could act for climate: instead of a battle and a war, what if we are creating and repairing a quilt? What if environmental action can be something more feminine, nurturing, and caring?"

As a girl, I always cried silently into my old-fashioned orange life jacket as I left Millie's cabin, hands trailing in the v-shaped fan of water that flew out of the side of the motor boat like a flock of geese flying desperately to return home. Looking at the Lost Channel now on a map, I am struck by how little is captured by the digital bird's-eye view of the place. On the rectangle of my computer, blue uniform water squeezes through nondescript, beige land that surrounds it, a crude representation of the heavy water that laps at craggy shores. The digital map misses the sensation of racing, exhilarated, in the motor boat towards the trees, looking for all the world like you'll head right into shore because of some visual deception. At the last moment, the channel reveals itself and you curve with the shore, cool water splashing at your face, upturned in the mist. The map fails to capture the sensation of sliding down a massive rock with your duffel bag in your seven-year-old hands, running with the push of gravity and excitement towards the dock. The map misses the fine details of living moss under your feet, the miniature olive forests which you collect carefully and gather in a small cardboard box to bring home to your townhouse bedroom window, where you water it liberally, if inconsistently, but cannot manage to keep it alive, away from its wild home. It misses the drips of water falling from bathing suits hanging on the line onto a stretch of pine needles, the sight of a water snake sliding down through the cracks of the dock into the reedy water below, and the sound of a loon calling across the bay before she disappears into the dusky lake.

An ancient animal, loons lived among the fossil record with mastodons and sabre-toothed tigers. Different from other birds, their haunting and mesmerizing howls across a misty morning lake conjure up millions of years of living history. Hearing their calls across the water of the Lost Channel, my body changed, growing both more alert and calm. Loons lived here for millions of years before human beings did. Essayist Stephen Marche wrote, "The loon was making the call you hear before great apes had evolved for us to evolve from. The call of the loon makes the puniness of the mere 300,000 years of Homo sapiens apparent. The sound was waiting for us, for you, from the beginning and before the beginning."

The loon's call often painted the mornings at the Lost Channel, a haunting sound that flew across the bay into bedrooms where cousins slept in 1980s pajamas and a kitchen where coffee dripped into the waiting pot. Carved wooden loons and paintings of loons surrounded the orange and brown living room, echoing the bird living only metres away. We children rubbed our eyes in bed, or the more wakeful adults, like Millie, heard the call from within the gunnels of a canoe as they skirted silently through the lily pads in a sunrise paddle. Millie watched from the canoe, her breath held as she paused to listen to the loon's call, as drops of lake water rolled down the edges of the paddle before dropping back into the infinite lake.

Marche writes about the efforts of early conservationists to eradicate the loon, as they did with the wolf — an animal with whom they equated the black and white bird, on account of their howls. Settler hunters and fishers saw the predator loon as a competitor. "Diverse Indigenous cultures — from Inuit to Anishinabek — tell stories about loons as kin, highlighting their vision, perceptiveness and call. In contrast, early European settlers had their own reactions to the primordial call of the loon, reactions of violence and control."

Loons connect us with the ancient past, and at the same time, connect us with other ecosystems. They spend time in both oceans and in-land lakes, and changing between the two diverse environments causes their eyes to turn red when they return to lakes like the Lost Channel. Loons share space with us in our above-water world, and also live in the depths of deep water, connecting us with habitats we never see. For both known and mysterious reasons, including a warming world and changing acidity in lakes, loons now face threats to their existence. Marche wrote that data forces us to "confront the possibility of loonless lakes; they would be sadder, lonelier places." The possibility fills me with deep sadness and also numbness, causing me to question how many tragedies a human being can possibly understand and grieve. Does the sadness of extinction know any limit?

Millie's quilts often draw inspiration from the Lost Channel loons, depicting a tranquil tangle of lily pads, the arc of a loon's back, or the silhouette of a lone canoeist. One quilt she made in 2005, called *Ancient One*, shows a loon racing across the surface of the water, full of movement as it takes off into the sky, its legs blurred by speed, its sleek black head and beak in profile racing off the side of the quilt as though it will leave the tapestry if you blink. The white of the loon's belly flies nearly perpendicular to the water, and his one red eye stays steady and calm, even in motion. Black wings, dotted with white stars like an ancient starling, trail off the top of the frame. Monet-like pastel rectangles form the lake behind the loon, the shades of green and blue fading and overlapping like strokes of paint. Bursts of water spray up across the quilt from left to right, splashes made by the feet of the ancient loon as it runs across the lake and up into the sky over the Lost Channel.

Our love of that beloved place and her loons is not the only similarity connecting Millie and I. While Millie is her middle name, her first name, like mine, is Alice. She and I belong to a long line of firstborn Alices, stretching many generations into the past. Owl's middle name is Alice, continuing to stitch the connection into the present and future.

My draw to the intersection of soil, textiles, and sheep led me to Rebecca Burgess, a farmer and writer whom I hoped to visit in California. Because pregnancy, pandemic, and other interruptions caused me to cancel two trips to California, I instead called Rebecca over Zoom.

"Today I farmed from six to eight a.m. That's how I start my day, and that's how I'm going to end my day, every day. I have to do it before *work*-work," she explained, referring to her critical role in helping to advance a statewide and worldwide movement to establish fibersheds. This movement offers a much-needed alternative to the fast fashion system I learned about in Portland. "The farm reminds me of the real experience of being on the planet."

An indigo farmer, weaver, dyer, and community organizer, Rebecca spent a full year wearing only clothing grown, designed, dyed, and created in her bioregion in California. That experience helped inspire her to write *Fibershed: Growing a Movement of Farmers, Fashion Activists, and Makers for a New Textile Economy*, and to become the Executive Director of Fibershed, a grassroots organization that builds on her work to decentralize natural fiber and dye processes to strengthen economic opportunities in her region. Rebecca has cultivated an internationally recognized network of farmers and artisans in the Northern California Fibershed to pilot this dream of a regenerative textile economy. Rebecca is working to create a fashion system that, from soil-to-skin, is good for people and for nature. Across the miles, we talked with one another about how we can topple outdated, extractive systems of the old economy, and in its place, rebuild the connections that knit together farmers, weavers, dyers, artisans, and wearers in resilient and regenerative communities.

I learned from Rebecca and her book that fibersheds resemble the farm-to-table movement, except the end product goes *on* our bodies instead of inside them. In this model, clothing would be grown, designed, dyed, created, worn, passed on, and eventually composted in our own regions. Like a watershed, where every stream, lake, marsh, and river connects in a whole, complex system, fibersheds bring independent features together in a mutually-beneficial textile system. Fibersheds provide stark opposition to the fast fashion system that relies on harmful chemicals and dyes, excessive water and land use, human exploitation, and ever-rising greenhouse gas emissions to produce clothing. In a fibershed, like the one Rebecca is helping to build and grow over many years in California, the way we make our clothing is carbon beneficial, regenerates soil, is healthy and safe for our bodies, and restores livelihoods to rural communities and economic sovereignty to regions. A fibershed takes into account nature's elegant cycles. Regenerative agricultural practices mean ethical treatment of animals, and decentralized processing and milling could help to support equitable food systems. A fibershed makes thoughtful use of the water cycle, and understands the importance of living in balance with the carbon cycle, working towards improved soil health and sequestration of carbon to help tackle climate change. The entire cycle of our clothing can be soil-to-soil, starting with how farmers tend to crops to how clothing composts at the end of its useful life. Natural dyes and materials mean decreased toxic dyes and chemicals in our ecology and our bodies. All parts of the supply chain, from growing crops to dyeing and weaving textiles to designing the clothing, happen in the region and benefit local workers.

Completely antithetical to an anonymous global fashion system where everyone wears the same mass-produced garments with a heavy reliance on fossil fuels, local fashion systems reflect the culture and landscapes of specific regions. Designers from the region create their own unique flair which reflects local culture, and in an ideal world, wearers of clothing learn who makes their clothing. Cotton, flax, hemp, wool, silk, and other natural materials are used based on the local growing conditions, and dyes from plants and flowers integrate the colours of the landscape into garments. As Rebecca wrote, a fibershed is "place-based textile sovereignty, which aims to include rather than exclude all the people, plants, animals, and cultural practices that compose and define a specific geography."

With society generally disconnected from the idea that our textiles, like clothing, towels, and sheets, come from agriculture, teaching people about fibersheds presents a challenge. The heart of that challenge is a reconnection with the land and our dependence on her. Rebecca's organization hosts a learning centre in the Black Mountain Ranch community of agrarians and artists located in Point Reyes Station, California, on traditional Coast Miwok Territory. The multi-use space provides demonstrations and allows for hands-on connection to dye and fiber systems, with opportunities to learn weaving, natural dyes, mud dyeing, spinning on a drop spindle, indigo extraction, and botanical printing. People interact with the seasonally grown crops for dyeing, pigments, and fiber-like wool, with plants from multiple ancestral lines and long classical breeding histories.

The space connects people from the burgeoning fibershed movement in their specific geography.

I asked Rebecca about fibersheds in different climates.

"What grows and how we farm are not universal across climates and communities. How much water a farm should use and what their cover crop seed mix should look like changes in different regions. Fibersheds come to life across different climates and places. Part of my undergrad looked at Indian cotton: what kind of textile patterns existed, what kind of antique processes were used, and how did the monsoon rains fit into those cycles? In many cases, it can be a rain-fed cotton, and that's perhaps why India has always had such great classical breeds. It had to be the right soil and the right rain cycle. They had cotton, before the British came, and that was an incredibly powerful crop. It was built into their food crops, meaning I'm going to grow what I wear and I'm going to grow what I eat on my five acres. And that's what my family has to eat and wear. You also see that same five acres in homesteading." Rebecca paused, looking concerned and mulling over her words. "I don't know, homestead is not the right word. That's a European term. But let's say self-sufficiency farming on five acres worked also in what we now consider desert conditions.

"In what is now called Arizona and New Mexico, they would also see monsoon rains. The Southwest of the United States does get summer, and it supported a beautiful cotton culture, so beautiful that the Spaniards saw the patterns of the Tiwa Pablo and other tribes, and they ripped the shirts off of the Indigenous people because they'd never seen anything so delicate, so refined. In talking to those in India who still are keeping some of those cotton breeds alive, even at a small scale, [one of those farmers] said, 'Well, our great-great grandparents did this on five acres,' but they received about eight inches of rain a year, versus monsoon rains that come in forty to fifty inches.

"I think about the climate of the north Atlantic, where my ancestors are originally from. And I think about the moisture in the air that allows you to grow plants that produce antimicrobial fibers like linen. That unique temperature and ambient humidity is so important for naturally taking pectin and letting the microbes eat the pectin, laminate, and leave the fibers. But then my European ancestors would have beautifully created flax into textiles that are completely dependent on humidity. So then when the north Atlantic settlers came here, they looked to places like Southern Oregon or Central Oregon to restart their flax traditions.

"The last thing is cochineal. We can grow a bunch of cactus, and there is more cactus drying out here. But if you go to Southern California, at the Santa Barbara Botanic Garden, there is a bunch of cactus covered in cochineal. So, not even a full latitude figure down, just three hours away, it survives. Three hours north, it is nowhere to be seen. Cochineal has such a powerful history as the color red or magenta or purple, whatever you can make, depending on the pH. It's magic.

"Weather patterns, soil types, and rainfall patterns are absolutely so cool. If we would honour them, life would be beautiful and diverse, right? Versus a unified homogenous fashion system where everyone buys this one shirt, with place-based textile economies you can almost picture the maps," Rebecca said.

"As you're talking about it," I commented, "I'm picturing the map from where your ancestors were to where you are now in California, with different fabrics and dyes, and reasons for each."

Rebecca nodded. "We need some level of protection against toxic materials coming into the country, and against products that are made by enslaved or indentured servitude labourers," she insisted. "We could in turn support places and place-based economies to have more of a level playing field. That levelling of the playing field is what national policy can do. It is human policy. But how you implement the actual restoration of the watershed, how you regenerate farmland, how you produce nutrient-dense food should be done in a way where money trickles back into these communities. Creating a fibershed today is about rebuilding. The infrastructure, the markets, the ideology. You're basically rebuilding the kind of fiber community you would have had a long time ago."

Rebecca's work rebuilding a fibershed rippled out beyond her farm and learning centre, and beyond clothing entirely. She embraced policy and advocacy, and worked to dismantle systems of extraction and waste, with the fashion industry as a hub of resource extraction, harmful chemicals, misuse of water and land, poor labour conditions, and extreme over-consumption and waste.

In the 2023 report *Stop Waste Colonialism!*, authors Liz Ricketts and Branson Skinner of the Or Foundation make an evidence-based plea for a justice-led circular textile economy. They want to see a system where producers like fast fashion companies are held responsible for the business model of overproduction, versus the current system where people in countries like Ghana, where the authors live, face unjust burdens when rich nations outsource the waste management of overproduction and overconsumption. The global second-hand clothing trade currently circulates over 4.5 million metric tons of second-hand clothing annually, a staggering volume that is hard to comprehend and harder still to manage. Ricketts' and Skinner's research shows that second-hand vendors in receiving countries like Ghana go into debt paying for bales of clothing that did not spark joy in wealthy countries, garments that hold no value for Ghanaian consumers as well. They write, "With under-resourced capacity and over-burdened infrastructure, much of what enters the global second-hand clothing trade may end up as waste, dumped or burned within sensitive ecosystems, causing significant harm to human and environmental health." Women and girls as young as nine years old carry the heavy bales of clothing, up to fifty-five kilograms at a time, on their heads, resulting in severe and irreversible spinal damage. Once the clothing reaches the second-hand market, forty percent leaves as waste anyways, piling up in a country facing climate change events from flooding to drought. As the authors write, "This has created an environmental disaster in Ghana, a disaster that has unjustly become the burden of communities that did not cause the problem."

One solution, Extended Producer Responsibility (EPR), would demand producers of textiles build in the cost of waste instead of passing it off to overburdened people, as a transitional policy from a linear to a circular economy. Global accountability must be central to such a policy to ensure justice, including accounting for losses and damages already caused by the fashion industry and excessive consumption by the wealthiest, as well as burdens borne by climate-vulnerable communities.

I spoke with Aja Barber, author of Consumed: The Need for Collective Change: Colonialism, Climate Change, and Consumerism. Aja powerfully critiques consumerism, and people gravitate towards her honesty and conviction. She pushes for the big brands to lose their chokehold over us, and urges us to organize and resist excessive consumption and injustice.

"Consumerism is embedded around these bad systems [of colonialism] and is connected to climate change. But what you can challenge yourself to do is say, 'I'm going to take a month off from buying.' You can challenge yourself and say, 'I'm going to try and buy six or seven items second-hand this year.' You know, setting goals that you can actually achieve is way more impactful than setting a goal that you're pretty much going to fail at, like saying, 'I'm quitting fast fashion tomorrow.' Unless you are able-bodied, thin, and have all the money in the world, that might actually be very hard. So I encourage people to set realistic goals and to not beat yourself up, if you have to get some work trousers from a place that isn't ethical or sustainable. And the more time we take, I think the better we get at this and the more we begin to understand our needs and how to achieve these needs in ways that don't hurt or harm someone else, human or planet.

"We're used to these systems being unfair. And I think we're primed for that in our society. One of the things I talk about, it's when parents will say to kids, 'Eat your vegetables, there are kids starving in this part of the world.' But even as a child, I was thinking that me eating my vegetables doesn't actually address the inequality that a child somewhere else is facing. Maybe we should actually just address the inequality instead of using this weird comparison game to guilt kids into eating peas. I think things like that really prime us to accept injustice instead of actually questioning why there isn't justice, as there is in a world that is so full of abundance and a world that could actually really feed and provide for all of us."

That reframing the world as abundant, versus the capitalist story of scarcity, felt transformative. Aja's vision of justice and mention of abundance brought me back to my conversation with Rebecca, the fibershed proponent from California, and something she said to me about redefining how we measure wealth. "Wealth is developed by the living, breathing ecological systems. Earth is doing the work to create prosperity. Photosynthesis is the work. The hydrological cycle is the work. That is work that is being done on our behalf. You're prosperous if you have clean water. You're prosperous if you have a dynamic ecosystem in your forest that is being well-tended to, and if your fisheries are intact. You have nutrient-dense food, clean air and clean water. That is wealth."

Ginger the shepherdess shared my fascination with fibersheds, so she introduced me to Marie-Eve Faust, a fashion professor in Montréal in the process of convening the first gathering to form a fibershed in Québec. Within days, I found myself driving a couple of hours and walking into the chic halls of the École supérieure de mode at the Université du Québec à Montréal. Far from the day-to-day reality of mucky fields and nuzzling sheep that I'd encountered at farms, urbane people in creative fashion spoke in French about the innovations, opportunities, and market forces facing the textile sector in our region. The room buzzed with researchers, entrepreneurs, economists, growers, and designers. Some people spoke the language of policy change or market signals, while others I met pulled tangles of wool from their pockets to display their sheep's coat, or showed me the dried blossoms of the flax they taught themself to spin into Québec-grown linen. Each person promised their own role to play in the development of a local, sustainable textile economy.

In my rusty, nervous French and through the haze of a medical mask, I participated in conversations, perched on a rotating stool at a twenty-foot-long design table. Mannequins adorned with everything from wool to chain mail circled the room, and in the middle we talked about challenges. How to grow linen and wool in our cold climate with short growing seasons. How to compete with global forces, knowing a local textile economy cannot compete on price, which is of crucial importance in times of crisis, inflation, and manufactured scarcity. How to take successful textile pilot projects and scale them so they make a meaningful impact. Like with many complex environmental problems, the reality facing us looked like a tangle of logistics, cost, time, weather, willpower, policy, and public support, with major global corporations and systems seemingly set up to obliterate local action. Like with the many regional and community solutions which are already available to us, the answers lie in creativity, cooperation, ideals backed by practical strategy, and dogged unwavering determination. Looking at the group gathered around the fashion design table, I saw the principles of Rebecca Burgess's book come to life, and I compared her experience of growing a fibershed in California to my own region. Fibersheds grew, stalled, and were reinvigorated across the world, in places like Ireland, Sri Lanka, and Spain. When I spoke with Malú Colorin, a Mexican natural dyer living in Ireland and one of the co-founders of Fibershed Ireland, she told me, "I don't think anything can happen in a movement such as this without a strong community. You know, as much as you try to single-handedly solve the problems of the world, you can't. And there's no point in tiring yourself out, thinking that you will. So we need one another." Lessons of building fibersheds could be shared across the unique specifics of our growing zones and regional cultures, stitching together local experiences across continents.

<hr />

Reflecting on the threads and throughlines that connected my quilt journey from Ginger's farm to Millie's studio to Rebecca's book to Aja's home to a fashion school in Montréal, I braided it all together. The first strand formed from my roots, through my conversation with Millie. The second strand was my present geography in rural Québec and passion for regeneration and caretaking discussed with Ginger while standing in the field of sheep and then with designers and innovators in nearby Montréal. The braid's third strand was our uncertain future of breakdown that calls out for repair and care, with conviction like that expressed in radical quilting. Roots, geography, and future, layered one over another, again and again, the different time spans and geographies intertwined. Ancestors and descendants, speaking in conversation, inextricably linked with a throughline of soil, textiles, and quilts.

Quilts offer us a way to think about rising to the crises and challenges that beset us. Quilts can express our own selves, roots, and places, and can be created communally by actions of community. They need to be repaired and attended to over time. Quilts are warm and comforting, while at the same time they can be powerful symbols of resistance. Just as our environmental and justice action needs to be, they are intergenerational and embedded with care. Quilts purveyed powerful messages and acted as conduits for radical action throughout history. Not only a medium for inspiring change, quilts also provide an analogy for the patchwork of actions and approaches that are required to tackle the complexity of ecological breakdown. Quilts have been under-respected as objects of artistic beauty and warmth because they are primarily feminine endeavours, just as caring and repairing have been largely ignored in climate conversations because our patriarchal society prefers electric vehicles and techno-fixes. As I deconstruct those viewpoints within myself, I come to terms with the fact that no one will save us but ourselves in collective action.

Ginger emailed a group of women, calling on her growing community to show up for her and her flock. On shearing day, I took my children to Ginger's to ostensibly help out, though coming with my trio of offspring meant we provided more of an energetic audience rather than assistance. Ginger's community gathered energetically to help sort the newly shorn wool. Witnessing the creation of a local regenerative textile community in my region was a beautiful honour. Devotion and sweat and persistence flowed from the people involved, with many hands required. I wanted to participate in some small way in the dream of a fibershed emerging where I lived, communing between the farmer, soil, sheep, knitters, shearers, millers, and wearers. In the words of Rebecca Burgess, "The emerging future is already starting to show itself, and all of us have a role in hastening its birth through our voices, actions, and consistent care."

We let ourselves into the barn, our eyes adjusting to the transition from the sunlit outdoors to the dark of the wooden structure. Sunlight sliced through barn boards in vertical lines, making visible the dust mites floating in the air. The place smelled clean and agricultural. The mud floor, dotted with the odd stalk of hay underfoot, connected to a perimeter of stalls lined with piles of hay on account of Ginger's dedicated work: hay laid with care for her sheep for birthing, a process which she midwifed in the middle of the night. Dozens of sheep milled around the barn and in the adjacent field, watching the shearing with curiosity from behind a closed gate that separated the sheep being sheared from the rest of the flock. For some of the younger sheep, today represented a new experience, and to the seasoned matriarchs, the ritual rang familiar. As soon as we arrived, we watched a big sheep shorn before she ran off, relieved to be finished and decidedly lighter without her winter's worth of wool.

"Her name is Alice," a kindly stranger informed us from her spot beside the barn door.

Returning home, I pulled from my pocket a grey-white puff of wool from Ginger's farm, a daily reminder of Alice and the eighty other sheep who help to regenerate soil, breathing the same air as me, connected to my patch of Earth in this region. The wool physically represented a dream of community gathering to be midwives to both an old and new way of being. I placed the untreated, oily wool in the basket in my closet, where I keep pieces of fabric for a one-day quilt, once I learn how to make one. It might be a matter of decades until I have the time. I'm collecting the fabrics from favoured childrens' pants with ripped knees, from a special dress that my daughter outgrew. Treasured fabric scraps, saved to be remade into a quilt for a descendent — perhaps an Alice's Alice — who comes next into an imperfect world requiring justice, repair, and intergenerational care.

15

THE LAST PASSENGER PIGEON

Extinction

"I'd follow love into extinction." **AYISHA SIDDIQA**

I walked down our gravel road with Bear, and he stopped to lay on his side. His white chest filled and emptied like a bellow struggling to keep a woodfire burning, and he looked at me from the sides of his eyes. *Help.*

"Come on, Bear!" I cheered him on, unsettled. "Here, let's go, Bear!" *It's probably the heat,* I lied to myself. *Always a stubborn boy.* I pulled his leash, half-heartedly and then fiercely, dragging him a foot along the gravel, his body limp as I tried to pull him into health. I remembered his wild self and my wild self on this road countless times — him pulling me, him accompanying me, him protecting me.

I thought back to a few years earlier. *My feet pound the gravel road, Bear running loyal at my side as I run. We quicken our pace, two wet creatures running across a canvas of fringed forest. I break into sobs as I run through the downpour, Bear keeping a steady pace and offering me unwavering love, even as I heave and weep, afraid to stop moving.*

I raised my voice, pulled harder, and then stopped, immensely guilt on account of dragging him through the dirt. He lay still, watching me, unable to move. I knelt on the ground, cried, and pet his white fur. My other dog, Sparrow, watched us, worried.

"I'm sorry, Bear, I'm sorry," I said weakly, looking at the valiant creature, pleading with me silently for help. After comforting him for a few minutes, I tried to encourage him to walk home, but he lay there miserably in the dust. I wrapped my arms under his heavy body, my forearms scraping along the small rocks, and struggled to lift one hundred pounds of sick creature to his feet. His torso arched up but I lacked the strength to carry him back to the cabin.

That winter, everything went backwards. Harmful algae in the Atlantic Ocean painted the coasts of Florida and Mexico red, killing scores of fish. In Ottawa, closer to me, residents waited for the canal to freeze like it did every year, so they could skate along the long spine of the ice as they had for decades. Weeks of hope finally died down as the water refused to freeze because of high temperatures, leaving residents in disbelief, unsure of how to fill the long winter months. Snow fell in Yosemite, causing the National Park to close because of unusual weather that became ever more usual, the boundaries of normal stretching like an elastic band that eventually must snap. Water across the Earth grew confused — running red, receiving chemicals and waste, falling as snow where it wanted to be rain, unfrozen and moving when it needed to pause. Local anomalies connected as one great climate-change terror, observed silently and worriedly by people and animals who shared the experience of watching as the world we knew disappeared.

A Costa's hummingbird in California watched the sunshine change, and he hungrily filled his tiny belly with nectar, storing fat to double his weight. He left his home, flying twenty hours a day over changing ecosystems to complete his biannual migration, entering a state of torpor where he slowed his metabolism and heartbeat, conserving energy for the wayward journey. But everything went backwards that year, including for him, and he migrated in the reverse direction, flying 180 degrees opposite to the usual route, flying as fast as he could for nearly two thousand kilometres, and finally ending up in a backyard in Saskatchewan just in advance of the coming winter. A chemist spotted the lost bird and rescued him, taking him into Living Sky Wildlife Rehabilitation, a centre created by Jan Shadick in her home until the rescued animals spilled out into every room and the neighbours complained. She then found a proper location to house hundreds of wild animals in need of her care. Yosemite Sam, as the humans called the displaced bird, spent the cold northern winter in Jan's nurturing care, as she fed him a special diet of fruit flies and protein in a humid environment designed to mimic California, anxiously trying to see him through to livable temperatures when he could hopefully return home. Maybe it made sense that Yosemite Sam migrated in the wrong direction, when the world itself reversed and altered — California under snow, a northern capital's canal unfrozen, and water running red with dead and dying animals. How could any of us creatures possibly know the right direction to fly?

Bear grew more sick. I play-acted the role of Hope, buying expensive kidney disease drops that seemed like snake oil, and rejoicing when I managed to convince him to eat a special home-cooked meal of rice, chicken, and carrots off a spoon, provided I held it for him long enough. He lost thirty pounds in a few weeks, the beads of his spine pressing against the fur along his back, and every day the bar for his health lowered. He managed to walk to the end of the road! He managed to eat a few bites of food! He barked at a truck that passed down our road! Like me, Bear lived each day as an overachiever, and he always barked far too much when no one asked for his help and he would do better by relaxing. I saw myself in his desperate need to protect, even when not required. He had often barked to the point where I screamed at him in frustration, unable to bear the constant barking over the overstimulating din of children, even though he simply did his job, protecting his family. Usually when the snow plow came, I gritted my teeth through the barking and the leaping at the windows, but in his illness he looked half-heartedly at the vehicle and then curled back up on his cushion. I now faced a world without him, and I knew his overachiever heart worried about leaving us alone.

"We are safe. You don't need to worry anymore," I told him. I whispered in his ears, "Everything will be okay," though I did not quite believe my words.

We took Bear's last loop in the woods, and my bones knew this would be the final time he could manage the route we walked so many times together. Over the snowbank, up the ridge with the eroded banks of the creek on our left, around the fallen tree, across the cracked wood of the foot-bridge, uphill around the basin of the valley in the middle of the woods, across the flat of the meadow, back into the relief of the forest, past where coyotes spilled the deer blood and fur, across the ridge, and down the hill to the road. Our loop. The walk that maintained my shredded mental and physical health.

The coming death of Bear made me fear other future losses. The losses and suffering seemed guaranteed, while beauty and life felt tenuous. Always so aware of endings, of the last time we do something, I mourned Bear leaving us and mourned all the other lasts. The last time my children tiptoed — or thundered — into bed because they've grown up. The last time I walked this loop. The heartache of preparing for his death reminded me of the fleeting honour of being alive.

That night, while Bear slept, skinny and struggling on his pillow, I watched Wren sleep sweetly upstairs in his bed. Watching his face, I saw what he would look like at thirty, just shy of 2050, the year with all those net-zero goals that won't arrive fast enough. I glimpsed what his face would look like at eighty, shy of the next century, a terrifying future I cannot imagine. Who will he love? What will he be like as an old man? Will he still be zany, spilling over with unpredictable laughter and joy? Will he face tragedy? Will he live to be very old, with grandchildren and friends around his bed, with someone holding his hand as he dies? Will there be birds? What of this Earth will be left?

Martha, the last passenger pigeon, died on September 1, 1914, the solitary final individual of her species. Passenger pigeons gravitate towards each other as their home versus a specific place, especially during nesting. Human beings gravitate towards each other as home, too. What have I been orienting to as home, throughout the many near-breakdowns and meager recoveries? My work? Accomplishment? Praise? What are all of us orienting to, at the expense of a geographic and community home — our phones, stuff, despair, online distraction? As a result of human activity in a newly colonized and stolen land, passenger pigeons dwindled, meaning their home — each other — disappeared. Our hubris told us that human excess would never possibly kill every last one. In *What is a Bird?*, the authors write: "Human actions threaten almost every extant avian species." *Every extant avian species.* Does that mean we threaten every bird? *Extant. Still in existence.* The *still* qualifying it, letting me know their existence is fragile, and that we expect them to disappear. Each species, ending with a Martha, a single sacred individual.

Great Auks, large flightless seabirds targeted by hunters in North America, stuffed our mattresses and provided meat and oil. The last known breeding pair was killed in 1844 on an island off Iceland, where fishermen not only killed the two birds, but also crushed their eggs, ushering in the end of a species. Today, a spotted owl in a vast rainforest in Spô'zêm First Nation in British Columbia is the fragile last of her kind. At the same time I grieved the absences and disappearances in my woods, Leyland Cocco wrote, "Only one spotted owl remains in the Canadian wild . . . Her precise location in the misty forests is a closely guarded secret and her lonely presence has become a symbol of the country's inability to save a species on the verge of destruction." He quotes species-at-risk expert Jared Hobbs, who said, "When I drive the highways and backroads here in their former range, all I see are ghosts. The owls we've lost, I know their stories. And those stories are gone."

My heart struggles to handle the ghosts and the grief, even as it continues around me under the name Normal.

On Bear's last evening, our family of five encircled him by the wood stove, and took turns sobbing into his fur, holding his paws, and telling him how much we loved him.

"You don't need to protect us anymore," Owl sobbed, falling forward onto his body, holding him. Had she heard that from me?

The next morning, we performed a subdued version of our morning routine of packing lunches and organizing backpacks. I opened the front door, and Bear looked up to Nik, waiting for permission to go outside. A good boy, checking in with his leader, even when we would have let him do anything he wanted. He always respected Nik, and he never really believed in me as his leader, though he sometimes pretended he did to humour me. He loved me, though. Nik took the children to school, and Bear walked out the front door, and without peeing, eating, or drinking, he lay simply in the sunlight against a snowbank a few feet from the front door of the cabin. His wisdom and readiness for death showed so clearly, bright in the winter sun. I bundled myself up in extra scarves, sat on the cold ice beside Bear, and lay blankets over both of us. My hand held his paw as his body worked to disappear slowly in waves, like the opposite of birth contractions, similarly mysterious and out of my control.

Snow drifted softly from tree branches in the sun, the snow-flakes' shadows below like swallows flitting across the road. Seeing his suffering, I willed his body to let go and die. I wanted him to lift his head, see a deer, and then run and chase it, wild and free through the woods until, just out of eyesight, he flew away over our forest loop, a free bird.

Who was Bear's mother, the dog who carried and birthed him down in Texas? How were they separated? I hoped they had time together when he was a baby, and that she was a good mother. I hoped I was a good mother to him, too. I struggled to mother him and give him attention when he was at his wildest and strongest. He took care of me more than the other way around. He protected me, and now my turn came to protect him. While I didn't mother him in birth, now he needed me to mother him in death.

"I love you, Bear," I whispered to him. "We are safe, we will be okay. You can go now. You do not need to protect us anymore. You have been such a good boy."

When Nik returned from the school run, he grabbed a blanket and sat on the other side of Bear, and we held each other's hand on top of Bear's breathing body. The three of us sat outside for hours in the cold between the cabin and the forest, partway between the domestic land of family and chickens Bear loved to protect, and the wild woods which he loved to roam, much to my worry. I lay on his chest, and for many minutes, his heart beat quickly, in perfect rhythm with the sharp caws of a nearby crow. *Caw caw caw. Beat beat beat.* I always suspected he would die fighting a bear to protect me and the children, but instead of the grandiose drama befitting a regal warrior, he suffered a sad process of failing kidneys. My childlike heart felt shock to see this majestic beast, as mortal as the rest of us, succumbing to a mundane disease. Bear died in our arms, with the help of a needle of the local veterinarian who does home visits. Nik held up his dear friend's body in his arms, sobbing desperately, trying to hold on for one more minute. I turned away, unable to see Bear's dead body sagging in his arms, and I fought the urge to throw up. When Nik could hold Bear no longer, we lay him on a sage-green blanket on a long plastic sled in the woodshed, and decorated his body with cedar boughs.

We picked up the children together, an unusual occurrence.

"Bear died today while you were at school," we told them as they sobbed. "We feel very sad. Whatever you are feeling is okay. Our bodies are safe. We love you."

At home, Nik asked them, "Would you like to see Bear's body to say goodbye?" All three children said yes, they wished to see him one last time. We walked to the woodshed, where the five of us sat around his body again, as we had the night before, but different. Once the children slept, and with the nighttime kitchen clean complete, I stripped Bear's soiled bed which smelled like illness, and placed his bedding in the laundry machine. I walked outside and said goodbye to Bear's bough-laden body before bed, a habit from when he lived. A futile goodnight to an empty body, before entering the house made quieter by his absence.

Our home, despite all its many living creatures, felt empty without Bear. We missed his slow walk to greet us at the door, his big and gentle head awaiting a pet in greeting. We missed his majestic stance on the crest of a six-foot snowbank, nose sniffing the wind for a deer to chase, a path to roam. What a wild soul. Our home looked cleaner, too. One less food dish. One less water dish. Marginally less fur on our clothes and in the vacuum filter, less near-springtime mud in the front hall. After years of complaining about the mess, I realized that our home looked messy because it was full of life. We only ever knew Birdsong Cabin with Bear, and without him and his steady presence, home felt less like home, and everyone seemed lost. I looked for his spirit in the forest but could not find it.

With all of my imaginations of animals, I struggled to imagine Bear. I could not see him. I ached to envision him chasing a deer along the ridge above the eroded valley. Sparrow searched for him too, running excitedly to each of his favourite places, expecting to find her best friend around the next corner and, when she finally walked back mutely to the house with her tail drooped to the snow in disappointment, she set off our tears again. The snowbanks melted as the freshness of loss became less raw. Sparrow's paw prints on the snow eventually covered all of Bear's until there were none of his left, as she also prematurely took over as protector. She looked to him for steadiness — we all did — and now she barked in odd ways, daunted by her newfound leadership responsibility. I showered her with all the love I couldn't give Bear, and took great joy in feeding her or removing a burr from her ear, finding the tasks turned into acts of love rather than chores.

Bear's death created a season of loss, and I could not find my footing without my protector. I tracked the spring migration of hummingbirds and, once they arrived in our region, I dutifully hung a feeder filled with sugar-water for them, but only ants crawled in, with no iridescent birds hovering at the sugary source. Ants emerged in the house, too, marching along the walls carrying boulders of salt or bagel, no matter how much we cleaned the crumbs, no matter how tightly we tied the rubber bands around the cereal bags in their family-sized Costco boxes, no matter how we attempted to chase the mess with our insufficient cleaning. Ginger sold most of her flock, to make the finances and the sacrifices make sense, keeping a few of her dearest sheep, whom she called the keepers of the faith. The heron didn't come home to the creek, for the first year since I moved to Birdsong Cabin. Every other spring, he returned to his thick pine branch that extended over the creek, standing majestically over the crashing water and fishing expertly in the fast-moving water. But in that fifth spring thaw in the woods, for weeks I sought him out, only to see an empty branch.

I knit the absences of the birds I knew best, and the sorrow of Bear's absence, to other sorrows. Sorrows from the past: the ant I vacuumed up as a child for no reason but to see what would happen, before immense guilt took over me. The rabbit I killed driving around a curve in the countryside at night as a teenager, with a *thud* as his body hit the tire under me. The pigeon I saw dying by the subway in my mid-twenties, whom I sat with while he suffered on the pavement, making myself late for work. The three chipmunks who ran behind my back wheels when I was a new mother with my two children in the back seat — three of them, three of us. The snakes and frogs we sometimes found squished on the gravel road on the way to Birdsong Cabin — their home, our home, their death by our violent life of convenience. I mourned the sorrows approaching in the future, and losing Bear ignited my acute awareness of all that we lose. The loss of the animals in our home, and in our woods. The loss of my children, other people's children, my husband, my parents, my sister, my home, my friends, me, the forest, the snow, the birds. The loss of ecosystems, the loss of animals I've never met, crushed under the weight of construction machinery in their burrows, or people fleeing forests on fire and wars, with nowhere to go. So much loss.

"But we breathe today," I tried to reassure myself and the children. "What a fragile and remarkable joy, to be alive!" with motherly, resolute cheeriness. Ephemeral creatures against a backdrop of infinite stars, rocks, and oceans.

Keep us safe.

An intense late winter storm found us, leaving the trees laden with a casing of heavy ice. Branches hung across the road in long arches, and the ominous arbour threatened to fall on us, cracking under the weight of ice and seismic changes. Power went out, leaving the whole region dark for days. I twisted a candle into a wine bottle until flakes of wax corkscrewed out of the thin line between the candle and the glass. The candle barely moved when I wiggled it, testing it for stability and safety. Something I could control. Wren took his puffer by candlelight, as he methodically ran a flashlight over his 100-piece glow-in-the-dark dino puzzle, piece by piece; by the time he got to about fourteen the first piece lost its glow, and he started again. The kids wrestled in their pajamas, and I spoke like a seasoned mother. "No horseplay by the candle!" We melted snow on the wood stove for water, for dishes and drinking, and used a pot of it to flush the toilets. Conserving water became a necessity rather than a nice-to-have environmental practice. We refrigerated our food in the cooler, worried about spoiling the food. After years of struggling with money, we'd finally lost financial security month to month, and we tried to extend our food until the next grocery shop. Financial struggles meant that taking environmental actions became an obligation rather than a fun project. Making our own deodorant and dishwasher tabs, reducing food waste, mending torn clothing, and reusing Ziploc bags meant hopefully making ends meet. My eyes opened more to the stark difference between the privilege of environmentalism as a hobby versus conservation and waste reduction as a true need. Some people enjoy the privilege of taking climate action as a concern, versus as an act of survival. I rested firmly in the former privileged group, but like many, I started to understand safety was an illusion, and we moved closer to that day when our struggle too would be survival.

A good friend in my community texted me, *I haven't heard from you in a while. Is everything okay?* and later, *Do you have power? Need anything?*

I replied, knowing thousands of people lacked power with hydro crews overextended. *We don't have power and I expect won't for a while, how about you?*

He replied, *Yeah we got power back a couple of hours ago. To tell you the truth I was hoping it would be out a little longer. I like the making do, the snowshoeing to the creek to haul back a bucket of water, working the BBQ in the snow, washing dishes and saving water. And candlelight is always nice. I do appreciate all the modcons — but at the same time I feel that I've made a pact with the devil, because I know full well that my chosen lifestyle is completely out of whack with Gaia and indeed the well-being of humanity itself. So it's fun to pretend for a day or two that none of that exists.*

Seasons came and went in odd orders, with the old natural cycles disrupted and gone. Spring allergies began before that ice storm. Wildflowers bloomed early, then died. Ice season melted into wildfire season, my first one. We woke up one morning to a hazy sky and orange sun, and when Wren opened the door to play outside before school, the smell of smoke filled our house. "Close the door, come inside!" I told him quickly, and went to pack his blue puffer in his backpack. Wildfire smoke from unprecedented forest fires in other parts of Québec coated the air and our lungs, turning the sky monotonous grey-orange, obscuring the clouds in the daytime and stars at nighttime. Late spring-time smelled not like moss and pollen and wildflowers, but like fire. I developed headaches, and Nik coughed through the night, unable to sleep. Sparrow ducked her head somberly when we let her outside, eyeing the sky nervously, and the animals in the forest seemed either absent or subdued from the smoke. Birds stopped singing, and we saw fewer birds, other than the ravens. We explained to the children that they couldn't go outside even though they wanted to run and play. The front hall — normally a mudroom caked with mud, snow, or leaves, reflecting the season outdoors — looked cleaner than usual. The fledgling beans in the garden, and the recently migrated birds in their nests, caused me worry. How small are the lungs of an infant robin, and what do they do when they cannot hide inside from the smoke? What about people without homes, air purifiers, and masks?

An official message came from the school board. *Schools are to remain open. Windows in schools are to remain closed, however they may be opened for short periods of time (ie. five-ten minutes) provided there are no students in the room (ie. before school, during recess breaks). Students are to remain inside the school during the school day; there are to be no classes or activities held outside (ie. Physical Education, noon-hour activities). Students may be taken out for a ten-minute walk during the course of the day. Students with asthma or other diagnosed respiratory problems should refrain from being outside at any time.* How do you convince a five-year-old child to refrain from being outside at any time?

The initial shock of wildfire smoke subsided as the air quality worsened repeatedly for weeks, and we learned to expect it. Parents contended with learning about wildfire smoke safety practices to add to our growing skills in Covid prevention and treatment, managing ice storms without power and the rest, while still showing up to work. "Air Quality Health Index. Oxides of nitrogen." *Are my children safe?* "High-resolution, interactive forecasts of hourly, daily average and daily maximum concentrations of PM2.5 smoke particles at ground level from wildfires." *Are my children safe?* We consulted an online map with puddles of yellow, tangerine, orange, russet, and dark brownish-red, looking for fire icons that indicated the locations of wildfires, trying to decipher how the smoke would find us.

I remembered Naomi Klein's 2017 essay, "In a summer of wildfires and hurricanes, my son asks 'Why is everything going wrong?'" Years earlier, her account of a summer of wildfires on British Columbia's Sunshine Coast disturbed me, linking global climate change with her family's experience being in a place blanketed by smoke. "For about four days, it's as if we are on a different planet, one with two red suns and no moon at all," she wrote, and her words struck me, but felt removed at the time. A West Coast reality, not one that I ever experienced. But smoke, of course, like climate change, filters freely across our false borders and imaginary securities, finding every place. Now, here. Our place, our lungs, our air.

Everyone started to turn the smoke into normalcy, because we can only hold so much fear. Our notable human resilience unfortunately allows us to absorb new realities and paint them ordinary, a talent that hinders us in the slowly unfolding emergencies of climate change and biodiversity loss.

We drove back from a camping trip and our tire popped, slowly deflating as Nik drove us over to the shoulder at the side of a steep hill. "Come on, kids, let's go have a picnic!" I announced cheerily, as Nik rooted in the trunk and we realized we had forgotten our spare tire. Outside of the van, our foreheads dripped in the oppressive heat as I led the kids away from the speeding highway traffic and around patches of poison ivy until we found a spot for our picnic blanket. Our water bottles emptied and our cell phone batteries drained as we called every tow truck in a three-hour radius. No one could come. The national car assistance line kept us on hold, with an automated message that informed us that extreme heat meant cars were breaking down and tires were popping with more frequency, and they could not support everyone who needed help along the roadsides.

This is what it will be like, I thought, on hold with a phone on one ear, listening to the voice of a robot on a loop. I opened a granola bar with my mouth, smiling at my children as I handed them snacks and trying to look like we knew how we would get home. *This is what it will be like when the systems we rely on start to fail us, because they aren't set up for a warming planet. What about the health system? The firefighters? Insurance? The food system?* Then I reminded myself that for many people, the systems had already failed them. Countless millions lived without the expectation of these supports, and have done so since long before I awakened to the climate crisis. In the end, it was not roadside assistance but a dear friend who offered to drive six hours to deliver us a spare tire, as night fell and we used our last ten percent of phone battery. Our communities will be our lifeline.

"This is the part where late stage capitalism blends into early stage apocalypse," I said to Nik matter-of-factly, in the kitchen once the kids slept. "The part where you get used to it." He grew accustomed to my statements like this, along with my improvised late night sing-song ditties about wildfires and flooding, to make myself laugh, to cope.

We got used to everything falling apart — *we* in our home, and *we* everywhere. The end of reliable schooling, with frequent cancellations for storms or our never-ending coughs and recurring illness and pandemic outbreaks. Checking air quality numbers from multiple sources while checking the weather. Moving kindergartners' birthday parties inside for safe air, after learning how to move them outside during the pandemic. Masks inside, masks outside. We learned to usher kids inside, with eyes flitting furtively to the sky, the same way we prompted them to wash their hands. Normal fires, normal floods, normal smoke, normal power outages, normal hundred-year storms every year. Routine fear and uncertainty, all a normal part of Owl's, Wren's, and Heron's childhoods.

Klein wrote:

> "[T]he idea that the entire planet has a fever that could get so high that much of life on Earth could be lost in the convulsions — that seems to me too great a burden to ask small children to carry. This summer marks the end of his protection. It isn't a decision I'm proud of, or one I even remember making. He just heard too many adults obsessing over the strange sky, and the real reasons behind the fires, and he finally put it all together."

This is good for them, I convinced myself, *a childhood of generators and masks and adapting to cancelled plans and no power for the foreseeable future.* Good preparation for adulthood in a tumultuous world, the way that typing class once provided a useful skill for the future. We are not raising children for a perfect world, or even a stable one, but rather a warming one, an aching one, an unmoored one. A world that is sorely out of right relationship and balance. "Rampant removal of groundwater for drinking and irrigation has altered the distribution of water on Earth enough to shift the planet's tilt," I read in an article, one of the hundreds that screamed for attention. The North Pole shifted four centimetres as a result of our pumping extreme volumes of water. My job, more than saving for my children's university, became preparing them for a world off its eternal axis.

Knowingly starting to expose our children to truths, in an age-appropriate way, starts preparing them for the world they inherit. The constant disruption evolved my mindset about raising children: instead of teaching obedience, good grades, and a linear path to success, I wanted to equip them for this time they live in. We are not raising them for the illusion of a stable past, but rather a turbulent future. A difficult time, a tragic time. A time rich with potential for change. Breakdown and breakthrough. A time that demands courage and resilience.

Elizabeth Bechard, author of *Parenting in a Changing Climate*, talked to me about how taking baby steps into climate action allowed her to engage during a very intensive season of life of mothering young children. "I would first offer deep compassion for how hard this is. Parenting is wildly undervalued work in our society," she commented. She outlined how she built confidence through tangible actions, like sending get out the vote postcards or engaging in child-friendly climate events with her kids during family time. "Every single one of us is required for this in our own way, versus a righteous few doing it perfectly," she insisted. "It helps me to not compare myself as much to other activists or other moms, right? Because, as parents, that comparison pressure is very strong at times, but our work is to show up for our kids, and it's the same with the climate crisis. All we have to do is what is ours to do. Not that that's a simple thing, but it is liberating."

I wanted my children to know self-sufficiency, the wonder of nature, compassion for suffering, self-love, and honesty to deal with grief and suffering. How to grow food, disobey authority, disagree with the powerful, and subvert harmful systems. How to work hard for something you believe in, how to resist the temptation of mass-consumption and distraction. How to rest and recuperate for the struggle. I strived to teach my children gentleness, resilience, and care for an era of sorrows. Harder still, I wanted to teach myself the same things.

But I still did not know how to care for myself, despite an acute awareness that I needed to. It's hard to learn. I became very sick, not from wildfire smoke but from lack of care, and I could not heal. I'd finally extracted too much from myself, my human body an analogy for the Earth. First, my heart kept racing and fluttering, causing me panic. I went to the doctor for heart pain — from anxiety, from heartache, from these sorrows? Then came inflammation and chronic illness. I lay in bed, unable to work or tuck my children into bed or eat, moaning in pain, with no signs of healing after days of illness. Scared I'd miss the future with my children because I worked too hard. Tried too hard. Pushed too hard. *Gentle gentle gentle*, begged my body and heart, insisting louder and louder until I simply could not ignore them anymore. My body was the Earth. Past real, non-negotiable limits, and breaking down and crying out, with tears and with smoke. When someone we know is gravely ill, we give care. When our mother is sick, we bear witness to her suffering and we extend to her our generous and loving care. I needed care. Our mother needs our care.

I did not work for a week, which is hard when you don't go five minutes without thinking about work. I slept. Drank water. Slept more.

Slowly my body gained strength, and I took Sparrow on the loop through the forest, with our new rhythm developed in the three months since Bear died. We came down the ridge, and she lifted her head, alarmed. We heard a bulldozer coming into the woods. The machine rolled up, rocking side to side with the effort of cutting a road through the meadow-like path through the forest.

I picked up the children from school and parked in front of the cabin, where Owl broke into tears, seeing the bulldozer and digger at the edge of the woods. "It is ruined!" she wailed, collapsing in the back seat.

"It is for a good reason," I consoled her. "The neighbour is creating this road so the forest can be surveyed, and then donated into a public trust, which means it will be protected." I crawled into the back seat and held her, but my rational explanation did nothing to reassure her.

I walked with Sparrow into the woods the next morning, stepping onto fresh gravel instead of the meadow path I walked for five years.

"Oh my god," I gasped.

Everything up the path was gone. Life, mown down in minutes. Tangles of thimbleberries. Clover, maple and oak seedlings, soil, mushrooms, coltsfoot, and poison ivy. Milkweed flowering with purple seeds arcing out in a sphere, offering itself to its monarch. The mossy fallen log on the western side of the ravine, from which I heard small cheeps days earlier, a nest crafted carefully in the presumed safety of the hollow trunk. The homes of frogs, worms, and dragonflies, all of whom heard a noise cutting through the morning stillness, before being crushed under the unforgiving wheels of the machine. Every day, life lived here, changed in front of my eyes, made space for my feet, Bear's paws, countless deer's hooves, the dog-like steps of coyotes. Now, gone. I shuddered, experiencing the loss in my body, my gut. I wept, wanting to turn around and go back to the cabin, abandoning the loop that offered me friendship and solace for years. Now, another road. My body heaved, and tears ran down my cheeks without stopping or slowing. One road opened me to the weight of the world, to the unstoppable scale of forests and habitats and the homes of creatures, all bulldozed for roads, toilet paper, and food to be shipped across countries by more trembling vehicles. How fast a machine can ruin life, and without ceremony.

My phone dinged, and a photo came through from a dear friend planting seedlings in our garden.

Is she still there?! I texted, excited.

Yep! he replied.

I ran down into the meadow, and to the garden, where the gates lay open. With my illness, nearly all the seedlings I'd carefully planted indoors in the winter died, and the garden lay bare of vegetables for the first time in five years, save for the tomatoes and peppers my friend started to plant. Instead of a lush garden, a dense wall of dandelion, coltsfoot, and thistle moved inwards over the beds of soil. The death of my fledgling garden was a necessary sacrifice as I attempted to do less — laundry piled in mounds around the dining table, evening meetings declined, seedlings under-watered, all in the name of sleep, food, and water. I took vitamins. The obvious basics of care, long neglected for myself in service of family and causes. I rested slightly more and did slightly less, with the messy imperfection of someone who does not know what she is doing. The messiness of my growth meant that the garden lay abandoned, like the mountains of unfolded laundry.

I saw her, a snapping turtle, lying still and watchful on the third hügel bed. I walked closer.

"Hello, turtle," I said, and kneeled a few feet from her. Finally, in a season of absences and losses, here, in front of me: a presence.

Her wrinkled neck curved downwards from her shell, and prehistoric webbed feet the colour of the sandy soil nestled lightly into the Earth. A pointed beak-like snout, almost the shape of a fish's head, held the grim straight line of her mouth, two nostrils, and unblinking, intense eyes that seemed to stare at me, not kindly. Fifteen scratched and worn plates formed her heavy carapace, with a stony perimeter surrounding the plates in an ancient oval. A long lizard tail with pointed ridges lay across the soil, longer and more reptilian than I expected. The beautiful being sat, and I marvelled at her existence, unmoving in the sun. How did she get in through the garden gate, how did she choose our garden to lay her eggs?

In the middle of the night, unable to sleep as I wondered about the turtle, I left the sleeping cabin and ran down to the garden, my phone in my hand with the flashlight lit, creating a small hazy triangle of light. I found my way to the garden, and flashed the light at the third hügel bed. No snapping turtle. Contemplating returning to the house, I started searching the other five garden plots and the thick perimeter of unwanted plants that enjoyed the neglected soil. Before every trod of my rain boots, I triple checked for the turtle beneath my feet, nervous to step on her in the dark. I gave up, and walked back through the recycled metal door, looking down as I walked.

"Hello," I said, startled to see her right by the gate, inches from where I stepped.

She looked at me. She arched her neck up, far, reaching and then swaying her head back and forth. Unlike her daytime stillness, the turtle moved almost wildly, awake in the nighttime.

"Goodnight," I said, after watching her for several minutes. Unsure whether to leave the gate open or closed, I left it ajar after considerable internal debate, wondering how she planned to return to the creek, whether she would make the trek that night, and how to protect her from predators. The next morning, she perched on top of the third garden bed again, where she had made two nests. She sat deeply in the second bowl-shaped nest, her back half-tilted down into the soil while she moved, slight motions from one side to the other. I spent thirty-six hours obsessed with her, visiting the garden in between work and parenting responsibilities. I tracked her movement around the garden, locating her at different parts of the fence and agonizing over whether she found herself trapped in the safety of the thirty-foot long enclosure.

Instead of a heron, the gift of a snapping turtle. Instead of a garden, a turtle-egg nesting sanctuary.

Again after midnight, I left bed and searched for her in the garden. Three times I circled the gate, anxiously watching for signs of her before stepping down with my rain boots, rooting through chest-high grasses and plants with more confidence as it became clear the turtle had found her way back home. I needed to see her once more. I left the garden gates open, hoping dozens of eggs lay buried in the soil of the sacred nest. I walked down to the creek, through the ferns as ancient as the turtle herself. Maybe I would see her at the creek's edge, I hoped wildly. Maybe I came at exactly the right moment to see her walking in, ready to be subsumed by the water. In the weak moonlight, I looked out across the creek. Every rock breaking through the water's surface looked like the grey round shell of a snapping turtle. Hundreds of mothers, coming back from their long journeys to birth their eggs in the safest place they could find, returning home.

After the summer of smoke, bulldozers, and absence, more presence started to appear.

"Is that a nest?" Owl asked, and we stood on our tiptoes to see the robin's nest against the front of our house, against the cedar siding on top of the hydro meter, behind the hydro mast. Three perfect blue eggs lay nestled in a home of grey down, mud, and twigs. For weeks the mother flew in and out of the nest, startling whenever our loud family opened and closed the front door. The eggs never hatched, but I took hope from them, and I decided I would save the nest and eggs, maybe to gift to my children when they one day graduated into adulthood.

Hummingbirds finally appeared, first periodically, and then they constantly flew towards the feeder I washed and filled with fresh nectar. I watched the returning humming-birds from the kitchen window. Flying in from the forest, their feathers flashed in the sun, and then turned drab brown when they flew into the shade. Frenetically, they filled their beaks, darting back and forth from the source of sugar, and then hovered in mid-air before disappearing as quickly as I could blink.

Only once I saw one of the hummingbirds rest on a branch on a nearby tree. It was startling to see the bird, ordinarily in constant motion, sit still. Even flickering hum-mingbirds rest.

Owl and Wren played at summer camp, where I had dropped them off in another eerie, nothingness sky of wildfire smoke.

"I'm going to play outside in the kiddie pool!" Heron exclaimed after seeing his older siblings pack their bathing suits and life jackets for a camp that ended up inside because of unsafe air.

"I'm sorry, my love, but we can't play outside today," I said again, now a normal phrase for a boy who, at age three, regularly asked us to check the air quality. After some tears, I convinced him to swim in the bathtub. He scooped bub-bles intently from measuring cups into a bowl, where he whisked the foamy suds into soup. I watched him, still part baby for a few more months at most. When done, he clam-bered out over the wet bathtub and curled up on my lap, his hair and body soaking my shirt as I embraced him. I looked at the pearls of his spine, running down his perfect back. Along my forearms, my moles showed, growing larger as

I grew older, against his smooth and flawless skin, raised with goosebumps from the cold and wrinkles from the water and bubbles. A happy mother and a happy child. We played k.d. lang's rendition of "Hallelujah" and sang together, unrushed. My body, pressed against his, still his home as we cuddled. Two sacred animals. I wondered if anyone had ever experienced such joy as this. We were no different than the turtle mother burying her eggs in the garden soil, or the deer mother and her daughter looking for food, or the bird mother with her nest in the log at the side of the road as a loud truck cleared the forest. I hoped they all made it safely. No different than the human mother, migrating as a refugee from climate change, while I held my son, safe for now at least, with eerie orange sunlight filtering in through the window over the place I love so dearly, looking beautiful in the smoke if you forgot the reason for the romantic haze.

16

"HOPE" IS THE THING WITH FEATHERS

Awakening

"'Hope' is the thing with feathers — / That perches in the soul — / And sings the tune without the words — / And never stops — at all —" **EMILY DICKINSON**

A great challenge in my quest became the search for hope during a dark time. Birds fell from the sky in India from dehydration in the ever-increasing heat, and people suffered. Birds vanished from North American skies, too, for other reasons, their bodies crushing against windows and their habitats destroyed so we could build more big box stores, with no plan to slow down. Every headline imprinted on me — *birds falling from the sky!* — and I never shook the new information, but rather kept adding more environmental heartache, fear, and grief.

The loss of birds crushed me. Our trusted, common companions, flitting in and out of our lives, our cities, our backyards, and our balconies. At the same time, they go beyond being commonplace to occupy a mythical reverence in our culture, stories, films, and music. Their nests symbolize our homes, and their flight represents the freedom that we all deserve. People go to great lengths to witness birds, or they stay at home to be with the familiar birds that share their patch of home. We watch birds to know when the seasons change, and we look to their safety as a harbinger of our own, respecting the canary's opinion. Working at my desk in the barn, I looked at the massive white pine tree outside the window, a home unto itself, the centre of a community of many birds — sparrows, flycatchers, robins — their lives interconnecting with mine. Sometimes they came right up to the window and we looked at each other, or in the case of the quick hummingbird, had no time to spare for me, and I watched her for a millisecond before she flew away to more important matters. When birds returned after the winter months, I daydreamed about where they'd been, the journey that they'd been on to come back. I revelled in seeing the birds, but alongside the beauty, I watched their homes go up in flames around the world, and grieved the possibility of their disappearance from our skies in the decades ahead.

Would Birdsong Cabin fall into silence? In 1962, to much scorn and disbelief, Rachel Carson wrote, "Over increasingly large areas of the United States, spring now comes unheralded by the return of the birds, and the early mornings are strangely silent where once they were filled with the beauty of bird song."

This old growth body felt the birds disappear and, swollen with sorrow, tried to make a home for them. My bones were made of old spruce. My cells and lungs expanded with the exhalations of trees, and my skin was harsh like flaking bark. My mind criss-crossed like a wild woodland. My womb flowered with blueberry and mountain laurel, my empty belly with echoing walls — a nest tended tiredly and lovingly for years — begged silently that all children find their way safely and freely.

In a world where birds fell from the skies and the coming of seasons themselves became unreliable, how could I possibly entertain hope? Hope seemed like an ignorant refusal of worsening environmental realities and a denial of suffering. Empty hope risked harming us, by allowing us to stay in a lovely house built in rising waters, where we close the windows tight in a futile attempt to keep despair and sorrow away, pretending we cannot be touched by the great forces that already crashed through the windows of our neighbour's home.

When I spoke with J. Drew Lanham, he reflected from his writing studio, "I think sometimes, instead of giving our hearts a soft landing on hope, we need to let them go ahead and break on despair. And then we pick them up and say, oh, this is what we're doing to create this situation, so let's do better."

In Rebecca Solnit's essay "We can't afford to be climate doomers," she wrote, "I wonder sometimes [if] people assume you can't be hopeful and heartbroken at the same time, and of course you can. In times when everything is fine, hope is unnecessary. Hope is not happiness or confidence or inner peace; it's a commitment to search for possibilities." Hope comes after allowing for acknowledgement of reality and the attendant heartbreak, and calls us to become our most courageous selves.

In their book *Active Hope*, Joanna Macy and Chris Johnstone delve deeply into this approach of a hope rooted in action:

> "Passive hope is about waiting for external agencies to bring about what we desire. Active Hope is about becoming active participants in bringing about what we hope for. Active Hope is a practice. Like tai chi or gardening, it is something we *do* rather than *have*. It is a process we can apply to any situation, and it involves three key steps. First, we take a clear view of reality; second, we identify what we hope for in terms of the direction we'd like things to move in or the values we'd like to see expressed; and third, we take steps to move ourselves or our situation in that direction. Since Active Hope doesn't require our optimism, we can apply it even in areas where we feel hopeless. The guiding impetus is intention; we *choose* what we aim to bring about, act for, or express. Rather than weighing our chances and proceeding only when we feel hopeful, we focus on our intention and let it be our guide."

Marine biologist and author Ayana Elizabeth Johnson encourages people to find their calling in the environmental movement through a triple Venn diagram. One circle asks, "What are you good at?", focusing on the skills, resources, and connections you offer. The second circle asks, "What needs doing?", and there are countless options, from ecosystem restoration to calling for policy change to public education. We each need to find the work that calls us in that circle, which sparks interest and passion. Finally, the third circle asks, "What brings you joy?", encouraging us to choose what enlivens rather than drains us, because environmental action needs to be sustained.

Focusing on a desire for a whole, balanced, and just Earth, and taking actions towards that reality *regardless of how everything turns out*, liberated me. The outcome no longer rested on my shoulders. Probably the worst fears would come true — the mounting evidence, both in reports and based on simply looking out the window, indicated that the worst would come to pass earlier than predicted. While my heart still broke, taking actions like planting a tree or joining a rally brought me into alignment with the world I hoped for. I could ask myself, "What do I know and believe to be true?" If the answer came back that people need to build relationships with place, or politicians need to make bolder decisions that rise to the scale of the emergency we face, then I worked towards those intentions. Active Hope could be my work, while the result, out of my hands, was not my responsibility. How could it be my responsibility, in a world so vast, with harmful systems and machines so complex? I practised something that, while maybe not hope, looked like Active Hope, or at least dogged determination that we do everything we can to restore balance and rebuild a world fit for birds and for us, regardless of how it all turns out.

The alternative to hope — hopelessness — felt dangerous. An abandonment of our humanity. Grace Nosek, climate justice scholar, community organizer, and storyteller, spoke with me from British Columbia about the perils of hopelessness, and how increasingly sophisticated narratives from fossil fuel companies and their public relations agencies wielded misinformation as a weapon.

"The narratives of the fossil fuel industry and their allies, could you tell me a little bit more about the stories we're up against?" I asked Grace.

"Right now, by far the most dangerous narratives are cynicism, doomism, and fatalism," Grace told me, based on her years of research studying and deconstructing the narratives and tactics of the fossil fuel industry. "It is not just the fossil fuel industry, but that is where the misinformation began. They've seeded it, and they've created the organizations and infrastructure with their money, and now the [climate obstruction] movement extends far beyond them, and comprises this right wing, populous media, lawmakers, and pundits, who are really expanding and amplifying these narratives that block and delay climate action by creating this sense that there's nothing we can do about this. Hopelessness is a destructive force, and one that is seeded by big companies to keep us numb and inactive.

"I see it in young people," she continued, speaking about her extensive work with youth. "Which is why I know it's this incredibly powerful one, because it just shuts people right down. They tune right out of any conversation around action or engaging with democracy or civic institutions, because there's this sense that it doesn't matter, that we've lost. We've lost the battle. The apocalypse is coming. Cynical fatalism is pernicious on all these fronts, and we have the empirical data showing that this is a popular narrative being used. We're seeing a surge in youth climate anxiety, and at the same time we know pro-extractivist actors are seeding narratives of cynicism, hypocrisy, and fatalism. The other reason this is so pernicious is that it takes the people who care the most, who feel that visceral empathy, and so they would be the normal leaders or the ones who would be doing the work on climate. These narratives absolutely shut them down and make them sit out."

I saw my younger self in her description — the empathetic, dedicated leader, hyper-involved in social justice and environmental action from a young age. The one sensitive to great sorrow, susceptible to succumbing to numbness because of the pain. Not alone, I knew many of us existed, volunteering our evenings and weekends, signing petitions, advocating for change at City Hall, shuffling responsibilities to stand at rallies, and volunteering on parent committees and boards. Spending scarce free time researching issues and reading books about the energy transition and biodiversity loss, trying to find ways to help. We are many. Imagining the most passionate and active people numb from sorrow and convinced of our collective doom — believing that all this dedication amounts to nothing, so why act anyways? — made me angry, and made me ripe for what Grace said next.

"I refuse to do the fossil fuel companies' work for them. I really try to challenge cynicism and fatalism in the work, but it's hard, right? Because you obviously also want to acknowledge the grief, the sadness, and the immense injustice and human toll that climate change is taking. The reason why I think this story is so dangerous is because it's going to get easier and easier to tell, right? As climate disaster becomes more common and more overwhelming, it's going to get easier to sell cynicism and fatalism, and [the idea] that governments can't do anything anyway."

"What, then, are the climate stories that we need?" I asked Grace. "Could you tell me a little bit more about the stories you want us to create?" She created her own hopeful climate narratives, such as the novel trilogy *Ava of the Gaia* and a graphic novel, *Rootbound*, aiming to push back against decades of industry narratives by centring justice, hope, community, agency, and collective action.

"We need to talk about how every point of a degree that we stave off matters, and will be felt in billions of human and animal lives, as well as in ecosystems. And if we really are doing intersectional climate work, we are building community. Climate action means calling each other in, building care, and being kind to one another, which has inherent value, even if we don't know whether it will lead to a reduction in warming. Making each other feel better in the present and near future is good and powerful. So, we can lean into narratives of joy, care, and love, and that everything matters on different time scales."

Fossil fuel narratives seep into our culture, media, politics, and minds like pesticides through soil, water, and food. It can be hard to know where these pervasive and damaging narratives started, or how to extricate them from our lives. Fortunately, we can create our own hopeful narratives of possible climate futures that run like fast-moving rivers from person to person. We do not need to push for a more hopeful climate future alone. We do not need to dwell in a place of crisis and fear all the time, though I personally need to visit those places often. We can find what Grace calls "the veins and rivulets of care that already exist" in the growing climate movement, and together rewrite the future to be one not of doom or empty hope, but one of collective care and power, no matter what we may face.

I abandoned my search for hope when, back at my desk, burn-out and crippling nervousness still plagued me. Why did I oscillate hourly between balance and panic? Colleagues and friends fawned over my organization and accomplishments — people have admired my work ethic and productivity my whole life — but on the inside I panicked daily. It was as though every tab always stayed open; as though every drawer and cupboard in a house lay ajar, with their contents strewn wildly around the house. Before media interviews, speaking engagements, and even regular team meetings, an overwhelming nervousness took over my body, to the point I could barely speak. My hands went cold, my heart beat fast, and I fought an overwhelming urge to fall asleep on the floor, as though my body shut down in fear. Sometimes, the nervousness began weeks before an important meeting or presentation, finding me in my bed at night or where I sat on the floor with my kids playing in the evening. On the day of a presentation, I could barely move or speak or eat, and nervousness overshadowed every facet of my day. People complimented me on my speaking ability and remarked on my perpetual calmness, oblivious to my truth, which I masked effectively after a lifetime of careful practice.

"It sounds like you have ADHD," my therapist suggested two or three times, and after dismissing the comments two or three times, I looked up attention deficit hyperactivity disorder in women and girls. *Anxiety. Hyperactive brain. Hidden chaos. The construction of a false self. Perfectionism.* I reflected on decades of excessive to-do lists created and never used. Moving too slowly as a child, as I dreamed and wondered and immersed myself in exciting worlds. Reading alone along the brick wall at the out-of-bounds side of the school, hiding from dreaded recess, unaware that a pack of girls watched me and laughed, seeing how long until I tore myself away from my book to notice their mockery. Intricate spreadsheets, piles of receipts and taxes squirreled away into drawers and boxes, litanies of missed bills, agreeing to do things mentioned in conversations I never heard because I could not bear to listen. Dividing my attention into a thousand tiny bubbles that floated away from me, while I struggled to stay connected with each of them, rein them in, control the chaos I created. The more I learned about my diagnosis, the more revealing and liberating it became, and I started to see I truly would never fit into a linear way of living. I compared myself to the blue jay, whom I saw everywhere that summer, that creature known for mimicking the voices of others but also whispering a song of his true self.

Four years into living in the woods, with my dancer and commuter lives in the distant past, I thought I would be a vision of calm and rootedness. But as I tried unsuccessfully to let go of perfection and performance, I finally unravelled. Even as my career and accolades rose, and even as I cultivated a relationship with the garden and forest, I kept pushing myself past my boundaries, trying to prove myself as worthy and productive. Keeping everything together for others — and for the sake of a false self, known for achievement and calm — made me chronically sick and nervous. The task of recovering from perfectionism reminded me of my long recovery from anorexia: in both cases, people and society applaud your illness, celebrating your skinniness or your achievement and perennial pleasingness, discouraging a healing process that will ultimately make you bigger, louder, less permissive, less pleasing. Bigger, more free. Proud of healing from anorexia over a period of years, I couldn't seem to recover from the addiction to perfection. I tried, but not having my perfect mask left me untethered and fragile. Without the safety of my perfect self who thrived in chaos, I faltered, unsure of how to love myself in all this imperfection.

What would it take to love myself enough that I began to take care of myself?

I crumbled daily, waiting for a full breakdown, or maybe this was in fact a messy breakthrough. But I knew I would never break down fully. Each time I was in labour, the midwives asked over the phone whether I could still talk, which they use as a measure of how far you are into active labour and whether they should come to provide care. All three times, I could continue to speak through the unspeakable intensity, and all three times the midwives barely made it on time, instead delivering their instructions over the phone to tell Nik how to catch the baby if they did not make it. Instead, I experienced a million breakdowns, a million revelations, and then I persisted and pushed too far again. Never enough until I hit too much.

My obsession with time harmed me more than anything else. I embodied our cultural sickness of maximizing time and minimizing space to breathe. Every day, I made impossible feats possible in small chunks of scheduled time, pleasing others and depleting myself until every night, I cried or screamed, from a place of dysregulation that lived far past my boundaries. In halls of professionalism, built on a patriarchal and capitalist approach to time, I thrived, but I didn't know how to do so without paying the cost of devaluing myself. Somewhere along the way, I absorbed patriarchal attitudes around motherhood and being "just" a mother, until becoming a mother to Owl showed me that being a mother in fact became my greatest joy and a whole, valuable endeavour unto itself. This private realization challenged me, as it has challenged so many of us in a culture that degrades women's work and worth, while we kneel down before the altar of productivity.

I oscillated between joy and challenge in giving fully to my children while giving fully to my work, like breastfeeding Heron during my meetings, nourishing him with food and medicine, just like the Earth gives us our food and medicine. I thought back to breastfeeding Owl during meetings seven years earlier, when I returned to work when she reached six weeks old, because I, like so many women, could not get maternity leave. I had no choice in the matter, and I needed to be home in my nest with my newborn, but instead I faced the screens and conferences. I longed to be like hummingbird mothers who tend their nests in June, like many human mothers who immerse themselves in nest-making and caring for tiny babies, dedicating themselves entirely, out of sight and often alone, not without struggle and loneliness, until they are ready to re-emerge. Or flamingoes, who lose their pink colour after becoming a parent on account of the nutrients they give graciously to help their babies survive; their rose hue returns later when their children reach independence. I forced myself to be pink nearly the whole time, because others demanded it, because I let them, or because I demanded perfect pinkness from myself. I asked myself every minute of every day to give too much. There is a saturation point, a limit, to how much a mother can sacrifice and give of herself. Our collective mother is no different, and I recognized myself in her; we've asked her to give us too much.

Maybe I will never feel calm and sorted, I realized, unsure what that meant for a human lauded for calmness and togetherness. Who would I be, without the construct of perfection? Maybe when left to my natural state, there would also be an element of chaos, energy, and wild motion. A brain like a quilt, a patchwork of patterns and colours, instead of the placid calm of a cream linen sheet. Maybe I needed more care, quietness, rest, and play than I ever allowed myself to know. Everyone called me calm, and I thought I sought calm, but maybe calmness was not my destiny. Perhaps I was wild and beautiful, and I found myself on a search for earthly exuberance.

I walked down to the garden in the middle of the night, as autumn started to slide in under the crack at the bottom of the door between seasons. The tallest sunflower stooped like a dishevelled wedding guest at two in the morning, messy and wilting in the jarring and unnatural light of a camera flash. Presumably she looked composed and majestic hours ago, but now her head hung messily at my breastbone. Later it dropped to my navel. Hers was a false yellow, artificially overexposed in the beam of my headlamp as I picked lettuce and kale in the dark. Under the full moon, the sight of the feral, dwindling garden told me that summer too was finishing. It pained me to see the vegetables, lovingly tended, now falling into disrepair. As I left the garden with the bowl of greens in my arm, I stepped on a wayward tomato, and it squished under my boot. The next day, the sunflower's once-grand golden head, with her petals chewed by mice, fell to the soil.

Everyone loves a garden in springtime, with the smell of fresh soil, the drip of melting snow, and the promise of warmth. In the summer, people tend to their burgeoning plants in between too many social plans, and proudly pick a tomato and hold it lovingly to their face, remarking that this is what a *real* tomato smells like. In fall, though, the gardens remain in our backyards and balconies, but without the same excitement or pride. They devolve into eyesores, or maybe reminders that warm months and bright days are behind us. Rather than simple green, my garden boasted yellow, red, brown, green, and crispy black. I watched how her wayward tangles of zucchini leaves handily overtook their neighbours, even as the celery stalks stayed stunted. The celery never really grew, though the previous year's had thrived tall and wide. Tomato vines ran riot, breaking under the weight of their own productivity and success, and I recognized myself in them. Cucumbers played creatively with shape and prickles. I watched curiously as the plants in the garden engaged in conflict and debated the seasons: the dry, curled brown leaves of the leeks argued that it was indeed fall, as the cold mornings suggested. The abundant tomatoes, on the other hand, seemed to side with the warm afternoons and the song of crickets, all in agreement that summer still reigned.

A few days after I spent my night with moonlight and the fallen sunflower, I again trekked down to my wayward ADHD garden, this time in cold rain. On this grey and soupy Sunday, two p.m. resembled dusk. Determined to salvage what food I could from the generous and gracious garden, with Owl, Wren, and Heron dressed in rainsuits and rainboots, I twisted twelve or more zucchinis from their stalks, piling them in a wheelbarrow that filled to the brim with rainwater as the hours passed. We gathered bowls and bowls worth of tomatoes; the red ones fell easefully into our hands and we scooped the green ones before they found themselves squashed underfoot. I stripped witchy, wet, dead leaves — their texture like seaweed — from vines and stalks, carefully tending to the garden in a way I had not when she thrived. Her brittle beauty grew sweeter in the downpour, as the rain washed the muddy vegetables clean.

Soaked to the bone, I harvested vegetables in the rain, after their months of soaking up sunlight. I discovered carrots I had written off as a failure, and found long-forgotten onions and garlic. Radishes which I presumed to be too woody turned out to be sharp and delicious. Cabbages finally started to mature, and Swiss chard grew yet another surprise harvest. The fall garden, which I mistakenly dismissed as dying, actually swelled with vibrant life when I took the time to watch curiously and clear out the old weight. In the words of Robin Wall Kimmerer, "Even a wounded world is feeding us. Even a wounded world holds us, giving us moments of wonder and joy. I choose joy over despair. Not because I have my head in the sand, but because joy is what the Earth gives me daily and I must return the gift."

I walked barefoot between the overgrown beds of abundant life, my feet prickled by thistles and coltsfoot that grew between them. Lessons waited for me, as always inside the garden gates. The lessons, usually heartening, grew melancholy at the crossing between summer and fall. Unclear and muddy like the garden herself. Some lessons were sad. You can give your love and not be able to hold onto vitality and summer health. Even the most cared-for homes fall into disrepair when it's time.

Some lessons came as questions. Did I let the sunny summer pass me by? My sacred garden time, now gone. Did I focus on the right things, or let myself get distracted by noisiness? Is my dying garden a microcosm of the planet I love dearly?

Some lessons rang wistfully. The passing of time, the essential and undeniable truth of cycles. How to graciously accept endings and the passing of seasons. How the Earth still worked to provide even in her waning autumn moments, reminding me that — before growing again — she required a wintry rest. Winter kept coming around to remind me about rest, whispering, "How can you succumb to your waxing and waning cycles of productivity, rest, and dreaming?"

And some lessons brought me peace. The tangle of messy life reminded me that I am worthy of love in my messy imperfection. The opposite of perfection is not imperfection, because imperfection is merely the absence of perfection — a poorly defined, negative space. The real opposite of perfection is wholeness. It is the bumps and ridges of a thing, accepted in its entirety, just as it is, rather than the sharpness and precision of perfection. Perfection is harsh, rigid, and unattainable. It can only look one way, and anything else is failure. Wholeness is a wild forest that changes over time and looks many ways. Wholeness allows me to just *be*, as I am, through my many cycles of growth, blossoming, decaying, and becoming fallow, like the forest sopping in the spring, buzzing in the summer, maturing in the fall, and freezing in the winter. Gazing at the autumn garden surrounded by a tangled forest, I recognized myself: not always pretty, but always beautiful. Never perfect, but always whole.

With the vegetables harvested, gathered, and piled on the old painted white table, ready for jarring and sauces, I took another walk through the beds of the garden. The snake who lived in bed four slithered away as I approached. The beds looked fresh. Cared for, perhaps for the first time all year. I stopped at the lone sunflower, her headless stalk still curved over towards the soil from the weight she used to bear. I wondered where her once-august bloom landed. I looked casually around the tall stalk, and not seeing the flower head, knelt down in the mud and began to search more vigorously. I pulled watermelon vines and the lily pad leaves of nasturtiums to the side, gently at first and then wildly, unable to find the golden flower. I grew obsessed, for her or maybe for me, and started pulling uninvited coltsfoot out of the ground to expose the soil. Still I could not find the sunflower. Had it disappeared?

I paused and caught my breath, and leaned closer to the Earth. Black shells, burgundy-tipped flesh, yellow petals. Chewed into thousands of pieces, barely discernible from the Earth, the sunflower already halfway to becoming soil again. The mice must have found the flower in the garden beds, delighted at the gift from above and relieved to be spared the journey up the eight-foot stalk. I picked through the debris, the hundreds of husks of chewed shells, made lacy by the teeth of mice. I found what I searched for: the beginning of next year's garden. A reminder that so much life exists, not only in seasons of warmth and bounty but also in times of heartbreak and change. I picked it up and placed it in my hand: one whole and perfect seed.

Today we were here. We spotted what looked like Bear's fur woven into a bird's nest. Sparrow and I lay in the meadow at the top of the forest loop, supported by Mother Earth, this sacred home, who provides supporting embrace and the company of sparrows. Wildflowers opened with joyous, unreserved beauty in the meadow around us, though they too will soon become a road. I saw beauty everywhere.

"Those who contemplate the beauty of the Earth find reserves of strength that will endure as long as life lasts," wrote Rachel Carson, and through all my heartbreak, I believed I would continue to find reserves of strength for the uncertain years ahead. What am I to do, except revel in beauty while it exists?

A blue jay called from the old pine that stands in front of the barn, those birds who embody their true self, find their voice, help plant trees. We are alive right now, and so we are the right people to solve this, to replant and regenerate. We are the only people who can restore a regenerative way of life and put an end to the extractive mode. We are the people to do this, for humanity and the planet. The people who can remember what matters, even in the face of every imaginable distraction. The people revelling in nature rather than levelling her. The people who can relearn how to co-exist and converse with our fellow species. The people who reconnect with the animal part of our being, the biological pieces that make up our whole selves, the ones whose breath can be taken away by the sight of a waterfall, redwood or canyon. The humans that can hear bagpipes playing and allow the music to swell in our chests and the tears to roll down our faces.

I walked over to a patch of soil, clover, fern, and mushrooms at the edge of the forest, with a backstory of ancestors behind me and descendants relying on me to learn how to take care of myself. I lowered myself to my knees, despite the stains I would surely imprint on my jeans. Kneeling on the good and gracious Earth, I leaned forward and kissed the soil — with thanks, with knowing, with gentleness, with care. With an ephemeral sense of hope that, depending on the headlines and the wind, visited or vanished.

How do we find and cultivate a sacred home, when our home is eroding and changing under our feet? What is home when the walls are coming down, when the seasons are unpredictable, when home is changing in front of our eyes and vanishing?

On my quest, I found the greatest sources of hope in the individual humans and their communities who reimagined the world, despite a gloomy picture, and worked creatively to uproot harmful ways of life and root regenerative dreams in their place. Regenerative agriculture, rewilding, fibersheds, and regenerative fashion in particular filled me with hope, deep in my gut, knowing that we have real ways of bringing soil back to health, feeding and clothing one another from the land in our own regions, and returning near-vanished species to rewilding homes.

I do not want to numb myself for the apocalypse, rather I want to be awake for the revolution — a revolution where, no matter how it all turns out, we revel in the beauty that still exists. I'll call that hope. We generously give care of every type — self care, community care, Earth care. Care can sound toothless, but in fact it is a powerful radical community endeavour on a scale so grand that we have no precedents to guide our way. Greeting breakdown with love is the work of our lives.

17

WOLF NO. 7

Songbirds

"It often seems easier to stay in winter, burrowed down into our hibernation nests, away from the glare of the sun. But we are brave, and the new world awaits us, gleaming and green, alive with the beat of wings. And besides, we have a kind of gospel to tell now, and a duty to share it. We, who have wintered, have learned some things. We sing it out like birds. We let our voices fill the air." **KATHERINE MAY**

I needed to make a big decision, one I had mulled over for months. Was I ready? It took me months, maybe years. Maybe the first nine years of my motherhood.

In the summer rain, Nik, Owl, Wren, Heron and I paddled on the river and into small inlets around the riverbanks, with life jackets up to the kids' chins as we cut through the still water and bullfrogs croaked. Long reeds, the ones that look like hot dogs on long sticks ready for roasting over a campfire, pushed up against the sides of the red canoe. The light rain stopped. We came to shore and set out an evening picnic.

I decided to leave my job that I loved in environmental economics, to take a leadership role in a grassroots environmental activist nonprofit, to immerse myself in advocacy and organizing in our nation's capital. I had supported the five of us for our first years in the woods, which meant immense pressure and also gave me pride, being able to feed my babies. Nik had made it possible through his work in our home, and now he supported me by going back to work.

I threw myself into my new leadership role and loved the work, but I continued to quietly deal with burnout and unwellness that became all-consuming. I repeatedly grew sick, endometriosis flared up, and my chest pain worsened. Pride kept me from telling many people. *I can do this.* I saw how my unhealthy patterns followed me to the woods and how they followed me through my career. I felt unable to address them while I held immense responsibility and worked at a relentless pace. The kids needed me more than ever, with their own frequent illnesses, hospital visits, and growing mental health struggles, and I frequently left meetings to answer phone calls from the school office, asking me to pick them up early from school. Guiltily and frantically, I tried to attend to their needs while giving media interviews, meeting with partners and government officials, and leading a team. I struggled to give everyone what they needed, least of all me.

Over my career, I believed deeply in the mandates of my organizations, but believing in the work was not enough to sustain me through my self-inflicted overwork and exhaustion. Like with anorexia, our culture — or maybe it was me — celebrated how much I could create and how fast I could go, with so little nourishment. A human cactus. But even cacti express basic needs, and they do not go without water: rather, they store rainwater in their stems for extended dry periods. They need to sustain themselves in order to provide a habitat and even survival for birds and other animals. I used my stored water up, repeatedly, scraping the bottom of my life source, and I began to understand dry periods as normal. Did I really love this work, the way I was doing it — burnt out after too many exhausted years, nervous, forcing myself onwards with a pit in my stomach?

Leaving my career trajectory terrified me, after fifteen years of a linear climb on an upward path, along which I equated my worth with productivity and results. All of those years later after Gombe — where I awoke to my fixation with deadlines, bottom lines, and finish lines — I still struggled to tear myself away from illusory lines on a circular planet. And years after recovering from anorexia, I still struggled to let go of the perfection, control, and image concerns that thrived in secret behind a facade, like an eating disorder. After hanging my identity on a skeleton of titles and external validation, I worried I might fall apart. People would judge me and say I lost my momentum, or that women cannot be leaders. They might say I was just a mother, or just a writer, or just this or that. I worried I might be just a mortal human. Would leaving be a public humiliation, or a grand liberation? My mind put up all sorts of protests. But you're so good at it! But you'll be letting everyone down! You've never quit anything! I succumbed to the stories, panicked, and then paused and responded to myself: Just because you can, doesn't mean you should. Staying will mean you let everyone down — yourself, your husband, your children, your colleagues. And you have done something like this before: remember when you healed from anorexia over a period of years, when it seemed impossible you would survive it? Remember when you redefined your identity and future after your dance accident? Remember when you left your life to follow your heart to the woods, and you found your home?

With my throat closed with nervousness and my pulse racing on a Monday morning, I sent in my resignation, not for a promotion or a bigger job, but for the unknown. For myself. I chose my motherhood and my well-being, and decided to try to heal my patterns of burnout. Of course I still needed to work to make ends meet. Most importantly, a significant part of my work ahead looked like uprooting perfectionism and obedience, and in its place, rooting a mothering relationship of care — for myself, one another, children, and nature. It meant offering the Earth a deep act of care that I personally am more deeply equipped to offer because of my motherhood experience, and which had to begin in me.

In my search to find my place in a humanity-wide effort to care for the Earth, I finally accepted the message of my soft animal body: that my unique role was as a mother, artist and communicator. Seasons changed, but my heart wanted me to do this, at least right now. With a crisis so massive, there was space for me to do what I loved. The environmental movement needs all of us — economists, artists, scientists, parents, builders, spiritual leaders, philosophers. Everyone.

The day after announcing my resignation publicly, I flew to Montana via Colorado. The journey happened five years after my first visit to Colorado to visit Hunter Lovins for my first interview. In the five years since that eager conversation,

I had interviewed more than sixty activists, scientists, artists, farmers, economists, entrepreneurs, community leaders, communicators, and builders, learning from their diverse perspectives on uprooting extractive systems and rooting regenerative ones. My worldview changed from an individualistic approach to systemic changes requiring each of us working in interconnected, complex relationships. I learned that I never was alone in the woods, a solitary Walden who lived in mythic independence from the rest of the world. I was always nested in community, connected to others who made life possible and rich. Cheap fossil fuels allowed me to travel to see my loved ones, warm my home, access cities, take my children to school, and build a life in the woods that was not lonely. During that first interview, I had carried my third baby in my belly, and now we registered him for kindergarten in the coming fall, a new season for him and me. Over those years, a pandemic breathed its way around the world, multiple horrific global conflicts happened and persisted, wildfire smoke and floods flowed through our ecosystem, and the amount of snow around our cabin dwindled compared to that first winter.

After arriving in Bozeman, Montana, I left the plane, found my rented car, realized I forgot my suitcase in the airport, and retrieved it from some backroom airline office. I rolled the bag away in a cloud of ADHD shame, part of my mundane daily experience of apologizing to strangers after I've made some silly mistake like losing my shoes or forgetting to pay my bill. I returned to the black Jeep, and set out of the airport parking lot towards Wyoming, with a pile of printed maps on the passenger seat beside me. Years had passed since I travelled internationally, and alone. Despite my reticence to leave my children, I journeyed to Yellowstone

National Park, which I'd read about repeatedly. The place earned wide recognition internationally as a rewilding triumph because of its reintroduction of wolves in the 1990s and the ensuing decades of research into wolf lives. My trip was a search for meaning in a sacred place that I revered, with its myths informing my understanding of wild spaces and the role of humans in restoring them to health.

After being villainized and facing elimination by the 1920s, wolves were reintroduced to Yellowstone in 1995, after much controversy and debate. Particularly in the pandemic, the beautiful story of wolves in Yellowstone proliferated, explaining how the reintroduction of the apex predator into a large ecosystem transformed everything. As Montanan freelance writer Cassidy Randall wrote for *The Guardian*:

> "The need for restoration was glaring. In the seventy years of the wolves' absence, the entire Yellowstone ecosystem had fallen out of balance. Coyotes ran rampant, and the elk population exploded, overgrazing willows and aspens. Without those trees, songbirds began to decline, beavers could no longer build their dams and riverbanks started to erode. Without beaver dams and the shade from trees and other plants, water temperatures were too high for cold-water fish. . . . Scientists always knew that as the top predator, wolves were the missing piece in this ecosystem. But they were astonished at how quickly their return stimulated a transformation. The elk and deer populations started responding immediately. Within about ten years, willows rebounded. In twenty, the aspen began flourishing. Riverbanks stabilized. Songbirds returned as did beavers, eagles, foxes and badgers."

These stories filled me with wild hope. Photos of wolves running in packs across the landscape made me tear up, as did the photo by Jim Peace of the National Park Service. He photographed Wolf Number 7 in January 1995, twenty-nine years to the month before I visited the park. The dark wolf holds her nose downwards, caramel eyes glistening in the circles of sunlight that come in through the holes of a shipping container, where she stays before being released to a holding pen and later to the wilds. What is the experience of that wolf? I anthropomorphized and saw myself in her, a "beautiful reddish-gray wolf" referred to as Rosie. My shipping container is my expectation that I am a perfect and productive servant; my wilderness is the acceptance of my ridges and scars, and my beauty and power, too. I sit, nose down, eyes looking up and out, lit up by small circles of sun. Ready to run wild and free.

In my Jeep, I drove past treeless crest lines, and slammed my foot on the brake pedal as a red fox stared at me from the roadside, maybe six feet away. We looked at each other and waited, until I inched forward, watching him. In my rear-view mirror, I saw him look both ways before trotting across the highway. At a sanctuary along the drive, I visited a 1,100-pound grizzly bear named Max, as magpies landed near him to peck at his food. When I returned to my drive, dusk fell. Herds of elk and mule deer dotted the foothills to my left, and a big-horn sheep looked at me from behind a guardrail, closer to me than the fox earlier.

Seeing the majestic fox and big-horn sheep up close at the roadside reminded me of my conversation with Amanda Stronza, an environmental anthropologist who studies human relationships with animals. She also memorializes animals killed by cars, recovering their bodies from the roadside in Texas and taking them to a nearby natural spot where she adorns their bodies with Spanish moss, snail shells, leaves, and flowers. Her memorials invite us to witness these animals, despite our distraction and fast pace. Instead of objectifying the animal as roadkill, her memorials call on us to see animals killed by cars not as objects called "roadkill" but rather as worthy lives. Amanda told me, "It's a being, that was a life. I stop for an animal and lift her from the asphalt, and find a quiet place. There is a meditative process of finding whatever is beautiful around. And then it's always a quiet moment, and I am just so attentive to that animal while I'm doing that. The honouring gives me catharsis, and it gives me peace. These memorials ask us to see, to look, to not be afraid. To look at that animal on the road, to look close and to care, and to feel, and to be emotionally connected to the animals who live with us." Amanda's witnessing of animals can be seen in connection to Robin Wall Kimmerer's encouragement of the pronoun ki and kin for animals, inviting us to expand personhood to our animal family.

I drove carefully through the winding roads, worried more animals would approach the car in the falling dusk. I stopped for groceries and packed my bags of food into the trunk, standing across from a neon lit-up cross on a mountainside above the Super 8. I called my babies, missing them immensely, 3,600 kilometres away. They yelled and cried chaotically on the phone, speaking over each other and begging me to come home as I drove into the park. As they wailed, my phone service cut out. Silence. I cried as I made my way along winding roads in the dark. Feeling like a terrible mother, having just left my job and gone away, I wondered, *Why am I here?*

My purpose in Yellowstone was to observe ravens, or maybe to try and comprehend why they fascinated me. Raven experts John and Colleen Marzluff would guide me and some other students. The married couple spent decades studying the birds, as well as other corvids. Since starting to learn about the birds, and seeing them around Birdsong Cabin even when other birds and animals were scarce, I grew obsessed and wanted to learn more. Winding my way through Yellowstone, rattled from the call with my kids, the GPS informed me, "You have arrived at your destination." I looked outside nervously, surrounded by blackness with no cell service, and no sign of the ranch where I would spend the night. My printed maps beside me looked feeble, but I consulted them when driving, and sighed with relief a few minutes later when I saw the glow of lights coming from Lamar Buffalo Ranch, home of the Yellowstone Forever Institute. I parked the car in the snow, grateful to find my bearings after twenty hours of travel that began at two in the morning, my bones and blood disconcerted from travelling over vast distances.

Inside the main building, I found a group of welcoming raven enthusiasts gathered around a horseshoe of folding tables. The room boasted a projector with a screen, learning materials, and a trio of playful dogs. The other students and I met each other, sharing one-by-one what brought us to the raven course. We reviewed our plans for the next few days, with our itinerary written on a chalkboard at the front of the classroom wedged between a communal kitchen and a room filled with birdwatching and wolf tracking books.

In my introduction, I expressed my interest in learning more about the birds, and cited the example of ravens sharing with wolves.

"Well," said John knowingly, "they don't necessarily share. Some of the stories can be overblown. Often, ravens are quite calculating and self-interested, and what looks like sharing is something else entirely." Humbled only minutes into entering the course, I called into question what else I thought I knew about birds and wolves. About humans, and the stories I loved about our sharing economies and altruistic ways of living. Was I too naive?

After our first session, I warmed a can of soup on one of the gas stoves in the communal kitchen. An old map of Yellowstone and photographs of bison and wolves decorated the walls, along with an old-fashioned manual pencil sharpener beside the window. Plastic bins on wooden shelves held instant oatmeal, soups, pasta, fajitas, and granola bars, each bin labelled with a strip of tape inscribed with a participant's name. I devoured my comforting dinner alone after everyone went to bed, and then I walked to my log cabin bunkie, mindful of our guide's instructions to use a headlamp because bison walk through the camp and can disappear in the dark.

When I woke, I felt afraid: far from home and unable to be in contact with my children. Here I found myself on a grand adventure, my first solo trip in years, and the fear of my big life transition and distance from my babies kept me in bed, hiding under a rented green sleeping bag in a bottom bunk. I cowered, reaching out occasionally to turn off the snooze function on the alarm clock on my phone, which lay on top of a pile of books about ravens and other corvids. Eventually I pulled back the blue gauzy curtains and saw the landscape I drove through the night before in the dark. Rolling low mountains surrounded us in a ring, under blue-grey clouds in a wide sky. Tangled tufts of sage brush stood upright, their shaggy, wrung trunks winding up through the layer of snow that covered everything. Craggy bison chewed food, unrushed, gathered in herds up the sides of the hills we could see from the ranch windows. A dream opportunity lay outside my window, but perhaps I was the *rabenmütter*, away from my children. Female ravens are observed to be more willing to disperse to new places than their male counterparts.

On our first early morning of observing ravens, we heard a group of coyotes howling close by. Wolves responded across the valley. Guides set up our spotting scopes, and over the next few hours, we watched a pack of wolves after they devoured a kill, as they rested and prowled, looking out over the land. Ravens danced in and out from the slim remains of the prey, negotiating dynamics between territorial birds and subordinates as they looked for scraps that were too insignificant for the wolves and their full bellies. Magpies landed around the edges of the scene, and a bald eagle landed at the centre of the scraps, unperturbed by the ravens who circled and darted as they watched him. One wolf climbed to the top of a rock and howled, repeatedly, as her family slept around her. A duo of the wolves carried a sizeable hide up the hill and left it near the peak. In the distance, a group of buffalo walked in a line, their hulking frames moving slowly in single file. When the wolves disappeared briefly, a quick coyote came and took the hide, back and out of sight.

Once the scavengers left, we explored the winterkill site, finding clues that told the story of what happened: the elk tracks down one hill and up another; the wolf tracks back and forth; coarse grey and brown fur spread over a span of twenty feet, with blood and rumen in the snow; small remnants of bone, and a set of mandibles picked clean, with the teeth still intact other than the missing back molars, indicating the animal was under a year old. While I slept the night before, a mother elk lost her baby right here, while another mother and her pack earned food to sustain their family. Raven tracks dotted the periphery of the scene, up and over rocks, showing where they came sidling in, looking for food. This landscape had seen its keystone predator exterminated and disappeared at human hands, and now it sang again with the presence of animals, reintroduced by humans.

I learned from John that, before 125,000 years ago, we humans were not a major force on the planet, but rather an opportunistic scavenger like ravens. What a relief to think of us as a part of an ecosystem, rather than a dominant, self-appointed king reigning over all other species. We competed with animals like ravens and wolves, but also provided for them as we became more efficient hunters. We affected the food chain, until their diets resembled ours as they relied on our kills, or as we saw in Yellowstone, they relied on our dumps and trash for food. I thought of the ravens back home in Québec, gathering around a skunk's dead body or a picked-over garbage bag on the roadside. Our relationship with wolves and ravens was made over the course of 50,000 years, and continues still.

During lectures, I learned much more than I had from my earlier book research. Ravens have foresight and solve problems. They do not migrate, but they do disperse, so instead of moving out in one direct line from south to north, they meander and float to take advantage of resources. Being in roosts at night allows them to share information, a process humans are still learning about. With a range of vocabulary and sounds, they give out hungry calls, and other ravens fly towards the sound to find food. Like us, some ravens want to live in a pair and others prefer to be unmated, and like us they create nests in a variety of situations, from trees and cliffs to nooks behind vents. The inside of their mouths are red when they are young and they grow black as they grow older, but if a raven is subordinate its mouth stays pink longer, versus a dominant baby whose mouth grows black sooner. They learn what to say from the noises of their ecosystem, growing an understanding of the important elements of where they live.

The raven is the largest songbird.

Back in my bunkie that night in my pajamas, I leaned against the wooden wall of the bottom bunk, like I was fourteen years old. Maybe the bed reminded me of the bunks at the Lost Channel, or maybe it was the simplicity of my day, stripped of demands and distractions, giving me a taste of a pre-Y2K life that came before career, readily available internet, cell phones, artificial intelligence, or awareness of climate change. Or perhaps I felt young because I'd enjoyed a rare full night's sleep. Before bed, I pulled on a pair of thick socks, and then took them off, changing the feet and putting them back on. Right, left. Left, right. I repeated this a couple of times, an OCD behaviour I show especially when I am far from home, as though I can control the worry of being in an unfamiliar place. The action reminded me of a dog or a wolf, circling and reversing neurotically, as it beds down on the earth for the night.

On my last evening, I left Yellowstone, and stopped the car on a bridge because a herd of bison ambled across the road in front of me. I sat for thirty minutes, watching them, undisturbed in their homeland. We heard that it is a misconception that wolves are the "saviours" of Yellowstone, but rather what matters is having an intact ecosystem. I came to watch ravens, but could not see them out of context; I could not understand them without understanding the wolves, or without seeing the bison, bald eagle, magpies, fox, and coyote. After all my adoration of rewilding, here I had the great fortune of seeing it in action — not a mystical, impossibly romantic dream, but reality, one that was possible in other places around the world.

The next morning I convinced my body to board the plane, with a myopic goal of seeing my children. Flying over Montana, I imagined a hummingbird mother who flew thousands of miles over habitats with a memory, sharp, that allowed her to remember every field and forest's edge, and through powers of recollection, she knew when a flower's cup would refill. Tiny and inconsequential though she appeared — and fearful of the journey — she flew fast and strong through the sky, her acorn-sized chest rising and falling with the effort of living as she retraced her route from last autumn when she left our home. Her sons and daughter followed after her, over the turtles in the lakes, bison on the plains, worms in the soil, and herons in the reeds of a marsh.

As a young female bird, she imprinted on the stars and the sun to learn how to find her way. Now she migrated north, using a combination of blood memory and the recognition of landmarks over which she soared. How precisely she found our home again is a mystery that only she knows. Once arrived, she carefully crafted a nest made of dandelion and thistle down, which she sewed together with spider's silk to keep her babies safe in the belly of the forest. She warmed them into life, fed them, stewarded them from nestling to hatchling to fledgling, and they learned how to fly without her. She stayed close by to make sure they were safe. Something deep inside their genetic material would tell them when it was time to fly wild, over a wide, wounded, wondrous home. They would need to migrate alone and find a home for themselves, dodging falling stars to find their place as everywhere changed, even over the heartbeat time span of a hummingbird generation.

I swooped my children up in my arms, and covered their foreheads and hair with kisses.

The next night, nervous and excited, I walked out of the Québec winter cold into our town's art space, converted from a church. I stood at the front of a wide open room with wooden floors, the room that once formed the sanctuary, and fourteen adults from my community watched as I guided them through a contemporary dance class. I returned to dance after many years. As the music of drums, strings, and piano pulsed, my toes worked their way over the wooden floors in *tendus*, *dégagés*, and *grand battements*, each movement surprisingly familiar. My body remembered what to do. *Blood memory* — the name of the memoir of infamous modern dancer Martha Graham, as well as the name of a book about the tragic decline and improbable resurrection of the American buffalo. Most of the students were beginners, and I encouraged everyone not to worry about perfect technique, but rather to express themselves freely. People moved trepidatiously at first, then eventually melted into the divine expression of dance, an outlet for freedom we find few places in life. My voice called over the music, as torsos curved and spiralled, and the dancers jumped, rolled, reached, and soared. We closed the class with choreography I developed on the plane rides back from Montana. Rehearsing the movements together, we all extended our right arms — on account of it being the one I can still straighten — and slightly out of time with each other, we pulsed with the beat of wings.

18

AINÉ

Epilogue

"We are all mothers here." IRENE SOLÀ

Animals visit me in my dreams lately. Bears — maybe ten of them — some black and some brown, walking towards me through an abandoned building. One of them tried to crawl on its stomach, under the door. On a different night, a rangale of deer made an appearance, and the number of individual deer — six — stood out as a clear detail, as note-worthy as the creatures themselves. The night before last, I dreamed of a hummingbird, lifting up a blue jay by its beak, carrying the much-larger bird and flying upwards.

Before bedtime, I lie in a bottom bunk, cuddled in a marshmallow duvet, with a son on either side. They ask about their births, and about death, a common bedtime conversation. Wren tells Heron we become zombies after we die, a myth I quickly dispel.

"When we die, we become rivers, trees, bears, and butter-flies," I explain knowingly. Hopefully. Wren's eyes widen.

"We become animals?" he asks in wonder, and I nod and kiss his forehead. We fall asleep talking about how we will be gorillas together in a thousand years. Tonight I let myself believe large primates will wander freely through rewilded landscapes in a millennia.

The next day I watch from the barn window as a deer mother and her daughter come to curiously look at the garden with its closed gate, wondering why their source of cabbage has been denied by our flimsy fence. I look away, guilty, as they sniff the barrier slowly before walking away. (From time to time, I toss tomatoes and cabbage over the weak wall, towards the creek, hoping that they come at dusk to eat them with pleasure.) Later, I walk barefoot through the meadow, after leaving the garden gate open for the two deer. In the cabin, I sit with my own daughter at the dining table, where she focuses on an ambitious science experi-ment of her own design. I watch her wrestle with getting it perfect, and I try to help support her in what is her own journey.

"You know, Owl," I remind her for the thousandth time, trying to be helpful. "Nobody is perfect."

"No, Mama," corrects my Owl, always quick to set me straight. "Everybody is perfect."

I do the unthinkable, and I email a realtor and look at another house, without telling Nik. We never keep secrets. Unlike our quirky cabin, the house boasts straight walls, ample storage, and a bedroom for each child. It is a house built for three growing children who look like teenagers in a hoodie and headphones, or with the right expression on their faces. It's like I'm cheating on Birdsong Cabin.

Nik and I walk on the forest loop with Sparrow. While I walk and daydream, Nik stops me from trodding on a snake as we walk down a hill lined with trees. I confess that I looked at another home, a more practical choice for our family than our cabin, and we contemplate the decision.

Undecided, we turn to the left to head up the hill to our cabin. "Should we walk through the meadow?" I ask.

"Sounds nice," he replies, and we turn around and walk in the other direction, away from our usual route to prolong the walk. We make our way across the meadow.

"Stop!" he shouts, and points down to the grass.

A baby snapping turtle. She nestles in the grass, under a shell barely larger than a nearby clover. She measures half the length of my thumb, plus a short tail narrower than a blade of grass. Scaly charcoal arms, wrinkled just like her mother's, extend out in a V in front of her, with tiny claws pointed towards the creek, directly as a compass pointing north. Both brand new and ancient, her eyes look out from underneath hooded eyelids the colour of a burnt match. The baby's shell resembles a rock, with shades of grey in irregular ridges, surrounded by perfectly uniform rectangles in a ring. All the parts of a snapping turtle, in perfect miniature. I burst into tears. *Life. Against the odds. She doesn't know that the planet is warming, or that there are fewer animals than there were decades ago. She is born into wonder.* She blinks slowly, and turns her head to the side, watching me, reminding me of her mother when I observed her under the moonlight months earlier. A miracle, born from that snapping turtle mother's arduous migration from the water to land — the only time she leaves the water — to make her babies' first home.

We search the surrounding meadow, each step hesitant, and find six more miniature turtles, each one imperceptibly making their way towards the waiting water of the creek. These babies grew in their eggs over ninety-nine days, incubating under the smoke of wildfires, before breaking open their shells and making an epic quest across a meadow blanketed by wildflowers.

"Never mind that other house," I say to Nik, crouched beside a baby turtle, looking at her as intently as I gazed at my own newborn babies years earlier. "This is home."

Author's Note

Research, interviews, memory, and imagination informed *Homing*. I have in some cases played with time and altered the sequence of events for the purposes of clarity and storytelling. I have endeavoured to accurately portray the information and opinions entrusted to me. Any errors belong to me.

Acknowledgements

I am grateful to many people who helped *Homing* come to life.

Thank you to the dozens of people who generously shared their time, expertise, and stories with me. I learned a great deal through our interviews in their ranches, farms, studios, and homes. Many of these interviews are included in the book, while others were instrumental in helping to expand my understanding of the diversity of ways in which people are living regeneratively. Collectively, these interviewees helped enlighten me on the fact that there is no one "right" way to do this work. The full list of interviewees can be found following these acknowledgements, and I am thankful to each of them.

Thank you to the writers and artists who have generously permitted me to share their words: Rebecca Solnit, Aja Barber, Robin Wall Kimmerer, J. Drew Lanham, Kerri ní Dochartaigh, Malcom Ferdinand, Alice Vincent, Hunter Lovins, Mary Annaïse Heglar, Katherine May, Daniel Rodriguez, Elizabeth Sawin, Amelia Langas, Jess Bailey, Stephen Marche, Rebecca Burgess, Liz Ricketts and Branson Skinner, Leyland Cecco, Elizabeth Bechard, Grace Nosek, Cassidy Randall, Amanda Stronza, and John and Colleen Marzluff. Thank you to Catherine Dawson March, editor of *First Person*, and the *Globe & Mail* for publishing three essays which I later integrated into this book: "Cutting my family's hair has taught me a lot about caring for them", "How will my children remember this pandemic?", and "Everyone loves a garden in springtime but what about in fall?".

Thank you to my agent, Marilyn Biderman, for finding a home for *Homing*. I appreciate the trust and patience that has been shown to me (as well as our shared love of dance). Thank you to Transatlantic Agency for welcoming me. Thank you to the wonderful team at Freehand Books — it has been a true delight to work together. Thank you to my editor, Debbie Willis, for her empathetic, skillful editing, and for helping me see that a memoirist doesn't need to be fully healed to write a memoir. Thank you to my publisher, Kelsey Attard, for believing in this story and for expert guidance. Thank you Natalie Olsen for beautiful cover design and typesetting. And thank you to Colby Clair Stolson for helping this book find its readers.

Thank you to those who reviewed chapters early in the proposal and writing process: Caroline Warrior, Rachel Sentes, and Amanda Lewis. Thank you to the Conseil des arts et des lettres du Québec for a literary grant to help work on an earlier version of this book, which allowed me to focus on interviewing community members in my region. Thank you to June Park and the English-language Arts Network (ELAN) for guidance on grant writing. Thank you to cartographer Garnet Whyte who illustrated a beautiful map of Birdsong Cabin, capturing the fine details like wild strawberries in the meadow.

My friends and family have offered emotional support, as well as practical support in the form of time spent with my children so their busy mother could write a book. I'm very grateful for this community. Thank you to our parents — Anne Marie, Christopher, Garry, Nanci, Roswitha, and Wade — for believing in me for a very long time, and for supporting me and our family. Thank you to my sister Imogen for every sustenance possible, and for understanding it all. Thank you to Meagan, Sarah, and Yvonne for listening to and celebrating book updates on our group chat. Thank you to my therapist, Dr. Line St. Pierre, for helping me understand, "Just because you can, doesn't mean you should," among many other lessons that influenced the path I detail in this book. Thank you to many friends and colleagues who have shown support and interest through the writing process. Thank you to the countless people who allowed me to write in their coffee shops, restaurants, bars, airplanes, rental apartments, and hospital waiting rooms. Thank you to Ross and Danielle for reading the manuscript on tattered paper printed at the local library. Thank you also to Ross for a hundred forest walks talking through my ideas, and for being an important unnamed character in the story who taught me about microseasons and introduced me to snapping turtles.

Thank you to the beautiful places that welcomed me along my quest, especially: Oregon, Colorado, Wyoming, and Montana in the United States; Chelsea, Wakefield, Montreal, Ward's Island, and Haliburton in Canada; Helsinki, Finland; and Gombe National Park in Tanzania. Thank you to the folks at Yellowstone Forever and Lamar Buffalo Ranch. Thank you to Birdsong Cabin for changing my life, and helping me find home in myself. Thank you to the turkeys, herons, turtles, hummingbirds, cedar trees, and creek who are my neighbours, and who accept me in all of my imperfection. Thank you to Bear and Sparrow for forcing me to leave my work to go into the woods, where I am able to think, and to my cats for keeping a sleepy watch while I wrote into the night.

Above all, thank you to Nik, my husband who has flooded me with love and support, and helped make my dreams come true. He listened to me talk about this book every day for years, encouraged me to fly away to write, and led the practical steps that made the gardens and chickens possible. He loves me in all of my light and dark, and is a true partner in the arduous but joyful work of cultivating our lives according to our values. A heartfelt thank you to my Annie Alice Owl, Julian Ross Wren, and Ciarán Keith Heron for generously giving my life great joy and meaning, and for choosing me to be their mother.

Interview List

Aja Barber. Author of *Consumed — The Need for Collective Change: Colonialism, Climate Change, and Consumerism*. United Kingdom (virtual). February 2, 2022.

Elizabeth Bechard. Author of *Parenting in a Changing Climate: Tools for Cultivating Resilience, Taking Action, and Practicing Hope in the Face of Climate Change*. Vermont, United States (virtual). February 27, 2022.

Lisa and Christopher Binns. Farmer–chef duo, Stush in the Bush. Free Hill, Jamaica (virtual). November 19, 2021.

Bryanna Brown. Originator of Land Back and Labrador Land Protector. Canada (virtual). December 17, 2021.

Rebecca Burgess. Executive Director and founder of Fibershed; Author of *Fibershed* and *Harvesting Color*; weaver and natural dyer. California, United States. June 14, 2021, and January 19, 2022.

Ann Cavlovic. Passive house homeowner and environmental policy professional. Chelsea, Québec, Canada (virtual). June 11, 2021.

Kai Chan. Scientist, professor, and cofounder of CoSphere, a Community of Small-Planet Heroes. British Columbia, Canada (virtual). May 20, 2022.

Tameeka Chang. Beekeeper; creator of The Black Beekeeper. Hillsborough, New Hampshire (virtual). May 31, 2023.

Kamea Chayne. Host and producer of the Green Dreamer Podcast. (Virtual). February 14, 2022.

Charles Clover. Executive Director of the Blue Marine Foundation and author of *Rewilding the Sea: How to Save our Oceans*. United Kingdom (virtual). September 13, 2022.

Malú Colorin. Founder of Talú and co-founder of Fibershed Ireland; natural dyer and designer. Ireland. June 22, 2023.

David Côté. Co-founder of LOOP Mission. Montreal, Canada (virtual). November 5, 2021.

Larissa Crawford. Founder and Managing Director, Future Ancestors Services; published Indigenous, anti-racism, and climate justice researcher, policy advisor, and restorative circle keeper. Calgary, Canada (virtual). October 20, 2022.

Millie Cumming. Quilter and textile artist. Fergus, Ontario, Canada (virtual). March 22, 2022.

Danielle Daniel. Author of *Forever Birchwood* and *Daughters of the Deer*; illustrator. Little Current, Canada (virtual). May 12, 2022.

Leticia Ama Deawuo. Executive Director of SeedChange (at time of interview); filmmaker. Ottawa, Canada (virtual). September 29, 2022.

Janet Gunter. Co-founder of the Restart Project. United Kingdom (virtual). January 19, 2019.

Erin Krekoski. Regenerative farmer, Rock's End Farm. Farrellton, Québec. December 9, 2021.

Hunter Lovins. Economist and regenerative rancher; President and founder of Natural Capitalism Solutions. Longmont, Colorado, United States. February 22–23, 2019.

Kerri ní Dochartaigh. Author of *Thin Places* and *Cacophony of Bone*. January 23, 2024.

John Hausdoerffer and Gavin Van Horn. Co-Editors of *Kinship: Belonging in a World of Relations*. United States (virtual). January 20, 2022.

Isaias Hernandez. Creator of Queer Brown Vegan. United States (virtual). January 14, 2022.

Ginger Howell. Regenerative shepherdess. Wakefield, Québec, Canada. June 16, 2021.

Arounna Khounnoraj. Author of *Visible Mending: Repair, Renew, Reuse the Clothes You Love*; co-founder of bookhou. Toronto, Canada (virtual). January 17, 2022.

J. Drew Lanham. Author of *Sparrow Envy*, *The Home Place*, and *Joy is the Justice We Give Ourselves*; ornithologist, wildlife ecologist, poet, and professor. South Carolina, United States (virtual). March 10, 2022.

Erica Violet Lee. Poet, scholar, and community organizer. Canada (virtual). December 20, 2021.

Amanda Lewis. Author, *Tracking Giants: Big Trees, Tiny Triumphs, and Misadventures in the Forest*. British Colombia, Canada (virtual). June 7, 2023.

Tamara Lindeman. Musician; front person and singer for *The Weather Station*. January 13, 2022.

Andrea and Todd Lithgow-Allen. Round home builders. Haliburton, Ontario, Canada. 2019.

Sara Lopez. Co-founder of The Jungle Journal; social entrepreneur, creator, artist, writer, and culture worker. September 6, 2022.

Steven Lovatt. Author of *Birdsong in a Time of Silence*. South Wales (virtual). May 30, 2023.

Debbie Patterson. Woodworker and educator. Wakefield, Canada (virtual). December 17, 2021.

Clémentine Mattesco. Regenerative farmer, alpaca and permaculture farm. Wakefield, Québec, Canada. January 3, 2022.

Aditi Mayer. Council of Intersectional Environmentalist and State of Fashion; sustainable fashion blogger, photojournalist, and labour rights activist; National Geographic Digital Storytelling Fellow. Los Angeles, United States (virtual). January 24, 2022.

Ingrid Mertens. Bushcrafter and harvester of wild fibres. British Colombia, Canada (virtual). December 13, 2021.

Brendon Nesbitt-Rathwell. Regenerative farmer, Grassroots Farm. La Pêche, Québec, Canada (virtual). June 18, 2021.

Grace Nosek. Author, *Ava of the Gaia* trilogy and the Rootbound project; climate justice scholar, community organizer, and storyteller. September 16, 2022.

Chúk Odenigbo. Expert in climate justice, oceans, anti-racism, public health, and decolonization. Canada (virtual). November 12, 2021.

Tao Orion. Author of *Beyond the War on Invasive Species: A Permaculture Approach to Ecosystem Restoration*; permaculture designer. Southern Willamette Valley, Oregon, United States (virtual). June 20, 2022.

Antonious Petro. Executive Director of Régénération Canada, and a Masters Candidate in Soil Science. Montréal, Canada (virtual). January 23, 2024.

Beth Rattner. Former Executive Director and Current Head, Design for Transformation, at Biomimicry Institute. Co-author, *Nature of Fashion*, Biomimicry Institute. August 23, 2020.

Bradley Robinson. Green builder. Chelsea, Québec. June 11, 2021.

Jad Robitaille. Founder and owner of Mini-Cycle. Montreal, Canada (virtual). October 29, 2021.

Emma Rohmann. Founder of Green at Home; environmental engineer. Toronto, Canada (virtual). January 29, 2019.

Rebeka Ryvola de Kremer. Artist, illustrator, activist, creative learning specialist, writer, and host of The Heart Gallery podcast. Washington, United States (virtual). June 16, 2022.

Anna Sacks. Waste expert; creator of The Trash Walker. New York City, United States (virtual). November 12, 2021.

Elizabeth Sawin. Founder of the Multisolving Institute; systems thinking expert. Vermont, United States (virtual). April 13, 2022.

Megan Schuknecht, co-author, Nature of Fashion, Biomimicry Institute. August 23, 2020.

Jan Shadick. Wildlife rehabilitator, and Executive Director of Living Sky Wildlife Rehabilitation. Saskatchewan, Canada (virtual). June 9, 2023.

Jean Sharp. Natural dye-maker and local textile expert. Ottawa, Canada (virtual). June 11, 2021.

Jess Sherman. Holistic Nutrition Practitioner; Author of Raising Resilience; Former off-the-grid homeowner. Wakefield, Québec (virtual). June 18, 2021.

Amanda Stronza. Environmental anthropologist. Texas, United States (virtual). May 31, 2023.

Cheyenne Sundance. Farmer and Farm Director of Sundance Harvest. Toronto, Canada (virtual). April 8, 2022.

Barbara Swartzentruber. Strategist and ecosystem builder; Executive Director of the Smart Cities Office at the City of Guelph (at the time of interview). Guelph, Ontario, Canada (virtual). August 23, 2022.

Stacey Tenenbaum. Documentary film and TV director. Toronto, Canada (virtual). April 15, 2022.

Tori Tsui. Author of It's Not Just You: How to Navigate Eco-Anxiety and the Climate Crisis; climate justice activist and organizer. United Kingdom (virtual). June 9, 2023.

Juniper Turgeon. Regenerative biodynamic farmer, Juniper Farms. Wakefield, Québec. June 16, 2021.

Alice Vincent. Author of Why Women Grow: Stories of Soil, Sisterhood and Survival and Rootbound: Rewilding a Life. United Kingdom (virtual). January 30, 2023.

Bettina Vollmerhausen. Co-founder and Executive Director, Ottawa Tool Library. Ottawa, Canada. February 4, 2019 (interview) and January 14, 2019 (repair café).

Various individuals. Sustainable Fashion Forum. Portland, Oregon, United States. April 26–27, 2019.

Britt Wray. Author of Generation Dread: Finding Purpose in an Age of Climate Crisis; science communicator and researcher. California, United States (virtual). March 15, 2022.

Sophia Yang. Founder and Executive Director of Threading Change. Vancouver, Canada (virtual). October 22, 2021.

Bibliography

EPIGRAPH

Lanham, J. Drew. "Field Mark 1: Love for a Song." *Sparrow Envy: A Field Guide to Birds and Lesser Beasts: poems.* Edited by John Lane, 67. Chelsea, Michigan: Hub City Press, 2021.

ní Dochartaigh, Kerri. "When You Could Hear the Trees." *Emergence Magazine,* November 9, 2023. https://emergencemagazine.org/essay/when-you-could-hear-the-trees/.

FLEDGLING

Stonich, Kathryn. "Hummingbird Nests 101: A Beginner's Guide." *American Bird Conservancy.* May 6, 2021. https://abcbirds.org/blog21/hummingbird-nests/.

THE SWALLOWS LEAVE IN SEPTEMBER

Bull, John, and John Farrand. *The Audubon Society Field Guide To North American Birds: Eastern Region.* New York: Alfred A. Knopf, 1977.

BIRDSONG CABIN

Tempest Williams, Terry. *Erosions: Essays of Undoing.* New York: 2019.

"*ker- (1)." Accessed January 15, 2024. https://www.etymonline.com/word/*ker-.

"Japan's 72 Microseasons." Accessed March 12, 2018. https://www.nippon.com/en/features/h00124/.

Leon, Natalie. "Forget the Four Seasons: How Embracing 72 Japanese 'Micro-Seasons' Could Change Your Garden (and Your Life)." *The Guardian,* May 11, 2024. https://www.theguardian.com/lifeandstyle/article/2024/may/11/how-embracing-72-japanese-micro-seasons-could-change-your-garden-and-your-life.

Hovane, Mark. "The 72 Japanese Micro-Seasons." *Kyoto Journal,* Spring 2023. https://www.kyotojournal.org/uncategorized/the-72-japanese-micro-seasons/.

"What is Rewilding?" Accessed June 1, 2024. Rewilding Europe. https://rewildingeurope.com/what-is-rewilding/.

Tree, Isabella. *Wilding: The Return of Nature to a British Farm.* London: Picador, 2018.

Daltun, Eoghan. *An Irish Atlantic Rainforest: A Personal Journey into the Magic of Rewilding.* Hachette Books Ireland, 2022.

Ferdinand, Malcom. "Behind the Colonial Silence of Wilderness: 'In Marronage Lies the Search of a World.'" *Environmental Humanities*, March 1, 2022; 14 (1): 182–201. https://doi.org/10.1215/22011919-9481506.

Cronon, William. "The Trouble with Wilderness." *New York Times*, August 13, 1995. https://www.nytimes.com/1995/08/13/magazine/the-trouble-with-wilderness.html.

Oliver, Mary. "Sleeping in the Forest." *Devotions: The Selected Poems of Mary Oliver*, 403. New York: Penguin Press, 2017.

BELONGINGS

Oliver, Mary. "Wild Geese." *Devotions: The Selected Poems of Mary Oliver*, 347. New York: Penguin Press, 2017.

Wynes, Seth, and Kimberly A. Nicholas. "The Climate Mitigation Gap: Education and Government Recommendations Miss the Most Effective Individual Actions." *Environmental Research Letters*, July 12, 2017. https://doi.org/10.1088/1748-9326/aa7541.

New Jersey Institute of Technology. "Downsizing the McMansion: Study gauges a sustainable size for future homes." *ScienceDaily*. Accessed June 1, 2024. www.sciencedaily.com/releases/2020/03/200305203533.htm.

Heathcote, Edwin. "Why Tomorrow's Architecture will Use Yesterday's Materials." *Financial Times*, January 13, 2020. https://www.ft.com/content/191c2f50-3395-11ea-a329-0bcf87a328f2.

Vincent, Alice. *Rootbound: Rewilding a Life.* Edinburgh: Canongate, 2020.

Guggenheim. "Frank Lloyd Wright and Nature." Accessed May 28, 2024. https://www.guggenheim.org/teaching-materials/the-architecture-of-the-solomon-r-guggenheim-museum/frank-lloyd-wright-and-nature.

Badger, Emily. "The Missing Link of Climate Change: Single-Family Suburban Homes." *Bloomberg*, December 7, 2011. https://www.bloomberg.com/news/articles/2011-12-07/the-missing-link-of-climate-change-single-family-suburban-homes.

Janjic, Ksenija. "The Environmental Impact of Single-Family Homes." *United States Environmental Protection Agency*, March 7, 2014. https://blog.epa.gov/2014/03/07/the-environmental-impact-of-single-family-homes.

Asdrubali, Francesco, Francesco D'Alessandro, and Samuele Schiavoni. "A Review of Unconventional Sustainable Building Insulation

Materials, Sustainable Materials and Technologies." *Sustainable Materials and Technologies*, Volume 4, 2015: 1–17. https://doi.org/10.1016/j.susmat.2015.05.002.

Brown, Allen. "8 Surprising Benefits of Straw Bale Construction." *Green Building Canada*, December 5, 2022. https://greenbuildingcanada.ca/benefits-straw-bale-construction/.

"About Passive House." Accessed March 5, 2024. https://www.passivehousecanada.com/about-passive-house/.

"15-Minute City." Deloitte. Accessed February 25, 2024. https://www.deloitte.com/an/en/Industries/government-public/perspectives/urban-future-with-a-purpose/15-minute-city.html.

Whittle, Natalie. "Welcome to the 15-Minute City." *Financial Times*, July 17, 2020. https://www.ft.com/content/c1a53744-90d5-4560-9e3f-17ce06aba69a.

Kucharek, Jan-Carlos. "Carlos Moreno: 15 minutes to save the world." *The Riba Journal*. December 16, 2021. https://www.ribaj.com/culture/profile-carlos-moreno-15-minute-city-obel-award-plannin.

Unbuilders. "Demo Done Better." Accessed March 7, 2024. https://unbuilders.com/.

THE BORROWED NEST AND THE OWL

Carson, Rachel. *Silent Spring*. New York: First Mariner Books, 2002.

Hawken, Paul, Amory Lovins, and L. Hunter Lovins. *Natural Capitalism: Creating the Next Industrial Revolution*. New York: Little, Brown and Company, 1999.

Lovins, Hunter, L., Stewart Wallis, Anders Wijkman, and John Fullerton. *A Finer Future: Creating an Economy in Service to Life*. New Society Publishers, 2018.

Itzkan, Seth, interviewer. "L. Hunter Lovins, A Finer Future: Outspoken Advocates of Soil Restoration as a Climate Solution." Soil4Climate (podcast). August 13, 2018. https://podcasts.apple.com/us/podcast/l-hunter-lovins-a-finer-future-august-13-2018/id1525993453?i=1000486784246.

"Hunter Lovins on the circular economy of the soil." Circulate (podcast). May 30, 2016. https://www.ellenmacarthurfoundation.org/podcasts/hunter-lovins-on-the-circular-economy-of-soil.

Penniman, Leah. *Farming While Black: Soul Fire Farm's Practical Guide to Liberation on the Land*. White River Junction, Vermont: Chelsea Green Publishing, 2018.

Gardiner, Karen. "How Canadian Bison have Been Brought Back from the Brink in Saskatchewan." *National Geographic*, June 3, 2023. https://www.nationalgeographic.com/travel/article/canadian-bison-brought-back-saskatchewan.

Burns, Ken, and Dayton Duncan. *Blood Memory: The Tragic Decline and Improbable Resurrection of the American Buffalo*. Alfred A. Knopf, 2023.

"Regenerative Principles." *Regeneration Canada*. https://regeneration canada.org/en/why-soil/#regen-principles.

"Guide to Regenerative Agriculture." *Kiss the Ground*. https://kissthe ground.com/regenerative-agriculture/.

June, Lyla. "3000-year-old solutions to modern problems." TEDxKC video. August 2022. https://www.ted.com/talks/lyla_june_3000_year_old_solutions_to_modern_problems?language=en.

IF RAVENS SHARE

Defebaugh, Willow. "As the Crow Flies." *Atmos*, March 12, 2021. https://atmos.earth/ravens-crows-symbolism-behavior/.

Buy Nothing Project. "About." Accessed March 7, 2024. https://buy nothingproject.org/about.

Heinrich, Bernd, and John Marzluff. "Why Ravens Share." *American Scientist* 83, no. 4 (1995): 342–49. http://www.jstor.org/stable/29775481.

Williams, Tony D., ed. *What is a Bird? An Exploration of Anatomy, Physiology, Behavior, and Ecology*. Princeton, New Jersey: Princeton University Press, 2020.

Bird, David M., ed. *Birds of Eastern Canada*. 2nd ed. Toronto: Penguin Random House, 2019.

Livingston, John A. *Birds of the Northern Forest*. Toronto: McClelland and Stewart Limited, 1966.

Williams, Tony D., ed. *What is a Bird? An Exploration of Anatomy, Physiology, Behavior, and Ecology*. Princeton, New Jersey: Princeton University Press, 2020.

Pokémon Super Extra Deluxe Essential Handbook. Scholastic Inc, 2021.

Hamilton, Samantha. "What's Mine Is Yours: The History of U.S. Tool-Lending Libraries." *School of Information Student Research Journal*, 11(1). May, 2021. https://doi.org/10.31979/2575-2499.110104.

"About Repair Café: Repairing for a Sustainable Future." *Repair Café*. https://www.repaircafe.org/en/about/.

Klosowski, Thorin. "What You Should Know About Right to Repair." *The New York Times*, July 15, 2021. https://www.nytimes.com/wire cutter/blog/what-is-right-to-repair/.

Tusikov, Natasha. "Giving Canadians the 'right to repair' empowers consumers, supports competition and benefits the environment." *The Conversation*, April 9, 2023. https://theconversation.com/giving-canadians-the-right-to-repair-empowers-consumers-supports-competition-and-benefits-the-environment-203302.

"How to support Right to Repair in the UK." The Restart Project. https://therestartproject.org/right-to-repair-uk/.

Evans, Steven. "Is the German insult 'Raven mothers' holding back women at work?" BBC, March 11, 2011. https://www.bbc.com/news/business-12703897.

Marzluff, John M., and Tony Angell. *In the Company of Crows and Ravens*. New Haven and London: Yale University Press, 2005.

MY HAND-STITCHED WINGS

Heglar, Mary Annaïse (@maryheglar). "The thing about climate is that you can either be overwhelmed by the complexity of the problem or fall in love with the creativity of the solutions." X, April 9, 2020. https://x.com/MaryHeglar/status/1248306300821307394.

"What is Permaculture?" *Permaculture Research Institute*. https://www.permaculturenews.org/what-is-permaculture.

Sweetser, Robin. "What Is Hügelkultur? Building the Ultimate Raised Bed." *The Old Farmer's Almanac*, May 21, 2024. https://www.almanac.com/what-hugelkultur-ultimate-raised-bed.

"What is Circular Fashion?" *The Sustainable Fashion Forum*. Accessed June 1, 2024. https://www.thesustainablefashionforum.com/pages/what-is-circular-fashion.

"A new textiles economy: Redesigning fashion's future." *Ellen MacArthur Foundation*, 2017. https://www.ellenmacarthurfoundation.org/a-new-textiles-economy.

Newbold, Alice. "Why We Should Be Asking #WhoMadeMyClothes? Before Every Purchase." *British Vogue*, April 26, 2019. https://www.vogue.co.uk/article/who-made-my-clothes.

Banwell, Eleanor, Megan Schuknecht, Beth Rattner, Natasja Hulst, and Brian Dougherty. "The Nature of Fashion: Moving Towards a Regenerative System." *The Biomimicry Institute*, June 30, 2020. https://biomimicry.org/thenatureoffashion/.

Barber, Aja. *Consumed: The Need for Collective Change: Colonialism, Climate Change, and Consumerism*. New York: Balance, 2021.

"Wonders of the Columbia Gorge." *Friends of the Columbia Gorge*. Accessed

June 2023. https://gorgefriends.org/about-the-gorge/wonders-of-the-columbia-gorge.html.

"Multnomah Falls-Wahkeena Loop Trails" (Map). *Friends of Multnomah Falls*. Accessed June 2023. https://friendsofmultnomahfalls.org/directions-trail-maps.

Kimmerer, Robin Wall. *Braiding Sweetgrass: Indigenous Wisdom, Scientific Knowledge, and the Teachings of Plants*. Milkweed Editions, 2013.

Goodall, Jane. *In the Shadow of Man*. London and Glasgow: Fontana Books, 1971.

McDonough, William, and Michael Braungart. *Cradle to Cradle: Remaking the Way We Make Things*. New York: North Point Press, 2002.

THE 37-DEGREE ISOTHERM

Plath, Sylvia. "Love is a Parallax" (Poem.) Accessed June 4, 2024. https://allpoetry.com/Love-Is-A-Parallax.

Erickson, Laura. "Robin Migration." *Journey North*. https://journeynorth.org/tm/robin/facts_migration.html.

Williams, Tony D., ed. *What is a Bird? An Exploration of Anatomy, Physiology, Behavior, and Ecology*. Princeton, New Jersey: Princeton University Press, 2020.

"What is a Circular Economy?" *Ellen MacArthur Foundation*. https://www.ellenmacarthurfoundation.org/topics/circular-economy-introduction/overview.

McDonough, William, and Michael Braungart. *Cradle to Cradle: Remaking the Way We Make Things*. New York: North Point Press, 2002.

Benyus, Janine M. *Biomimicry: Innovation Inspired by Nature*. New York: William Morrow, 1997.

Laker, Benjamin. "Redefining Leadership: The Rise And Evolution Of The Sharing Economy." *Forbes*, July 6, 2023. https://www.forbes.com/sites/benjaminlaker/2023/07/06/redefining-leadership-the-rise-and-evolution-of-the-sharing-economy/.

Eckhardt, Giana M., and Fleura Bardhi. "The Sharing Economy Isn't About Sharing at All." *Harvard Business Review*, January 28, 2015. https://hbr.org/2015/01/the-sharing-economy-isnt-about-sharing-at-all.

Raworth, Kate. *Doughnut Economics: 7 Ways to Think Like a 21st Century Economist*. White River Junction: Chelsea Green Publishing, 2017.

Hilton, Carol Anne. *Indigenomics: Taking a Seat at the Economic Table*. New Society Publishers, 2021.

Davis, Sam. "What is a Regenerative Economy?" *The Dogwood Alliance*, February 1, 2023. https://dogwoodalliance.org/2023/02/what-is-a-regenerative-economy/.

"What is a Wellbeing Economy?" *Wellbeing Economy Alliance*. *https://weall. org/what-is-wellbeing-economy.*

"What is Degrowth?" *Degrowth*. https://degrowth.info/degrowth.

"A History of Degrowth." *Degrowth*. https://degrowth.info/about/history-of-degrowth.

"Economy." *Merriam-Webster*. Accessed April 5, 2023. https://www.merriam-webster.com/dictionary/economy#word-history.

Hersey, Tricia. *Rest is Resistance: A Manifesto*. Little, Brown Spark, 2022.

Hersey, Tricia. *The Nap Ministry's Rest Deck: 50 Practices to Resist Grind Culture*. Chronicle Books, 2023.

Davis, Angela Y. *Women, Culture & Politics*. New York: Vintage Books, 1990.

WHEN ROTTEN GRASS BECOMES FIREFLIES

"Japan's 72 Microseasons." Accessed March 12, 2018. https://www.nippon.com/en/features/h00124/.

V (formerly Eve Ensler). *In the Body of the World*. Random House Canada, 2013.

Klein, Naomi. *This Changes Everything: Capitalism vs. The Climate*. Alfred A. Knopf Canada, 2014.

Klein, Naomi. "Let Them Drown: The Violence of Othering in a Warming World." *London Review of Books*. Vol. 38 No. 11. June 2, 2016. https://www.lrb.co.uk/the-paper/v38/n11/naomi-klein/let-them-drown.

COYOTE AND WREN

Daniel Rodriguez of Elephant Revival, "Birds and Stars," track 1 on These Changing Skies, Itz Evolving Records, Recorded at Bear Creek Studio, 2013.

Gier, H.T. "Ecology and Behavior of the Coyote (*Canis latrans*)". In Fox, M.W. (ed.). *The Wild Canids: Their systematics, behavioral ecology, and evolution*: 247–262 New York: Dogwise Publishing, 1974.

Bull, John, and John Farrand. *The Audubon Society Field Guide to North American Birds: Eastern Region*. New York: Alfred A. Knopf, 1977.

THE PEAR TREE AND THE SHREW

Sawin, Elizabeth (@bethsawin). "Everything and everyone that I love is a carbon-based life form connected inextricably by cords of flowing energy and matter to oceans, tundra, coral reefs, and prairie soils." X, April 15, 2020. https://x.com/bethsawin/status/1250540965905010699.

Bentsink, Leónie, and Maarten Koornneef. "Seed dormancy and germination." *The arabidopsis book* vol. 6: e0119. 2008. doi:10.1199/tab.0119.

Pausas, Juli G., and Byron B. Lamont. "Fire-released seed dormancy — a global synthesis." *Biological Reviews.* 97 (4): 1612–1639. August 2022. doi:10.1111/brv.12855.

Kavanagh, Jim. *Les Oiseaux du Québec/Quebec Birds: Un guide de poche bilingue sur les espèces familière/A Bilingual Folding Pocket Guide to Familiar Species.* Waterford Press, 2013.

Lanham, J. Drew. "My Wild-Like Refuge." *Emergence Magazine*, August 31, 2022. https://emergencemagazine.org/essay/my-wild-like-refuge/.

Bull, John, and John Farrand. *The Audubon Society Field Guide to North American Birds: Eastern Region.* New York: Alfred A. Knopf, 1977.

"John James Audubon: A Complicated History." *Audubon.* https://www.audubon.org/content/john-james-audubon.

Langas, Amelia. "The Mystery of the Missing John James Audubon Self-Portrait." *Audubon*, April 26, 2019. https://www.audubon.org/news/the-mystery-missing-john-james-audubon-self-portrait.

Lanham, J. Drew (guest) and Alice Irene Whittaker (host). "Rewriting Wildness." Reseed (podcast), April 10, 2022. https://www.reseed.ca/listen/rewriting-wildness.

LION'S TOOTH

Klein, Naomi. *On Fire: The Burning Case for a Green New Deal.* Alfred A. Knopf Canada, 2019.

Lanham, J. Drew (guest), and Krista Tippett. "Pathfinding Through the Improbable." On Being (podcast), March 24, 2022. https://onbeing.org/programs/j-drew-lanham-pathfinding-through-the-improbable/.

Odenigbo, Chúk (guest), and Alice Irene Whittaker (host). "Redefining Environmentalism." Reseed (podcast), December 3, 2021. https://www.reseed.ca/listen/redefining-environmentalism.

Sundance, Cheyenne (guest), and Alice Irene Whittaker (host). "Rerooting Farms in the City." Reseed (podcast), April 19, 2022. https://www.reseed.ca/listen/rerooting-farms-in-the-city.

QUEEN MOUSE AND CEDAR WAXWINGS

Johnson, Ayana Elizabeth. "Be Tenacious on Behalf of Life on Earth." TIME Magazine, June 2, 2023. https://time.com/6283728/be-tenacious-on-behalf-of-life-on-earth/.

Bailey, Jess. *Many Hands Make a Quilt: Short Histories of Radical Quilting.* England: Common Threads Press, 2021.

Harrap, Liam. "Revelstoke Students Sewing Giant Quilt for Climate Action." *Revelstoke Review*, February 8, 2020. https://www.revelstoke review.com/community/revelstoke-students-sewing-giant-quilt-for-climate-action-4277143.

Kimmerer, Robin Wall. *Gathering Moss: A Natural and Cultural History of Mosses.* Corvallis: Oregon State University Press, 2019.

Marche, Stephen. "The Call of the Loon." *Canadian Geographic*, March 10, 2023. https://canadiangeographic.ca/articles/the-call-of-the-loon/.

Cumming, Millie. "Ancient One" (Quilt). 2005. https://www.millie andgraeme.ca/millies-galleries.

Burgess, Rebecca and Courtney White. *Fibershed: Growing a Movement of Farmers, Fashion Activists, and Makers for a New Textile Economy.* White River Junction, Vermont: Chelsea Green Publishing, 2019.

Burgess, Rebecca (guest) and Alice Irene Whittaker (host). "Regenerative Textile Economies." Reseed (podcast), January 31, 2022. https://www.reseed.ca/listen/rewriting-wildness.

"Fibershed Learning Center." Fibershed. https://fibershed.org/programs/education-advocacy/learningcenter/.

Ricketts, Liz, and Branson Skinner. "Stop Waste Colonialism! Leveraging Extended Producer Responsibility to Catalyze a Justice-led Circular Textiles Economy." *The Or Foundation.* February 14, 2023. https://stopwastecolonialism.org/stopwastecolonialism.pdf.

Barber, Aja. *Consumed: The Need for Collective Change: Colonialism, Climate Change, and Consumerism.* New York: Balance, 2021.

Barber, Aja (guest) and Alice Irene Whittaker (host). "Resisting Consumerism, Reclaiming Power." Reseed (podcast), March 28, 2022. https://www.reseed.ca/listen/resisting-consumerism.

"The Fibershed Quebec Mission." *Fibershed Quebec.* https://fibershed.uqam.ca/en/.

Colorin, Malú (guest) and Alice Irene Whittaker (host). "Reconnecting with Land and Community through Slow Fashion." Reseed (podcast), December 22, 2023. https://www.reseed.ca/listen/malu-colorin.

THE LAST PASSENGER PIGEON

Siddiqa, Ayisha. "On Another Panel About Climate, They Ask Me to Sell the Future and All I've Got is a Love Poem." *On Being*, June 10, 2022. https://onbeing.org/poetry/on-another-panel-about-climate-they-ask-me-to-sell-the-future-and-all-ive-got-is-a-love-poem/.

Ajasa, Amudalat. "What is red tide and why is it killing fish in Florida?" *Washington Post*, March 6, 2023. https://www.washingtonpost.com/weather/2023/03/06/red-tide-toxic-algae-fish-florida/.

Longo, Audette. "If We Can No Longer Skate on Ottawa's Rideau Canal, We Must Change the Climate Conversation." *National Observer*, March 7, 2023. https://www.nationalobserver.com/2023/03/07/opinion/can-no-longer-skate-ottawa-rideau-canal-must-change-climate-conversation.

Toohey, Grace. "Yosemite Breaks Decades-Old Snowfall Record, Closing National Park Indefinitely." *Los Angeles Times*, March 1, 2023. https://www.latimes.com/california/story/2023-03-01/yosemite-national-park-closed-indefinitely-historic-snowfall.

McLernon, Will. "The Tale of Yosemite Sam: How a California Hummingbird Got Lost and Landed in Saskatoon." CBC, February 6, 2023. https://www.cbc.ca/news/canada/saskatchewan/the-tale-of-yosemite-sam-how-a-lost-hummingbird-made-its-way-to-saskatoon-1.6737930.

Shadick, Jan (guest) and Alice Irene Whittaker (host). "The Hummingbird Who Lost His Way." Reseed (podcast), May 6, 2024. https://www.reseed.ca/listen/hummingbird.

Williams, Tony D., ed. *What is a Bird? An Exploration of Anatomy, Physiology, Behavior, and Ecology.* Princeton, New Jersey: Princeton University Press, 2020.

Cecco, Leyland. "There's Only One Spotted Owl Left in the Canadian Wild. Can She Be Saved?" *The Walrus*, June 2, 2023. https://thewalrus.ca/last-owl/.

Klein, Naomi. "In a Summer of Wildfires and Hurricanes, My Son Asks "Why Is Everything Going Wrong?" *The Intercept*, September 9, 2017. https://theintercept.com/2017/09/09/in-a-summer-of-wildfires-and-hurricanes-my-son-asks-why-is-everything-going-wrong/.

Yarber, Aara'L. "Humans have used enough groundwater to shift Earth's tilt." *The Washington Post*, June 27, 2023. https://www.washingtonpost.com/science/2023/06/27/groundwater-use-planet-earth-tilt/

Bechard, Elizabeth. *Parenting in a Changing Climate: Tools for Cultivating Resilience, Taking Action, and Practicing Hope in the Face of Climate Change.* Brasstown: Citrine Publishing, 2021.

Bechard, Elizabeth (guest) and Alice Irene Whittaker (host). "Remaking Parenthood for the Anthropocene." Reseed (podcast), March 7, 2022. https://www.reseed.ca/listen/remaking-parenthood.

"HOPE" IS THE THING WITH FEATHERS

Dickinson, Emily. *Hope Is the Thing with Feathers: The Complete Poems of Emily Dickinson.* Gibbs Smith, 2019.

"Dehydrated Birds Falling from Sky in India Amid Record Heatwave." *Al Jazeera,* May 12, 2022.

Aponte, Veronica I., Marie-Anne R. Hudson, and Adam C. Smith (eds). "The State of Canada's Birds 2019." *North American Bird Conservation Initiative Canada (NABCI Canada),* 2019. http://nabci.net/wp-content/uploads/2019-State-of-Canadas-Birds-1.pdf.

Carson, Rachel. *Silent Spring.* New York: First Mariner Books, 2002.

Lanham, J. Drew (guest) and Alice Irene Whittaker (host). "Rewriting Wildness." Reseed (podcast), April 10, 2022. https://www.reseed.ca/listen/rewriting-wildness.

Solnit, Rebecca. "We Can't Afford to be Climate Doomers." *The Guardian,* July 26, 2023. https://www.theguardian.com/commentisfree/2023/jul/26/we-cant-afford-to-be-climate-doomers.

Macy, Joanna, and Chris Johnstone. *Active Hope: How to Face the Mess We're in without Going Crazy.* Novato, California: New World Library, 2012.

Johnson, Ayana Elizabeth. "Climate Action Venn Diagram." Accessed January 7, 2024. https://www.ayanaelizabeth.com/climatevenn.

Nosek, Grace (guest) and Alice Irene Whittaker (host). "Rejecting Fossil Fuel Narratives, Rewriting Climate Futures." Reseed (podcast), October 31, 2023. https://www.reseed.ca/listen/rewriting-climate-futures/.

Stonich, Kathryn. "Hummingbird Nests 101: A Beginner's Guide." *American Bird Conservancy.* May 6, 2021. https://abcbirds.org/blog21/hummingbird-nests/.

Ling, Thomas. "Flamingoes aren't born pink. Here's the (very bizarre) reason they take on that colour." *BBC Science Focus,* September 14, 2023. https://www.sciencefocus.com/nature/why-are-flamingos-pink.

Kimmerer, Robin Wall. *Braiding Sweetgrass: Indigenous Wisdom, Scientific Knowledge and the Teachings of Plants.* Milkweed Editions, 2013.

WOLF NO. 7

May, Katherine. *Wintering: The Power of Rest and Retreat in Difficult Times.* Riverhead Books, 2020.

Randall, Cassidy. "A Rewilding Triumph: Wolves Help to Reverse Yellowstone Degradation." *The Guardian,* January 25, 2020. https://

www.theguardian.com/environment/2020/jan/25/yellowstone-wolf-project-25th-anniversary.

Stronza, Amanda (guest) and Alice Irene Whittaker (host). "Witnessing the Lives and Deaths of Animals Among Us." Reseed (podcast), October 2, 2023. https://www.reseed.ca/listen/witnessing-animals.

Kimmerer, Robin Wall. "Speaking of Nature: Finding Language that Affirms Our Kinship with the Natural World." *Orion Magazine*, March/April 2017. https://orionmagazine.org/article/speaking-of-nature/.

Marzluff, John M. and Tony Angell. *In the Company of Crows and Ravens.* New Haven and London: Yale University Press, 2005.

Burns, Ken, and Dayton Duncan. *Blood Memory: The Tragic Decline and Improbable Resurrection of the American Buffalo.* Alfred A. Knopf, 2023.

EPILOGUE

Solà, Irene. *When I Sign, Mountains Dance.* Translated by Mara Faye Lethem. Minneapolis: Graywolf Press, 2022.

GENERAL READING

Bateson, Nora. *Small Arcs of Larger Circles: Framing through Other Patterns.* 3rd ed. Axminster: Triarchy Press, 2018.

Buller, Adrienne. *The Value of a Whale: On the Illusions of Green Capitalism.* Manchester: Manchester University Press, 2022.

Hetxw'ms Gyetxw (Brett D. Huson). *The Raven Mother.* Highwater Press, 2022.

Heinrich, Bernd. *The Homing Instinct: Meaning and Mystery in Animal Migration.* Mariner Books, 2015.

Macfarlane, Robert, and Jackie Morris. *The Lost Words.* House of Anansi Press, 2018.

Macy, Joanna, and Molly Brown. *Coming Back to Life.* New Society Publishers, 2014.

Maloof, Joan. *Nature's Temples: The Complex World of Old-Growth Forests.* Portland: Timber Press, 2016.

McKibben, Bill. *The End of Nature.* Random House, 1989.

Monbiot, George. *Feral.* Allen Lane, 2013.

Morton, Timothy. *Being Ecological.* Pelican Books, 2018.

Oakes, Lauren E. *In Search of the Canary Tree: A Story of a Scientist, a Cypress, and a Changing World.* Basic Books, 2018.

Schapiro, Mark. *Seeds of Resistance: The Fight to Save Our Food Supply.* Hot Books, 2018.

Simard, Suzanne. *Finding the Mother Tree: Discovering the Wisdom of the Forest*. Allen Lane, 2021.

Suzuki, David, and Amanda McConnell and Adrienne Mason. *The Sacred Balance: Rediscovering Our Place in Nature*. Greystone Books, 2007.

Wray, Britt. *Generation Dread: Finding Purpose in an Age of Climate Crisis*. Knopf Canada, 2022.

Index

Alice Irene Whittaker is an author, mother, and environmental communications leader. She is the creator and host of the *Reseed* podcast. She has been a finalist for all three CBC Literary Prizes, and her writing has been published in national and international publications. Alice Irene has spent over a decade in leadership and executive roles in nonprofit organizations. With her husband, three children, brood of chickens, trio of cats, and a dog, Alice Irene lives in a cabin in the woods on unceded Algonquin Anishinaabe land in Québec. *Homing* is her first book.